Esther Delisle

MYTHS, MEMORY AND LIES

By the same author

The Traitor and the Jew: anti-Semitism and extremist
right-wing nationalism in Quebec, 1929-1939

Canadian Cataloguing in Publication Data

Delisle, Esther, 1954-
Myths, memory & lies : Quebec's intelligentsia and the fascist temptation, 1939-1960
    Translation of: Mythes, mémoire et mensonges.
    Includes bibliographical references

    ISBN 1-55207-008-5

    1. Fascism - Quebec (Province) - History. 2. Quebec (Province) -
History - 1936-1960. 3. Nationalism - Quebec (Province) - History -
20th century. 4. Intellectuals - Quebec(Province) - Political activity.
5. World War, 1939-1945 - Quebec (Province). I. Title.

FC2924.9.F3D4413 1998   320.53'3'09714   C98-941370-5
F1053.D4413 1998

Look for our complete catalogue on the World-wide-web at
http://www.rdpppub.com

Esther Delisle

MYTHS, MEMORY & LIES

**Quebec's intelligentsia and
the fascist temptation
1939-1960**

Translated by Madeleine Hébert

ROBERT DAVIES MULTIMEDIA

Ordering information

USA/Canada:
General Distribution Services,
1-800-387-0141/387-0172 (Canada)
1-800-805-1083(USA)
FREE FAX 1-800-481-6207
PUBNET 6307949
or from the publisher:

Robert Davies Multimedia Publishing Inc.
330-4999 St. Catherine St. West
Westmount, QC H3Z 1T3, Canada
☎ 514-481-2440
▤ 514-481-9973
e-mail: rdppub@netcom.ca

The publisher wishes to thank the
Canada Council for the Arts,
the Department of Canadian Heritage,
and the Sodec (Québec)
for their generous support of its publishing programs.

To A.L., with affection and tenderness

Table of Contents

Acknowledgements

I would like to thank the Social Sciences Research Council of Canada for having granted me a post-doctoral research fellowship which allowed me to prepare this book. My particular thanks go to Professor John Hellman, with whom I had the privilege of collaborating during my time at the Department of History at McGill University. His frank criticism, his erudition, tireless curiosity and willingness to defend unpopular ideas make him an original and inured historian. I also thank him for having afforded me the opportunity to give a workshop on comparative history jointly with him. The freedom of expression and the lively quality of the exchange of ideas that characterised that workshop made it into an ideal research laboratory.

Thanks also go to the Fondation Raymond Garneau which gave me a grant to allow me to complete this book. The meandering ways of research, like those of the life they are part of, holds a number of real surprises. I thus thank Jean-François Garneau for his friendship, his passionate interest in my work and his judicious suggestions for future research. Ramsay Cook read each of the essays that comprise this book and found some merit in them, and Chris Heppner helped to improve the quality of the writing of the ones I initially wrote in English. I sincerely thank them for their help.

My gratitude also goes out to René Aubé and Me François Morin, for facilitating certain steps in my work that saved me considerable time and energy.

Introduction

The recent history of Québec resembles a tragicomedy : the manifestations of repressed memory are often comical while the past that is strenuously denied is tragic. A three-and-a-half metre high statue of the late premier Maurice Duplessis, who for sixteen years ran the Province of Quebec, can disappear without a trace, and not even a commission of inquiry can discover its whereabouts. And a world war (the Second) can cover the planet with blood and flames, but no one in Quebec seems to recall it.

At the beginning of the 1960s, the young guard of the Quebec sovereignty movement and the older, federalist guard, together created the myth of the Quiet Revolution and its necessary corollary, the Great Darkness. The former were anxious to dissimulate the extreme right-wing ideological origins of their political views; the latter wanted to forget that in their youth they had shared them. It was an exercise in occultation of the recent past which gave both groups want they wanted. The young sovereigntists could pose as revolutionaries having broken with the clerical obscurantism, while the federalists could pretend that they led the way by their opposition to the Duplessis regime. These two groups are the architects of the official memory of Quebec. Their success is astonishing when one thinks of the size of the mystification, and can be explained in part by the fact that both the sovereigntist and the federalists had the wind in their sails during the sixties and were settling in to command positions of political and intellectual power. The myths they created and which served them so well would, however, quickly turn into an orthodoxy as "quiet" as it was tenacious.

Viewed from the outside, the generation of René Lévesque and Pierre Elliott Trudeau seems to be a generation that had no youth. But it was not banal to be twenty years old when World War II broke out. What did they think of this conflict without precedent in human history, what were their feelings, which belligerents did they support ? Reading the memoirs of Pierre Elliott Trudeau, Gérard Pelletier and Gérard Filion, among other French Canadians promised to prestigious careers, one could conclude that they saw nothing, heard nothing, and said nothing at the time, and that they were only interested in (and marginally, at that) in the struggle against conscription. René Lévesque became a war correspondent in Europe, but would lie about some of his activities of that time. It is remarkable to find that both Pierre Elliott Trudeau and René Lévesque express in very similar terms their regret at not having participated in what they perceived as the great adventure of the men of their generation. Nevertheless, there is more to the silence and lies than a simple narcissistic scratch. There is the need to hide positions which the Allied victory made unspeakable. These men would have to forget, and make others forget their attraction to the siren songs of fascism and dictatorship in the worst cases, and in the best, their lack of opposition to them.

Omission and lies became the principal tools used to conceal the facts of their youth. They were well served in this demeanor by the lessons of their intellectual guide, Lionel Groulx, and of their mentor, André Laurendeau. In his memoirs, Groulx covers the war in but a few pages, an astonishing feat when one thinks of his exalted pre-war pro-Mussolini, pro-fascist tirades, and he clearly shows the way by speaking only of the referendum on conscription and the Bloc populaire canadien.

In the same perspective as that adopted by Lionel Groulx, André Laurendeau would write the quintessential tragicomical book, *La Crise de la conscription 1942*.[1] In it, trying to justify his lack of criticism of the Vichy regime, he resorts to lying absurdly, pretending to have been ignorant of the conditions of life in occupied France. Laurendeau then appropriates the drama of which he is apparently ignorant and writes, quite seriously, that Québec also sunk beneath the fascist yoke during these terrible years. In the words of this able magician, Canadian prime minister William Lyon MacKenzie King takes on the role of «führer» or «il duce», and Adélard Godbout (premier of Quebec) has the attributes of a «collaborator». Of which abominable crime were these two guilty ? According to Laurendeau, it was nothing less grave than legalizing a system of universal unemployment insurance. While the poor Europeans were shaking at the thought the Gestapo might come knocking at midnight in their occupied lands, Quebeckers were apparently trembling at the mere thought that an unemployment insurance cheque might show up in their mail boxes ! Different countries, different fears, one must believe ! Laurendeau became less and less rational as the years went by, saying to the national convention of the Bloc Populaire Canadien on February 4, 1944: «This meeting is taking place in tragic circumstances, in the middle of a war that has sown disorder, misery and death.»[2]

There is something indecent in the appropriation of the misfortunes of others, all the more so when one also supports the agent of their ills. In the same year of 1944, the same André Laurendeau harangued the masses, pushing for a National and Social regime for the Province of Quebec which would free it from the nightmare of the parliamentary system and give due punishment to its politicians. The use of the expression "National and Social" regime (as in National Socialism), pronounced in 1944 only a few short months before the Normandy invasion, is hardly innocent, especially when it comes from the lips of a political leader who was the head of a nationalist magazine, a man who had lived for some years in France during the crucial 1930s. The journal of the Bloc Populaire Canadien, of which he was secretary, overflowed with admiration for the Portugese dictator Salazar, and described the war as the work of the Anglos and the "kikes." Can we believe that Laurendeau never read the publications of his own political party? More credible is another explanation, that the people who joined the ranks of the Bloc Populaire Canadien, motivated by their hatred of the old parties and by their nationalism much more than by simple opposition to conscription, were not mistaken in choosing a party that had a similar agenda. In fact, the Bloc Populaire Canadien was founded after the referendum on conscription, which clearly shows it had other fish to fry. The truth of the matter is that Laurendeau would use the war to renew the fascist convictions of his youth, if in fact he had ever abandoned them in the first place.

By characterising the conscription issue as the principal, if not the only one surrounding World War II that concerned French Canadians, Laurendeau penned the fable around which would crystallise Quebec's historical memory. But he himself was not taken in by his own mystification. "In the full and formal sense, there was no conscription: was this long debate only in fact a sinister joke?[3]" he asks at the conclusion of *La crise de la conscription 1942*. Moreover, the book itself came out in 1962, at the very moment when the myths of the Quiet Revolution and the Great Darkness were being written. The mystification would be endorsed by older federalists about to become ministers in Ottawa and by the nationalist young Turks who believed they were moving in for good in the citadels of the provincial state and of the universities of Quebec. In their hasty attempts to recast a pure past for themselves and for the nation, their view of the conscription crisis quickly acquired the status of dogma. André Laurendeau, showing great prowess at conjuring information became, unsurprisingly, a political icon whose popularity was high in both camps.

But what were the noteworthy from the *Ligue pour la Défense du Canada* and the *Bloc Populaire Canadien* up to during the war, whenever they had a few minutes to spare from their noble combat against conscription? The archives of the State Department in Washington and the Royal Canadian Mounted Police in Ottawa offer a partial response to the question. We learn from the reports to the State Department of Rollin R. Winslow, American consul in Quebec City, that two young men, hardly twenty year old, were arrested in March 1942 for distributing Nazi propaganda. Raymond Chouinard and Lauréat Tardif belonged to a subversive clandestine organization with a sinister, evocative name: The Iron Guard. Documents seized at Tardif's home by the RCMP revealed that he and his accomplice were but the small fry in a movement run by some of the most eminent nationalist figures of the time: Lionel Groulx, Philippe Hamel, René Chaloult, Oscar Drouin and Paul Gouin, among others.

Raymond Chouinard explained to an RCMP agent that financing The Iron Guard posed no problem until the USA entered the war. From that time on, young Chouinard confessed, things became more difficult, but the organization was still able to obtain the funds it required. This information suggests that The Iron Guard was financed by a foreign power, and in fact the address book belonging to Lauréat Tardif contained the names and addresses of many foreign individuals and organizations. Among them was Eugène Deloncle, a former member of *l'Action française* and a highly-placed partisan of the Nazi order in occupied France who founded the *Mouvement Social Révolutionnaire* during the war in order to put his convictions into violent practice.

These activities took place on a background of Radio-Vichy and Radio-Paris short-wave radio broadcasts, easily captured in Quebec, which announced the progress in the struggle to eliminate the Jews of Europe, bragged of the formation of a chaste and virtuous youth under the guidance of Marshal Pétain and his National Revolution and constantly denounced an England rotted to the core by the bankers and consumed by its imperialist ambitions in Europe. Messages also travelled back the other way. Radio-Algiers reported the words of the rector of the Université de Montréal, Mgr Olivier Maurault, who announced the news of the creation of the *Ligue pour la Défense du Canada* and who reminded listeners in the same breath that in 1942, France and Quebec shared the same ideals, more so than ever. It is certainly not by chance that during this period the American consul Winslow observed a rekindling of fervour for Laurentia (an idealized kind of independent province of Quebec governed by a dictatorial regime) and for its unofficial flag, the Carillon.

Winslow and other observers feared the creation of an independent French-Canadian state modelled on European extreme right-wing or fascist regimes. It is more reasonable to believe that Groulx and his acolytes would only have been able to take power as Pétain had: in the suitcase of an invader. Winslow also believed that the Province of Quebec constituted a danger for the security of the North American continent, probably an unfounded conclusion. The consul's anxious exaggerations, however, do not mean that the currents he described did not exist in fact, nor that the acts and the activities of the people he observed did not take place. His interpretation of events, while interesting, was not necessarily exact and just.

In any event, it is very interesting to observe the consul at work. He had at his disposal a variety of means he could use to unmask spies and to obtain information on people suspected of being hostile to the Allied cause. Even J. Edgar Hoover, director of the Federal Bureau of Investigation, got involved : a reading of his agents' reports throws some light on the agency's procedures.

The fact that the partisans of Laurentia and Vichy were in many cases the same persons who welcomed and defended the French Nazi collaborators who sought refuge in the Province of Quebec after the war tends to confirm Winslow's interpretation of wartime Quebec nationalism.

During the war, these Frenchmen joined the ranks of the Militia run by Joseph Darnand, and swore to fight against «democracy, Jewish leprosy and dissident Gaullism». They were judged in absentia by the French courts established after liberation, and given various sentences, from death to loss of citizenship. In every case, their property was also confiscated. They hid in monasteries, obtained false papers and French Government Orders of Mission and/or received Canadian visas at the Canadian Embassy in Paris. Not just anybody had the connections to obtain these " Orders of Mission", nor for that matter the means to defray the cost of crossing the Atlantic. Where, one wonders, did they find the money needed to come to? Some possessed French passports with consecu-

tive serial numbers, all illegally issued by a single prefecture of police. Others, unable to find their way to such
"collaborative" prefectures, somehow received passports
from the Order of Malta, made out in the name of fictitious
persons.

It is difficult not to conclude that some well-placed
persons in the upper echelons of the French state apparatus facilitated the post-war evasion of these fleeing militiamen. Worse: when their situation became tenuous in
Canada, the government of France never officially requested the extradition of the condemned collaborators,
and the French Minister of Justice proved unwilling to
forward to the Government of Canada the information it
had requested concerning these war criminals who had
entered the country illegally. If the French government or
its officers did not actively assist their clandestine departure from France, it was now clear that there was obviously
no wish to bring these collaborators back to face justice in
their own country.

In almost every case, their narrow exit channel would
flow through the Canadian Embassy in Paris, which issued
them entry visas. General Georges Vanier was then ambassador of Canada in France; his biographer and his wife
recount the events as they took place in almost identical
terms, with one important exception: Pauline Vanier gives
herself the role that Robert Speaight maintains was played
by her husband. According to their story, a number of
people came to the embassy in Paris on an emergency
basis, proclaimed their innocence to Georges or Pauline
Vanier and asked for their assistance in escaping France.
The names of the fleeing collaborators were submitted to
French Justice Minister Pierre-Henri Teitgen, who made
enquiries and gave recommendations to one Vanier or the
other. Canadian visas were then promptly issued to the

innocent, while those guilty of minor offenses were advised to turn themselves in to the French authorities. Parties guilty of grave crimes were told that it would be better for them to hide for the time being. Pauline Vanier admits that the handling of the case of Jacques de Bernonville was a serious blunder. It is difficult to swallow the affirmation that an inquiry led by the French Justice Minister did not come up with the fact that Bernonville was (among other claims to infamy) military governor of Lyon, a superior of Paul Touvier and a member of the Waffen SS. Many hypotheses are possible in this affair: Teitgen was misinformed and in turn, misinformed ambassador Vanier; Teitgen knew the truth about Jacques de Bernonville and lied to the Vaniers; or, Teitgen knew the truth and so informed the Canadian ambassador, who under political or personal pressure, admitted Bernonville to Canada despite his crimes.

Another interesting case concerned a Doctor Michel-Lucien Seigneur, 42 years old, an important militiaman in the Vienne region of France. If the French Justice Minister was ever in fact consulted about this man, the inquiries made were of necessity quite lax. Using the assumed name of Vincent Desgarets, Seigneur obtained a student visa to pursue his studies at Montreal's Collège Stanislas, a private and well-known high school! It is frankly incredible that such an absurdity would not have been noticed by Vanier. In addition, Michel-Lucien Seigneur, like a number of other refugee claimants who knocked at the embassy's door, had been hidden at the Château d'Ars, and like the others, assumed the name of the lords of the manor which gave them refuge. This entire operation just could not have been conducted without the approval, be it tacit, of Georges Vanier. Finally, both the wife of Michel-Lucien Seigneur, Geneviève Seigneur, and Julien Labedan, for-

mer militia member condemned to death after the Liberation affirmed in a summer 1984 interview that Georges
Vanier simply pretended not to know that their papers
were fake.

The reasons that caused General Vanier to facilitate
these French militiamen's road to Canada remain obscure.
Vanier was a constant supporter of the allied armies
throughout the war and showed no sympathy for the Vichy
regime, the National Revolution, or Marshal Pétain. Was
he continuously duped or misinformed by Pierre-Henri
Teitgen, French Minister of Justice, who was his friend?
Or, as devout Catholics, were he and his wife showing an
obligatory Christian charity by assisting fellow Catholics
in trouble, who they believed had been unjustly accused
victims of the kangaroo court justice that sprung up in
France right after Liberation? Were they pressured by the
religious orders who were hiding and protecting these
militia members? It is quite remarkable to discover that
the Vaniers advised those guilty of grave crimes to hide,
rather than give themselves up to the police. In any case,
no thought seems to have been given to turning them in
to the French police authorities.

From 1946 to 1948, a rag-tag band of Nazi collaborators, French for the most part, arrived in Montreal. Among
them were a world-famous writer, a doctor (formerly Vice-
Mayor of Annecy and a friend of some very wealthy
Americans), an former military governor of Lyon, close to
Klaus Barbie and a superior of Paul Touvier, a Radio-Paris
journalist, a French Nazi propagandist from *Solidarité
française* (one of the principals of the antisemitic movement in the Alsace region before the war) and militiamen
protected by a family of manor lords who during the
nineteenth century were the protectors of the parish priest
of Ars.

In the Montreal area, the doors of the best houses in
Outremont and Westmount were flung open to the Nazis
collaborators. They were suddenly acclaimed as the real
heroes of the war. In Quebec City, some of them were
received in the panelled salons of the residences of René
Chaloult, Philippe Hamel and Noël and Frédéric Dorion,
the very same people who had only recently gaily toasted
the Vichy regime with the city's French consul. Out on the
town, these collaborators could always find a good table at
the celebrated Kerhulu Restaurant, owned by one Joseph
Kerhulu, an unconditional supporter of Pétain. Father
Simon Arsenault, former director of the newspaper *La
Droite* which saw its publication suspended in 1941 by the
RCMP, would often join these feasts. American war-time
consul Rollin Winslow's suspicions finally found a post-
war confirmation in these activities.

These elegant soirees of the "right" crowd would
soon be unfortunately disrupted when five former French
militiamen, instead of their anticipated Canadian residence visas, were served with deportation orders. A street-
fighter's trench war ensued, between the federal
government and the defenders of the collaborators; in the
end, four of the five fugitives were allowed to remain in
Canada. It is worth noting however, that the group of
fugitives who had arrived from the Ars Château were never
bothered by Canadian immigration authorities, and none
of them would ever receive deportation advices.

Through their defence of the French collaborators,
René Chaloult, the Dorion brothers, Philippe Hamel, André Laurendeau and Robert Rumilly exposed their pro-
Pétain, even fascist convictions, convictions apparently
not curtailed by the Allied victory. A curious re-writing of
history began to come to light: according to André
Laurendeau and Philippe Hamel, it was Poland, destroyed

by the Nazi blitzkrieg which found itself in the box of the accused, for having been too intransigent towards Hitler, who really had no other option but to attack, thus provoking the worldwide conflagration. Mindlessly repeating the ideological clichés of the Révolution Nationale so dear to Pétain, the fumbling Quebec defenders of the exiled collaborators lashed out at the Jews, the Communists and the fanatical Anglophiles who had it in for their proteges here and in France. André Laurendeau was aware of the contents of the police file concerning Bernonville; one would hardly suspect it from the way he supported this war criminal in the pages of *Le Devoir*. Philippe Hamel, for his part, wasted no time in rushing to the defence of Maurice Bardèche, the brother-in-law of Robert Brasillach, a man who had been the secretary of the publication *Je suis partout* and an unrepentant fascist, who was having problems, not surprisingly, with French justice.

Prime Minister Louis Saint-Laurent appeared reticent to become publicly involved in the business of the refugee war criminals in exile in the Province of Québec. He bent in the face of the combined pressure of French and Canadian prelates, of Quebec public opinion and of immediate political imperatives. After all, on the eve of the June 1949 federal elections, what good could possibly come from alienating all those devout and opinionated voters, especially since *Le Devoir* and Robert Rumilly did not conceal their intentions of using that particular card in the defence of the collaborators. Still, the question of who exactly protected these illegal immigrants who were never bothered by Canadian authorities remains open. As time went by, for example, the members of the Château d'Ars-sur-Formans group all abandoned the Desgarets pseudonym and began to use their real names in order to legalize their status in Canada. Their true identi-

ties were then out in the open, so why was there no attempt
made to deport them? Another question with no answer,
as yet: why were the contents of the criminal file on
Jacques de Bernonville never fully revealed in public? On
June 5 and 6, 1951, Immigration Minister W.E. Harris
swore under oath that the contents of the file were a state
secret and refused to divulge its contents in a Montreal
Superior Court. To this day, we still do not know the
precise and complete nature of the information in that
dossier.

Then there is the case of Paul Erwin Eberhard
Reifenrath, alias Paul-Éverard Richemont, alias Paul Dumont, alias Paul Leyzen, alias Paul Chambord, alias Tonton, who never tried to acquire permanent residency in
Canada. It didn't stop him from becoming the personal
and confidential ambassador to the Vatican of the premier
of Quebec, Maurice Duplessis. A Nazi propagandist in
war-time France, Paul Reifenrath arrived in Quebec after
the war using the name Paul Leyzen. He then assumed the
name Paul-Éverard Richemont and quickly became associated with the *Association professionnelle des industriels
(API)* and Maurice Duplessis in their struggle against the
Communists, the Jews, the freemasons, the Christian
democrats and all the other "subversive elements at work
in the world and in the province." The role Richemont
played as a paid Duplessis propagandist during the famous
asbestos strike shows him in a different light than the one
generally presented by historiography. Duplessis responded to this labour conflict by launching an ideological
war that took no prisoners and gave no quarter, aiming to
eliminate once and for all the subversive threat as he saw
it in the above description. As the many-tentacled beast
reached even into the very heart of the Vatican, according
to Duplessis, he decided to send Richemont to Rome in

order to throttle it. As Duplessis saw it, if a cat's paw segment of the Church in Quebec supported the asbestos miners' strike and lobbied the Vatican to denounce the collusion of the provincial government with the mining companies, the true puppet masters were surely those subversives hiding as much over there as right here in Quebec. Richemont's stay in Rome would be a lengthy one, and he tirelessly sought support for Duplessis from whichever cardinal who would listen to him. In the *Bulletin de Custos* that Richemont edited in Rome, he portrayed Duplessis as the Franco du Nord and the head of the "only Catholic government in North America," a phrase coined by Duplessis himself.

The astonishing thing about the propaganda penned by Richemont and his acolytes, be it in the Custos Report, the *Bulletin de Custos* or the diatribes of On. Lezaura, is its crude nature. Crude, first and foremost, was their methodology, for who would take seriously their articles signed with obvious pseudonyms, quoting anonymous sources? The arguments they used were equally simple-minded: the Comintern was controlling the asbestos strikers, and the Jews, in cahoots with Christian democrats were dragging the world down to ruin, and so forth and so on . That the premier of the province and eminent members of the clergy were content with such vulgar propaganda is stupefying. Our astonishment though, is tempered by the knowledge of the crude, virulent and vulgar antisemitism of *Le Devoir* during the thirties, which was also published using patently unbelievable pseudonyms. That the same tired methods were used over and over from one decade to the next still provide researchers with some surprises, not the least of which is to see how a third-rate Nazi propagandist and illegal alien could gain direct access to the cabinet of the premier of Québec.

Duplessis belonged to an icon of accepted dogma, the Great Darkness, and as such, was classified and any contradictory information consigned to dusty archives. His statue remained hidden for 16 years until, in 1977, the Parti Québécois erected it in a grand ceremony in front of the National Assembly in Quebec. The dignitaries invited to the event represented the mainstream of provincial politics: the Parti Québécois, Liberals, and Union Nationale all attended. On a cold and grey November morning, the children of the Quiet Revolution all recognized the Duplessis in themselves and in close ranks, formed a true "national union." They celebrated his defence of provincial autonomy and excused his dictatorial regime. One notable difference did separate the father from the children, though. In a break with the past the Union Nationale party name no longer referred to a political ideology but to the Nation, without, however, overtly naming it. The Parti Québécois, going a step further on the path opened by the Union Nationale, chose an ethnic denomination. Thus, while the Great Darkness put the idea of a nation on the political agenda, the Quiet Revolution, named it without defining it but rendered it exclusivist all the same.

Of course, this does not in any way mean that the Parti Québécois presented a clear political option. Many competing formulas were proposed, such as sovereignty, sovereignty-association, independence, autonomy, last-chance federalism, to name only a few, some even at one and the same time. Not wanting to be left in their dust, the political adversaries of the Parti Québécois came up with their own abstruse proposals: cultural sovereignty, special status, renewed federalism, asymmetric federalism, etc. During the sixties, the constitutional status of Quebec became a hive of business for a great number of Francophone intellectuals and politicians, and for a surprising number of Anglophones. Media access was virtually guaranteed to anyone with a word or two to say on the question, as long as they showed the serious demeanor the subject called for.

But the blush on the rose of the sixties has long since faded. The young sovereigntist rebels of that time now see the spectre of retirement approaching at a brisk clip; for some, the rubicon has already been crossed. But they want one last kick at the can before they go. The trouble is, they never stop kicking, and worse, they have taken on the pontificating tone of the priests who educated them and against whom they had the illusion of having rebelled. Their federalist elders, somewhat more on in years, see their ranks dwindling ineluctably, but never miss a chance to valiantly sing the old refrain whenever an opportunity presents itself.

On the eve on the new millennium, it is clear that the fables and the myths of the Quiet Revolution have long since become an orthodoxy riddled with dogma and hackneyed tales that even those who spout them no longer believe. But what thinking person would voluntarily relinquish such a lucrative trademark? The fables of the Quiet Revolution and the constitutional three-ring circus ensured the successful careers of a whole class of bureaucrats, intellectuals and politicians, who had no interest in considering other interpretations of history nor other political agendas. Their dust-covered orthodoxy now shivers with mean-spiritedness, and sees in any new idea a threat to its monopoly of the truth and to the fortunes of those whose interest it defends. Cringing, it fears for the future, and lashes out at those who challenge its tenets, like all orthodoxies that have run out of breath.

This behaviour resembles that of the Roman Catholic Church in the two decades before Vatican II. The Holy See had so often thundered against any heterodox idea that the simple mention of its name sufficed to gag any potential audacious spirit. In Quebec, the clergy rivalled the Holy See in its zeal, abusing its power so flagrantly that it looks comical in today's light. While the excommunications spewed in all directions and the speeches flew fast and furious, opposing currents of thought grew in influence until the day when Vatican II sounded the death knell of a power that its tenants had thought eternal. The triumphant trumpet call usually signals nothing more than the beginning of defeat.

The essays that compose this book were written during my two post-doctoral research years at the Department of History of McGill University. The subject of my research was the exiled French Nazi collaborators who had taken refuge in Quebec, which explains why the longest chapter in the book (*A Strange Sort of Hero*) concerns these people and their story.

According to an unwritten but implacable law of historical research, the historian often finds something quite different from what he or she was looking for. But this "something else" is more interesting than what the researcher was hoping to find. For example, I went looking for traces of collaborators exiled in Canada in the American National Archives, but came up empty-handed. However, I did discover the existence of a nestful of spies and fascist sympathizers in Quebec City that was reported by the American consul, Rollin R. Winslow, and this discovery formed the basis for Sleepless in Quebec City. The other chapters in the book *Sounds of Silence*, *A Tale of Two Statues* and *Loony Tunes* were written to order for academic journals. University publication being what it is, *Sounds* was not accepted because it was deemed too tract-like, with an "anti-scientific, polemical" tone where "gratuitous and unfounded affirmations ran rampant," the second was accepted but the special issue of the review in which it was to appear was pulled from publication sine die. As for *Loony Tunes*, it appeared in the distant and solicitous down under, in Australia, where a few hardy souls yet study the affairs of our nation.

Sleepless in Quebec City:
the Anxieties of an American Consul

Once upon a time there lived in Quebec City a very worried man named Rollin R. Winslow. From 1939 to 1942 he was the American consul in the capital of the province of Quebec. If he had believed that this backwater posting to an ostensibly quiet provincial town was to be a relatively peaceful one for a diplomat in a world at war, he quickly changed his mind. The picturesque city, established in 1608, was the theater of much covert and not-so-covert activity by suspected Nazis, other foreign agents and underground fascist organizations.

In some ways, consuls and ambassadors are *bona fide* spies for the country they represent. They closely monitor the media where they are posted, develop contacts with sources and meet with informants in order to draw as accurate a picture as possible of the situation in the city and country of their assignment. They then report their conclusions to the government of their country. They also fulfill administrative duties such as issuing visas, and they socialize extensively.

That is the routine that Rollin R. Winslow would follow. But the situation in which he performed his duties was extraordinary, to say the least. The world was at war, with the Allies pitted against the Axis countries. This heightened his sense of alarm and give a dramatic cast to his reports. In fact, Winslow's concerns grew steadily in the months and years to come. Once the United States and

Canada had joined the war against Germany, Italy and
Japan, any activity believed to be helpful to the Axis forces
became more worrisome than it had been during the
"phoney war," the years 1939-1940 when the belligerents
stood still on the edge of the abyss. This growing sense of
urgency is reflected in Consul Winslow's largely accurate
reports. The detailed information Winslow provides in his
reports was rarely wrong: yes, *Abbé* Pierre Gravel was *curé*
of St. Roch parish; yes, Canon Chamberland was director
of *L'Action Catholique*; yes, Father Ignatius Eschmann was
a professor at Laval University. But, here and there is a
minor inaccuracy: Eschmann was never head of the
School of Social Sciences as Winslow wrote. This kind of
mistake was not often found in the reports consulted for
this chapter more than fifty years after their writing.

The German victories on European battlefields, and
especially the establishment of the Vichy government
under the authority of Marshal Philippe Pétain encouraged many Quebec nationalists to support Vichy and to
sympathize with the Axis powers. At the same time these
events renewed their hopes that something similar was
possible in the province of Quebec. The conscription crisis
about which so much has been written appears almost
incidental to their global concerns. Behind opposition to
conscription there was support for the National Revolution in France and a faint yearning that such a new order
would see the light of the day on the banks of the St.
Lawrence river. Not surprisingly, Canon Lionel Groulx
and his dream of a fascist Laurentia — *Laurentie* being the
name of an independent province of Quebec — greatly
worried Winslow. Other names appearing in his reports
are those of prominent members of political parties or
movements inspired by Groulx's extremist nationalism,
like the "national" arm of the Action libérale nationale,

and during World War II, the League for the Defence of Canada and the Bloc populaire canadien. This is the case for René Chaloult, Philippe Hamel, Paul Gouin, Oscar Drouin and J-Ernest Grégoire. Father Simon Arsenault and *Abbé* Pierre Gravel were outright fascists while Noël Dorion and Antoine Rivard were prominent lawyers and high-ranking members of the Union Nationale of Premier Maurice Duplessis. Furthermore, the clergy largely supported Marshal Pétain and his National Revolution.

Did Winslow bestow too much importance to some of these political characters and their movements? These men believed they were important and, as nationalists, that their voice was the one and only true voice of French Canada. Winslow took them at face value. This led him to have an inflated view of their influence on Quebec society, an influence that might not have been as great as he believed: their self-aggrandizement fed his fears. At his most alarmed, when he expressed his concerns that blood could be shed here if the fascism of Lionel Groulx and his followers took power in the province of Quebec, and his worries that this brand of extremism had continental ambitions, he remained cautious enough to emphasize that these were his personal views only and not the ones he carried in his functions as American consul in Quebec City. Furthermore he was not the sole monitor of the situation in Quebec at the time: the Division of Foreign Broadcast Intelligence Service followed the plebiscite on conscription, the Office of Coordinator of Information (precursor of the Central Intelligence Agency) received an alarming report from a French politician of the Third Republic visiting Quebec, and, once in a while, J. Edgar Hoover, head of the Federal Bureau of Investigation, wanted to know more about some dubious characters. In other words, there was cause for concern.

Father Ignatius Eschmann

The first to arouse suspicion from Winslow was Father Ignatius (civil name: Theodor Karl) Eschmann, a professor of sociology at Laval University. After having become *persona non grata* in Nazi Germany, Eschmann had arrived in Canada in December 1938 in order to teach in the fledgling School of Social Sciences at Laval University. An erudite man, he had a world-wide reputation as a sociologist and philosopher. He was very tall and handsome with blond hair and brown eyes, and was an immediate success with the students.

One and a half years after leaving Germany, Father Eschmann experienced a moment of epiphany in his political convictions. With Hitler's panzers rolling through Europe, he felt an outburst of patriotism that quickly led to enthusiasm for National Socialism. In short order, Consul Winslow came to suspect him of being nothing less than an active Nazi agent.

In a report dated May 27, 1940 to the Assistant Secretary of State, Adolf A. Berle Jr., Winslow contended that Eschmann had devised a scheme to avoid censorship of his letters to Berlin.[1] A New York friend of Eschmann's had agreed to mail them from Manhattan to his relatives in Germany. The return address was "C. Peters," Hotel President, 234 West 48th Street, New York. That was the address German correspondents would use to communicate with Eschmann. These letters would be collected by the anonymous friend in New York and re-addressed to Mr. Peters in Quebec where someone else would receive them and deliver them to Father Eschmann. Eventually, the compliant New York friend got cold feet and decided to deliver some of the letters to the Canadian authorities.

One of these was addressed to Miss Ina Frank, 23 Luitpoldstrasse, Berlin W30, but began with a somewhat inappropriate salutation to "Dear Uncle." Authorities scrutinized the letter and came to the conclusion that it might contain double meanings. Double meanings or not, in that letter a homesick Eschmann clearly expressed his eagerness to return to Germany to serve the Fatherland and wrote that it was becoming difficult to restrain his rage.

One can safely assume that upon receiving the reports from Winslow, Assistant Secretary of State Adolf A. Berle Jr. requested the FBI to further inquire into the American ramifications of Eschmann's activities. On November 8, 1940, J. Edgar Hoover sent Berle a copy of a report by Special Agent L.A. Langille on the suspected espionage activities of Father Eschmann. "A discreet inquiry" at the Hotel President showed that no one by the name of C. Peters had registered at that hotel and that no mail had been received under that name either directly or as a forwarding address. The mail carrier and the hotel manager were thoroughly interrogated and assured Mr. Langille that if any such mail was received they would immediately communicate with the New York Division of the FBI.

While that inquiry was taking place, Father Eschmann's enthusiasm for National Socialism grew. In a letter to a friend he quoted exultantly from a Berlin broadcast to French Canadians saying that before long Hitler would have dinner at the Chateau Frontenac (in Quebec City).[2] After receiving a tip that Father Eschmann had bought sporting clothes and was getting prepared to leave for the United States by crossing the woods near Jackman, Maine, the police renewed their surveillance of him.

They could have spared themselves the trouble. Father Ignatius Eschmann was the main artisan of his own undoing. While the ecclesiastical Palace remained indifferent to his dubious political activities it reacted with the speed and might of a lightning bolt to the one misdeed Cardinal Rodrigue-Marie Villeneuve never forgave a priest of his diocese: having an affair with a woman. Canadian authorities had intercepted correspondence between Father Eschmann and a young French-Canadian woman temporarily living in New York. These letters convinced the authorities that they were engaged not only in a passionate love affair but also in subversive activities of a treasonous nature. On September 27, 1940 an upbeat Winslow reported to the State Department that Father Eschmann had been placed in close confinement in "a disciplinary camp of the Roman Catholic clergy in the northern woods of Canada."[3] The wandering Father was actually sent to the Dominican monastery in Ottawa where he remained almost incommunicado — *in pace* in the religious lexicon — for some time.

Six months later J. Edgar Hoover wrote Berle that a confidential source had informed him that Father Eschmann's conduct was "most satisfactory." For the last six weeks he had not communicated with a living soul outside the walls of the monastery: neither had he received nor sent any letter and no one had visited him.[4] Soon after, Father Eschmann left to teach at the Institute of Medieval Studies of the University of Toronto established by the French philosopher Étienne Gilson. He lived in Toronto until he died in 1968 .

The French Connection

French Consul Jean Ricard saw a golden opportunity in Quebec City.[5] He never lacked people to lend him assistance. For him as well as for some prominent nationalists in Quebec City, Vichy was a dream come true.

Winslow suspected that Ricard worked tirelessly to disseminate the Vichy propaganda he obtained, which was sent by diplomatic pouch in order to circumvent Canadian censors. On February 25, 1942,[6] a person deemed "reliable" by the American consul had informed him that Canon Joseph A. Chamberland, Director-General of the newspaper *L'Action Catholique* was "incensed by a recent visit from Consul Ricard who had presented him with a copy of Admiral Darlan's speech outlining French grievances against the English." Admiral Jean-François Darlan, then head of the French government and passionate advocate of co-belligerency with Germany ranted about the ever-perfidious England, which he claimed would lose the war anymay, for opposing France in its desire to join the new European Order by bombing its ports and attacking its navy in North Africa, not for fear the German army would use them, as they claimed, but to establish British imperialism over Europe.

One week later Winslow was fortuitiously seated next to Canon Chamberland at the Chateau Frontenac where both were attending a banquet in honour of a visiting curling team.[7] The ecclesiastical dignitary confirmed that he had received Admiral Darlan's declaration. However, he told him that it had not been handed to him by Ricard. Who then had given it to Canon Chamberland for his "use and information?" From an independent source Winslow learned that the guilty party was René Chaloult, a Liberal

member of the Quebec Legislative Assembly from the
Lotbinière riding. Described by Winslow as "an ardent
and sincere French-Canadian nationalist and an Anglo-
phobe of note," Chaloult was also an "intimate of the Vichy
Consul." A follower of Canon Groulx, René Chaloult had
been campaigning for a national flag for French Canada
for a long time. A former member of the fascist arm of the
Action libérale nationale, he had become a Union Nationale Member of the Provincial Parliament for the riding of
Kamouraska in 1936.

In the days following the banquet, a certain Paul
Bouchard called at the American consulate to apply for a
visa.[8] Paul Bouchard had been the young instigator and
director of the weekly *La Nation* which never reneged on
its fervent enthusiasm for fascism. Winslow, knowing very
well that Bouchard's political beliefs were similar to, and
possibly more extreme than Chaloult's, questioned him
about the circulation of Darlan's declaration among the
chattering classes of Quebec City. Bouchard denied having
seen the declaration although, according to Winslow, he
accurately knew its contents. He added that his friend
Noël Dorion and other of his acquaintances had also seen
the document.

Had he only known, he could also have added that in
June 1941,[9] a man named Charles Villeneuve had been
fined 50 dollars after he pleaded guilty to having distributed in Quebec City leaflets containing a declaration
against conscription by the Irish Cardinal Joseph Macrory
as well as this declaration by Admiral Darlan: *"C'est l'Angleterre qui fut l'instigatrice de la guerre. Nous n'avons été qu'un
jouet entre ses mains."* Charged under the Defence of Canada
Regulations with the same offense, another man named
Louis Tardivel had pleaded not guilty. Furthermore, the
murder of Darlan on December 24, 1942 created a consid-

erable stir among nationalists in Quebec. They believed
he had been assassinated on the orders of British officials
who were bent to eliminate sympathizers of Darlan and
the Vichy regime in North Africa.[10]

Winslow described Noël Dorion as "a nationalist and
anti-de Gaullist." He was a prominent lawyer, a high-ranking member of the Union Nationale and a pivotal figure
of the *beau monde* of the newly established suburb of Ste-
Foy. Some of his political associates were other lawyers:
Stanislas Germain, Antoine Rivard and Jean Blais. Antoine Rivard was another prominent member of the Union
Nationale who became a candidate for that party in the
riding of Québec-Centre in 1944. He was defeated, but had
better luck in the next election when he became Union
Nationale MPP for Montmagny in 1948. He would later
became Attorney General of the Province of Quebec and
Minister of Transportation and Communication. A reliable person had informed Winslow that Consul Ricard was
a regular guest at Dorion's home along with French-Canadian nationalists. Paul Bouchard confirmed this piece
of information when he told Winslow that the day before
he had indeed met Ricard at Dorion's place with a number
of his "nationalist" colleagues.[11] At that gathering, Jean
Ricard claimed that "contrary to popular belief the Government of occupied France was being administered from Vichy
except for matters affected by the terms of the armistice."[12]

At the same time, to compound the American consul's worries, Radio-Vichy, Radio-Algiers and Radio-Paris
specifically addressed pro-Axis broadcasts to French-Canadian listeners. Pétain was ritually praised, de Gaulle
always qualified as a "traitor," Jews routinely vilified,
Fascism and National Socialism extolled as the way of the
future.[13]

For example, on October 28, 1941 Radio-Vichy informed listeners of some activities of the Association of Anti-Jewish journalists of France and invited their brethren outside France to follow their example and serve Pétain:

> VICHY – October 28, 1941. Paris. The Association of Anti-Jewish Journalists placed a wreath on the grave of Edouard Raymond, on the anniversary of his death. Distant listeners, let us work patiently. Let us return to fundamental truths. Pétain is doing so and is rebuilding our fatherland, with strength and fortitude! Let us Frenchmen in France and abroad follow him and serve him! Slogan: Our duty, with Marshal Pétain, is to build a better homeland, for a better people. (p.1)

Any show of support from the Catholic hierarchy to the Vichy regime was duly emphasized:

> VICHY – October 29, 1941. The Archbishop of Paris is in Vichy. He was honoured at a dinner attended by many notables.

Another piece of good news: Europe was increasingly becoming *Judenfrei* :

> Bratislava: 1500 Jews have received the order to leave the city before November 1st. 1200 have already left. Budapest: 87 Jews were arrested for presenting medical certificates on the basis of which they had expected to be exempted from work.

Back in France a new elite was being created :

> (...) A talk was given on camps for children on the Côte d'Azur. It was called Côte d'Azur 1941. One sees no striped parasols, no fancy artists. Young girls are serious. No flirting, no swimming or showing off. A girl swims because she must have relaxation after her work or because it is

part of her course in training to become a physical instructor. All here is order and cleanliness. The French are at work preparing an elite.

Lest their listeners forget to hate Jews, Radio-Vichy broadcasted a long tirade by one René Joubet three days before Christmas:

VICHY –December 22, 1941. A strong tirade against Jews was launched by René Joubet. Jews he said, had gone over to the Christian faith for practical and material reasons. Jews never encouraged proselytism for the same reasons. In France they constituted a state within the state. Initial measures against them were instituted by Marshal Pétain on February 22 and October 3, 1941, eliminating them from administrative posts in the state, and shutting them out of the professions, so that their representation in them is now limited to about 2%. Jews are not permitted to own real estate other than the houses they live in. In the pre-war administration, out of 14 Jewish members of parliament only one was a member of the Right. The Jewish religion, it is easily seen, is not at all devoted to the spiritual but almost entirely furthers material interests. How many Jews were there in France before the war? In the district of Paris alone there were 300,000. They flocked to Paris because they could amass fortunes quickly there. In Bordeaux, there were 4,000. The Jews were against the welfare of the State. They ruined local businesses by their methods. (Note added by Winslow: The text was given to an announcer who read it very dramatically ending in a passionate crescendo of hate).

Marshal Pétain lavished attention and solicitude on New France:

FIRMIN ROSE(sic) - "The Pilot at the Helm" Pétain's robust hand is at the helm. He realizes that not only is Europe in turmoil, but the whole world. (...) Not only European

France but French islands and colonies beyond the seas are receiving the Marshal's solicitude and attention. (...) Pétain deplores the tragic difficulties in this respect which are produced by the great distances from the homeland and consequent lack of information in the colony. Who can understand this situation better than you, dear Canadian listeners? In the 18th century France possessed territory on the North American continent — New France. It was not a colony. It was just another province of France. Versailles chose the governors with great love and care. Great names like Frontenac, the Governor of New France; Talon, the brilliant intendent (sic; intendant); Montmorency Laval, the first Bishop of Quebec — these glorious names are ample proof of France's pride in her New France. The province was rich and beautiful, but we were too far from it to be able to hold it. Our history blames the government of that time and individual persons for our loss. Marshal Pétain is determined that this incident in our history will not repeat itself.

VICHY – December 30, 1941.Paris-Canada (notes): On Friday December 26th the Comte de Guedon lashed out at the Free French and Muselier in particular because of the occupation of St. Pierre and Miquelon. The islands, he said, have been French since the time of Jacques Cartier. Every Frenchman remembers that, just as he remembers that Quebec was once Stadecona and Montreal was Hochelaga, and that Jacques Cartier founded them. The French people resent seeing these "countryless mercenaries desecrating French soil." (...)

A message was read to the Pointe du Lac religious community. The reader said, "We know by your letters that you hear us and are anxious about us."

To look at the past was fine, but equally important was to work diligently toward a Fascist future:

VICHY – January 29, 1942. Staff speaker. The Fascist Revolution proceeded from the will of Mussolini. The National Socialist *Weltanschauung* sprang from the "mystic ardour" of Hitler. It is important to have a will, and having it, to act.

The "rotten" and "money worshipping" Englishmen were almost as nefarious as the Jews:

PARIS-CANADA, January 23, 1942. This is a transmission from Paris for you, to French-Canadian listeners: "We, in France, defend our morale which is so aptly exemplified by the Marshal's motto of Honour, Family and Fatherland."

Admiral Charles Beresford was quoted on the subject of the English nation: "The English are rotten to the core. Now they are led by their allies and dance to the tune of the plutocratic violins. They have abandoned everything and prostrated themselves in worship of the Golden Calf." (...)

Short-wave radio provided like-minded people an efficient tool to make their views known and to perhaps gain new followers for their ideas and organizations. Thus the rector of the University of Montreal, Monsignor Olivier Maurault, days after the Bloc populaire canadien was established had this to say on Radio-Algiers:

RADIO-ALGIERS, January 30, 1942. The Rector of the University of Montreal has urged the members of the newly formed organization to contact all who might be "susceptible." The French Canadians are a great "nation" and "though separated from the mother country, they are animated by the same ideals."[14]

The programs now included elements characteristic of German radio, for example, concerts, sports, reports and so on, reported Winslow. The object of this new extensive schedule was to "keep in touch with French racial elements, to develop closer relations with them and, where possible, to organize them," Winslow outlined.

He concluded his report by stating that opposition to conscription coupled with the activities of the French consul in Quebec City and these "hate-inspiring" broadcasts represented nothing less than "a serious menace to the order and security of this continent."

The Travels of Albert Briand

Another highly vocal Vichy supporter in Quebec City was Albert Briand, a 33 year-old French citizen and businessman who had left the French islands of St. Pierre and Miquelon in January 1941 to register, with his wife Mary Deminiac, as students at the School of Social Sciences at Laval University.[15] Briand soon became pals with the son of the Vichy consul, both endlessly extolling the virtues of Pétain's "new order." His poor attendance at Laval University aroused further suspicion: in 1941 Briand had spent more than 18 weeks in the United States, not to mention his numerous trips across Canada, all of them allegedly for "business reasons." Also, he had visited St. Pierre on December 16, 1941, a few days prior to the island being taken over by the Free French.

During a trip to Ottawa, on December 29 and 30, 1941, he tried to communicate with the Japanese Embassy in Washington (telephoning Decatur 0716) following the occupation of St. Pierre by the Free French, but was prevented from doing so by the censor. Although he had always carefully omitted to inform the American consulate that he would visit Washington during his trips south of the border, he later admitted that he had maintained close contacts with Jacques Dumaine, Counselor of the

Vichy Legation and with his successor, Guillaume Georges-Picot both, of course, in Washington.

On April 13, 1942 Albert Briand went to the American consulate in Quebec City to obtain a visa for his wife.[16]
He said he was planning a business trip and wished his
wife to accompany him.

On that afternoon, a cat-and-mouse game ensued
between Briand and Winslow, the latter trying to gather
more evidence to substantiate his suspicion that Briand
was in fact a foreign agent. Upon learning that the total
volume of Albert Briand's purchases in the United States
in 1941 amounted to a grand total of only $15,000,
Winslow suggested wryly that it did not amount to much
considering the numerous trips and considerable time
Briand had spent in the United States since his moving to
Quebec City. Briand replied unconvincingly that he had
simply taken the opportunity to visit friends and to contact people in order to continue his studies in the United
States.

Winslow wanted to know about the people Briand
had met while he was in Washington. At first Briand
denied having seen anyone else except a Father Farrell and
a Colonel Melville Gillett. Further grilled, he admitted to
have regularly visited Mr. William de Courcy of the State
Department. On his first visit, he carried a letter of introduction from Consul Maurice Pasquest stationed at St.
Pierre and Miquelon. At that point, Briand claimed that
William de Courcy was the only person he had met while
in Washington.

Becoming more inquisitive now, Winslow asked him
if he had ever gone to the French Embassy in Washington.
Briand retorted he had done so in order to see Commander
Denis de Bourgoing, the naval attaché, who happened to
be an old friend of his. Perhaps fearing he had said too

much, Briand recanted his statement soon afterward and said he had not known de Bourgoing before going to Washington. He had rather been referred to de Bourgoing by the French consul, who thought the naval attaché might be interested to learn more about the volatile situation in St. Pierre and Miquelon.

Asked again about the content of his meeting with de Bourgoing, Briand changed his story one more time. Following the capitulation of France he had experienced serious difficulties in getting money in St. Pierre and Miquelon and he just wanted to discuss the matter with his old friend de Bourgoing. When asked for the nth time if he had seen other people during his previous visits to the United States an angry and purple-faced Briand refused to answer any more questions, and rose from his seat. He said he would complain and Winslow replied that if Briand could not answer his questions "with perfect frankness" he would take steps to have his visa cancelled. Which he did a few days later.

In the days following his stormy conversation with Winslow, Briand was again interrogated by the police.[17] He denied having phoned the Japanese Embassy on December 29, 1941, although records of the telephone company showed in fact that he had placed a call to Decatur 0716. He later said by way of explanation that he had in fact tried to reach Georges-Picot, the Vichy Counsellor and not the Japanese, but changed his story minutes later. Now, he asserted that on that very same day he had made a business call to Denis de Bourgoing, the Vichy naval attaché in Washington.

To the Canadian Immigration officer in Quebec, Briand had said that his business had practically ceased to exist with the entry of the Free French into St. Pierre and Miquelon. In that case, Winslow pointed out, his claim that he wished to go to the United States on business for his firm was very questionable, wasn't it?

Briand told the police that the plebiscite that ended with the victory of the Free French in the islands of St. Pierre and Miquelon had been unfairly conducted and that more than half of their population supported the Vichy regime. Furthermore the economic situation had taken a turn for the worse: the islands were now deprived of the $60,000 per month from French assets in the United States which had been pouring in during the Vichy regime.

Following his stormy meeting with Briand on April 13, 1942, Winslow requested the opinion of the local president of the Free France movement in regard to this suspected foreign agent. Three days later he received a reply stating, rather unsurprisingly, that Briand was strongly in favor of the Vichy regime and that he had fiercely opposed the occupation by the Free French under the command of Admiral Muselier. He remained an active and ardent propagandist against the Free French and their allies and he even fancied himself as the future dictator of the islands.

The Iron Guard

Hostile consuls, suspected foreign agents or putative active Nazi agents, Vichy propaganda: these were not the only worries of Rollin R. Winslow. A homegrown subversive organization soon caught his attention.

In the early hours of Sunday, March 8, 1942, the Royal Canadian Mounted Police and the federal attorney general's department decided to cover a Saint-John-the-Baptist Society meeting held in Quebec City's Limoilou neighbourhood that evening.[18] Policemen would pick up all those found distributing subversive circulars. They would be interrogated and hopefully would reveal the name of the heads of their organization. The RCMP hoped to secure sufficient evidence to warrant their arrest. Approximately thirty policemen in plain- clothes and in uniform attended the surprisingly quiet meeting.

They nevertheless arrested a young man for printing and then distributing subversive pamphlets during the meeting but outside the premises. The 20 year-old taken into custody was Raymond Chouinard, a member of the Iron Guard (presumably named after the infamous Nazi Roumanian Iron Guard led by the sinister Codreanu).[19] He was arrested at his home in the parish of St. Roch of Quebec City's lower town.[20]

Entitled "CANADIANS! LEND YOUR MONEY!", the pamphlet seized by the RCMP ironically encouraged French Canadians to lend their money to the Canadian government in the war effort so that the RAF could kill their brothers in France. The author was alluding to the bombing of the Renault factories in France by the RAF. It continued:

"The London oppressors, 'these damn Jews' would have been better inspired to fight in France during the spring of 1940 instead of running away to London and New York to establish the Free French movement. England only wants someone who will fight with her so that the Jewish-English oppressors may keep their hold on colonies which they held in slavery, like Malaysia. (...) WAKE UP CANADIANS! The Germans are killing Communists in France who are guilty of sabotage but English kill, without discernment, women and children. (...) CANADIANS, REMEMBER THE RAID ON PARIS THE 3rd OF MARCH 1942. CANADIANS, REMEMBER ACADIA! (...) THE IRON GUARD! Join our guard, we number in the hundreds already, and tomorrow we will be thousands, we play our cards on the table."

God will help us. Hail France!

Following the arrest of Raymond Chouinard, the RCMP raided the home of one of his associates, Lauréat Tardif, who lived with his widowed mother on St. Louis street in the oldest part of the city. There they found valuable evidence in the form of notebooks and a diary which gave in minute detail the activities of extremist nationalists and named all the "higher-ups" (called The Committee) of its organization. They were, according to Tardif's papers and as reported by Winslow:[21]

Abbé Lionel Groulx of Quebec
René Chaloult, member of the Provincial Assembly
Paul Bouchard of Quebec (now in Mexico)
J.E. Grégoire, former Mayor of Quebec
Abbé Pierre Gravel, *curé* of St. Roch parish
Philippe Hamel, a Quebec dentist
Oscar Drouin, Provincial Minister of Trade
J. Ernest Drolet, Quebec journalist
Victor Barbeau, Quebec journalist
Hermas Bastien
Demet Baril of Montreal
Olivar Asselin of Montreal
Fernand de Haerne of Montreal
Paul Gouin of Montreal

The list reads like a Who's Who of Quebec nationalism in the thirties. *Abbé* Lionel Groulx, a fascist and an antisemite, was the nationalist mentor of the young intellectuals of that generation. He was a professor of history at the University of Montreal. Invited by the Saint-John-

the-Baptist Society to teach Canadian history in Quebec
City in 1937, he was not allowed to teach at Laval University so he went to the Palais Montcalm. This might explain
his regular presence in Quebec City in the following years.

Oscar Drouin, Philippe Hamel, Ernest Grégoire and
René Chaloult had all been members of the extremist-na-
tionalist wing of the Action libérale nationale (ALN), a
splinter group of the Liberal Party, before they established
a new party in 1937, the Parti National.[22] Their platform
was inspired by Charles Maurras' "integral nationalism,"
and Oscar Drouin's favorite rallying cry was: "Quebec to
the French-Canadians." After having left the Union Nationale in 1936, Paul Gouin, scion of a prominent French-
Canadian family, son and grandson of two of the province's
premiers, Lomer Gouin and Honoré Mercier, was still
head of the ALN the following year. The brand of nationalism the ALN fiercely advocated was very similar to the
one preached by the Parti National and both were the
political offspring of Lionel Groulx's teachings of "national doctrine." Hoping to create a national popular front,
Paul Gouin entered negotiations with Paul Bouchard,
editor of the openly and proudly fascist magazine *La
Nation,* but nothing came out of that endeavour because
Bouchard ran as an Independent Liberal in the Lotbinière
federal by-election of December 27, 1937.

By the time of the provincial election of 1939 Oscar
Drouin had left the Parti National and joined the Liberal
Party to be rewarded with the Ministry of Trade. Paul
Gouin resuscitated the ALN the day after the Third Reich
invaded Poland in 1939, to protest against the Jews and
the bankers that were allegedly leading the world into
another war. During World War II he was behind the
fascist and anti-semitic newspaper *L'Union* and he co-
founded the Bloc populaire canadien, writing its platform.

J. Ernest Drolet was a lawyer, an alderman in Quebec City and the publisher of the short-lived pro-Pétain magazine *La Droite* whose publication was forbidden in April 1941. The others mentioned on the list were mainly university professors — Victor Barbeau, Hermas Bastien — or long-time nationalist activists — Fernand de Haerne, Demetrius Baril — who were all close to *Abbé* Groulx and his Action française before World War II.

Abbé Pierre Gravel was a long-time friend of the Union Nationale's leader Maurice Duplessis and an ardent proponent of fascism. More intriguing is the case of the famous journalist and polemicist Olivar Asselin who died in 1937. Either his presence on the list is a mistake, or he was involved in the activities of the ALN or the Parti National which provided the nucleus of the Iron Guard.

The evidence found in Tardif's home showed that while he was a student at Laval University, he had come under the influence of *Abbé* Lionel Groulx, of *Abbé* Pierre Gravel and, *quelle surprise!* of Father Ignatius Eschmann. After Canada had joined the Allies, *Abbé* Gravel and *Abbé* Groulx had "continued to hold clandestine meetings with the young nationalist group of which Tardif was a member."[23] According to Tardif's diary, *Abbé* Gravel tirelessly expounded the advantages of National Socialism and other German superiorities. One evening when the *Abbé* Gravel was too ill to hold a meeting, his group met instead with Father Eschmann. That evening, Father Eschmann told his young followers that French Canadians shared nothing with the rest of Canada because of their superior culture and their different language and religion. They should remember as well that nazism was born out of Germany's misery under the Versailles Treaty.

The associates of Lauréat Tardif were, according to the seized papers: Father Simon Arsenault, s.v., *Abbé* Ed.

V. LaVergne, recently deprived of his parish by order of
the Cardinal, officials of the Socitété Saint-Jean Baptiste
such as Edouard Coulombe and many others whose names
Winslow didn't mention. These documents explained
"the formation of a Nationalist organization " and gave the
different names under which this organization went without Winslow mentioning them. Lauréat Tardif regularly
wrote to Italian consular officers and other Axis repre-
sentatives and ended all his letters with a "salute of 45
degrees." In his notebook, Tardif very often refered to Saul
Aguilar, Argentine Consul General in Ottawa. In Quebec
City, Commander J.E. Corriveau, Honorary Consul for
Argentina, 78 Moncton Street, was "a member of Father
Arsenault's new fascist order and a regular attendant at
Abbé Gravel's pro-Nazi convocations in St. Roch, Quebec."[24] One could find in other notebooks the names and
addresses of the Yugoslav, Italian, Polish, and Columbian
Consuls in Montreal.[25] Listed as well, the name and address of Eugène Deloncle, (2 avenue Rodin, Paris 16e,
France, entre de la Tour et Mignard), a prominent and
violent proponent of full collaboration with the Nazis who
had established in September 1940 the Mouvement social
révolutionnaire successsor to the Comité secret d'action
révolutionnaire (C.S.A.R.), known as La Cagoule, which
tried to overthrow the French government in 1936.

Also alarmed was the Press Censor for Canada. In a
letter to Inspector A. Drysdale of the RCMP dated March
13, 1942 he observed that the Iron Guard's leaflet was
vintage Nazi propaganda and "was based on exactly the
same technique used by the Germans in the Sudeten
countries and every country where there lives an important minority." He keenly observed that although the
pamphlet's style was foreign in its inspiration, it fell on
very favourable grounds. He warned that the success of the

war effort could suffer if distribution of such literature went on unabated. The authors and distributors of the Iron Guard propaganda should be handed a stiff sentence before a court in order to: "deter would-be imitators from spreading further Goebels (sic) propaganda."[26] Linking that leaflet to the well-known and established Nazi propaganda pattern and equally eager to know more about the Iron Guard was the Under-Secretary of State for External Affairs.[27]

Acording to the RCMP's files, the main suspect was 21 and employed in the managing of a confectionary stand. He boasted his organization had 2000 members in one district. When asked where he had found the money to meet the expediture incurred by writing and distributing circulars such as "CANADIANS! LEND YOUR MONEY!", the suspect replied: "Prior to the United States joining up with the Allies, we could easily get the money required, but since then, we are having some difficulties in getting it, but we are still in a position to get some."[28]

The commanding officer of the "C" Division of the RCMP, H.A.R. Gagnon, did not buy the suspect's story of the Iron Guard having 2000 members in one district. The total membership of the Iron Guard was no more than five or six youngsters, who would all be interrogated in due time. He believed that there was one nationalist organization using many different names to create the illusion of a momentum. For example, the League for the Defence of Canada, Social Credit, Ligue des Patriotes, Jeune Laurentie, that was all the same group. Contrary to the opinion held by Rollin R. Winslow, Gagnon firmly believed that these movements did not draw a large group of people and their leaders exerted very little influence. They were:

"such persons as (Name Witheld), former (Name Witheld) of Quebec City,[29] (...), the Reverend Gravel."[30]

Altough he held these organizations to be insignificant in influence and size Gagnon nevertheless believed there was sufficient evidence to curtail their activities. What he had in mind was internment rather than court trials because trials "will only assist in spreading the propaganda of this group." If the RCMP secured enough evidence the various supects — the higher-ups in the French-Canadian nationalist movement[31]— could be charged with conspiracy against the security of the State.

The higher-ups of the Iron Guard actually were never bothered. Before the RCMP could raid the homes of its leaders a local radio station and newspapers reported that raids were in progress; consequently, the other raids were useless.[32] "It is regrettable, but unavoidable," wrote a RCMP official, "because sooner or later the news would have been given to the newspapers by those who had an interest in hindering the investigation because of their involvement with that organization."[33] In Winslow's mind that was further evidence that "subversive" elements were extremely well organized in Quebec.

Raymond Chouinard and Lauréat Tardif bore the brunt of the RCMP's offensive against subversive activities in Quebec City. Chouinard was charged with three offences under Section 39A of the Defence of Canada Regulations. According to the RCMP, the suspect at first denied all knowledge of the source of the leaflets, but subsequently admitted full responsibility for their preparation and distribution. He signed a full confession and explained the reasons for his political activities. As a student he had come under the influence of teachers promoting "national disunity" — in the words of a RCMP officer. A priest — whose name is withheld in the reports

— was especially held responsible for the youngster's actions. He had exerted a strong and lasting influence on the suspect and on many other young men. Chouinard's steadfast claim that he had acted alone never convinced the RCMP which always maintained that the youngster had acted upon the instructions of someone else.[34]

On March 11, 1942 Raymond Chouinard appeared in court only to hear that the sentencing was postponed.[35] According to Constable Dubé, the primary suspect in the distribution of offensive circulars in Quebec City on March 7 and 8, 1942, although intelligent, bright, talented and well educated could be mentally unstable since he had seriously injured his spinal cord two years earlier. The Court had requested that he be mentally examined so that he would be handed an appropriate sentence. Mentally sound or not, the young man stated repeatedly to police officers that he strongly supported the Axis powers.[36] He finally was convicted on all counts and sentenced by Judge Thomas Tremblay to two months on each charge, the sentences to run concurrently.[37]

Chouinard may have not remained idle for a very long time. On May 19, 1942, Winslow reported that during one of his bi-monthly visits to Quebec City, Henri Coursier, the French consul in Montreal, who was in charge since the transfer of Ricard, had unsuccessfully endeavoured to contact the "Iron Guardist" Raymond Chouinard. Raymond Chouinard visited the consulate after Coursier's return to Montreal and was told by its secretary, Mr. Lorent, that Coursier had wished to offer him the thanks of France for the literature which he had distributed condemning the action of the British in the bombing of the Renault factories. He assured him that France would remember and would reward him after the war. In the meantime he should not hesitate to call upon consulate if he felt it could be of any service to him as it looked favorably upon the activities of the Iron Guard. Lorent expressed an oblique reservation when he suggested that Chouinard's group should cease the distribution of pamphlets because it represented visible evidence of their activities. They should instead organize many small but secret groups while awaiting the day when they could be utilized to better purpose.[38]

Because Lauréat Tardif was luckier, smarter or less gullible, he avoided going to jail. He pleaded not guilty and was sentenced to two fines of 25 dollars each. Winslow attributed that light sentence to the talent of Antoine Rivard and "to the strategy of the police in withholding evidence that might be useful in rounding up some of the leaders."[39] Interestingly enough, this unemployed youngster living with his widowed mother at 69 St. Louis Street was indeed defended by one of the most successful criminal lawyers in the city, if not the province: Antoine Rivard, close collaborator of Maurice Duplessis.

There were suggestions made to Louis St. Laurent that some nationalist leaders be interned during the war but they remained just that: suggestions. Winslow reported that in a private meeting with him, Colonel Leon Lambert, head of the Provincial Police, told him that he had made a special trip to Ottawa in 1941 to have *Abbé* Pierre Gravel interned but that he failed to persuade the Minister of Justice, Mr. Ernest Lapointe, to take action.[40]

Soon after these events Raymond Chouinard left for Montreal where he had a long and successful career in radio and television under the name of Jacques Normand. In a telephone conversation with the author, Jacques Normand denied being Raymond Chouinard, and stated clearly that it was not his real name. He had never heard of Lauréat Tardif and had not been living at 22½ Du Roi street in Quebec City in 1942. Interestingly enough though, in his own book *Les Nuits de Montréal* he corrected his sidekick Roger Baulu for having written that his real name was Jacques Chouinard. "Wrong one more time. It is Raymond."[41] As far as the Iron Guard is concerned, Normand said in two phone conversations that he had never dabbled in politics, that he was already living in Montreal in the year 1940. However, in his biography *De Québec à Tizi-Ouzou* he relates how he went to jail during the war for having written and distributed propaganda literature against the Allies.[42]

Laurentia nous voilà !

The activities of the parishless Father Lavergne, of Father Arsenault, "a fascist who was trained as such in Rome," of *Abbé* Pierrc Gravel or of *Abbé* Lionel Groulx, "the founder of a movement for an independent clerical Laurentia" were not curbed in any way during the war.[43] Father Arsenault was head of the Scholasticate of the Fathers of Saint Vincent de Paul and was very much involved with organizations like the Jeunes Laurentiens and the Société Saint-Jean-Baptiste (SSJB), and he was editor of the magazine *La Droite*. His extremist nationalist views coupled with strong anti-democratic overtones would again catch the attention of the RCMP a few months later when an agent reported he had forcefully expressed these views in a SSJB meeting gathering of some 400 people.[44]

On the contrary, these activities seemed to have gathered momentum as Europe was becoming more fascist with each passing month. The Carillon flag, the unofficial emblem of Laurentia, if seldom displayed in the first two years of Winslow's assignment in Quebec City (1939-1940) was two years later widely exhibited at every possible

occasion. "At French-Canadian fêtes and on national holidays, it flies over the Cardinal's Palace alongside the Papal
flag and on such holidays as Corpus Christi and Saint-
Jean-Baptiste, it is everywhere in evidence, some house-
holders and merchants having replicas large enough to
cover the sides of buildings." Individuals and organizations eagerly followed that trend:

> "All the more prominent French-Canadian nationalists
> such as René Chaloult, *Abbé* Lavergne, *Abbé* Gravel et
> cetera, wear small replicas of the flag in their lapels and at
> convocations of French-Canadian youth organizations
> and many other nationalist groups; the members swear
> allegiance to the flag and bear it in processions. It is now
> seen in the form of posters on the windows of automobiles
> and some nationalist groups, like SSJB, carry the flag on
> at least some of their letterheads.[45]"

The RCMP reported that on November 10, 1942,
André Laurendeau, General Secretary of the League for
the Defence of Canada had addressed a meeting of the St.
Jean Baptiste Society attended by almost 1300 people in
Quebec City. "At the opening, the chairman recited an oath
to the flag of Carillon with the audience saluting in the
fascist manner." In his speech Laurendeau conveyed "the
idea that certain legislation would be more fatal for the
French Canadians than the horrors of military defeat."[46]

To compound Winslow's growing worries, the people
he saw as friendly to the Allied cause were steadily losing
ground and, in some cases, ways of making their voices
heard. To his dismay, the great majority of the clergy sided
with Vichy — exceptions like Father Georges-Henri
Lévesque, "a highly respected figure here (...) whose activities were not in doubt"[47] were few and far between.
Supporters of the Allies in the clergy suffered a serious
blow when Canon Joseph Alfred Chamberland resigned as

director-general of *L'Action Catholique*. He gave as a reason his poor health but Winslow and his informers in Quebec City doubted this reason very much.[48]

There were rumours that *Abbé* Arthur Maheux, another supporter of the Allies, had been dismissed from his work as Professor at Laval University. At first, Winslow did not believe that piece of information, but learned from *Abbé* Maheux himself that it was indeed true. In the course of a private conversation, *Abbé* Maheux told him "that Monsignor Roy, the Rector, would not permit him to give any more lectures to which the public would be admitted." He feared they could raise too much controversy. Winslow believed that Monsignor Roy had been converted to the Vichy cause by former French consul Ricard. Earlier an "interesting conversation" had taken place between *Abbé* Maheux and Winslow.[49] *Abbé* Maheux had told Winslow that he had received anonymous threatening letters because of his book *Ton histoire est une épopée*. He confirmed the rumour that one large bookstore of Montreal — believed to be owned by *Le Devoir* —refused to sell his book. When asked the reason for such a boycott, *Abbé* Maheux explained that Georges Pelletier, editor-in-chief of *Le Devoir*, had once told him he hated the English because in the days following the Conquest, British soldiers had burned his ancestors' home near Rimouski. Maheux had sarcastically replied that one of his ancestors was killed on the Island of Orleans by the Hurons and that if he followed Pelletier's policy he should get a gun and kill the remnants of the Huron nation at Loretteville.

The results of the conscription referendum held on April 27, 1942, would not assuage Winslow's anxieties, with the population of Quebec voting roughly 77% No to Premier MacKenzie King's request to be freed from his promise of not enforcing conscription in Canada for over-

seas service. Like many observers, Winslow attributed the
defeat of the Yes side to the poor campaign conducted by
the federal government as well as to the fact that for a
quarter of a century the Liberal Party had been elected on
the oft-reiterated promise that it would never enforce
conscription of French Canadians like the treacherous
Conservatives had in 1917. To renege on their word at the
last minute was a sure recipe for failure. The confidence
that the United States would protect French Canada in
case of invasion played an important part in the victory of
the No side, as well as the conviction that Canadians could
successfully fight the war while remaining at home.[50]

The victory of the opponents of conscription gave
momentum to the brand of nationalism Winslow feared
most: the one championed by *Abbé* Groulx, *Abbé* Gravel,
Father Simon Arsenault, René Chaloult and Philippe
Hamel. He saw it as a very serious threat to the security of
North America, already threatened "more than ever in its
history" by foreign foes. In the conclusion which "repre-
sents the purely personal views of the writer" of a dispatch
to the American minister in Ottawa, Winslow shared with
him his concern that American investments were no
longer safe in the Province of Quebec:

> "(...) this vote, the plan to expropriate the power industry;
> the heavy public debt of the Province: the spread of totali-
> tarian propaganda through youth organizations under the
> leadership of such men as *Abbé* Gravel, Father Arsenault
> and a host of others, are all straws in a wind which bodes
> ill for American capital here. In Provincial bonds alone
> these investments amount to something like $70,000,000.
> National barriers could be erected that could hinder the
> trade between the two countries."[51]

French-Canadian "most selfish and narrow nationalism" had continental ambitions, warned Winslow: it tried

very hard "to retain its hold over French Canadians in the United States and Anglo-Canada" as was evidenced by the activities of the Saint John the Baptist Society and the French-Canadian clergy. "In the six month period, ending December 31, 1941, the Consulate issued 72 immigration visas to FC priests and nuns, few of whom spoke English." Winslow laid the responsibility for the growth of nationalism and of religious intolerance straight at the door of the Catholic Church. For instance, in 1941 the newspaper *l'Action Catholique* had claimed that the "(...) 'French-speaking Catholics were the only truly devout ones', thus upsetting the Irish to such an extent that it eventually amended its words."[52]

It was imperative, suggested Winslow, that schools stop teaching hatred of the British and give more importance to the teaching of the English language. Premier Adélard Godbout was trying to implement such changes but there was no guarantee of his success, and educational reforms would not suffice anyway to redress the situation. More needed to be done: "(...) at this critical time French-Canadians had to be plainly told where to 'head-in' and be made to 'play ball' with the rest of Canada and the United States."

Who could convince French-Canadians to play ball with the rest of North America? Desperate situations called for desperate measures and U.S. President Franklin D. Roosevelt would be the most effective speaker: "President Roosevelt is very highly regarded by French Canadians and, if he were to speak to them in a fireside chat for a few minutes in strong but friendly terms concerning the effect of their plebiscite vote upon the people of the United States it might, in fact I firmly believe it would, avert eventual bloodshed here. No time could be more ripe as something should certainly be done to check the present headlong rush toward separation."[53]

The Canadian government had failed to nip these dangerous trends in the bud and now found itself in a quandary. To intern nationalist tenor René Chaloult as Mayor Camilien Houde had been several years earlier, for instance, would be a perfect recipe for making him a martyr to the nationalist cause. Less effective, but obviating criticism of U.S. interference in Canadian politics would be an address of Roosevelt to the American people with only indirect references to French Canada. "Once the FC nationalist leaders learn from a high and authoritative American source that we will have no 'truck or trade' with their separatism they will lose some of the wind in their sails. A ten minute talk by President Roosevelt addressed in the French language to Quebec might change the course of history in the Province of Quebec."[54]

Pierrepont Moffat replied somewhat laconically to Winslow that "(...) Mr. Roosevelt is one of the few Americans who knows that particular situation in all its ramifications, and that Mr. King during their talk was surprised at his knowledge of the forces and counter-forces at play."[55] Moffat was concerned by the turn of events but was not panicky like his Quebec City counterpart. "The situation is sour and I fail to see the pattern of its improvement," he wrote, but he did not fear bloodshed or the establishment of a Vichy-style Republic on the banks of the St. Lawrence river.

Henry Torrès, French politician of the Third Republic, prominent lawyer and author of a book on Pierre Laval evocatively entitled *La France trahie* (France Betrayed) addressed a memorandum — The Fifth Column in French Canada — to the Office of the Coordinator of Information (forerunner of the CIA) in Washington in the spring of

1942. The OCI had in turn sent a copy to the Department of State.[56] Henry Torrès had spent some time in the province of Quebec in September 1941. He had been the guest of the Bar Association of Montreal at the opening of the session. He had also given a speech at Radio-Canada where he had vehemently attacked the Vichy regime and Admiral Darlan, immediately infuriating *Le Devoir* which did not waste any time informing its readers that *Maître* Torrès was Jewish and was wrong, in that order!

In *The Fifth Column in French Canada* Torres echoed many of the American consul's preoccupations. He believed that opposition to conscription was just one aspect of the autonomist movement in the Province of Quebec. Linking that movement to the autonomist Flanders and Alsace-Lorraine movements in Europe, he saw the three of them led by nationalist extremists working hand in hand with priests who wielded an extraordinary influence on an illiterate peasant population. Even though Bishop Villeneuve remained loyal to the Commonwealth and to Great Britain, as had remained the Archbishop of Malines towards Belgium and the Archbishop of Strasbourg towards France, he was as powerless as they were in influencing and controlling the lower clergy. French-Canadian autonomists were a dangerous threat to Canadian unity and might seriously harm Canada's effort at total war, warned Torrès.

Not only did the Vichy government "tune its propaganda to them but it generously contributed to their movement through diplomats such as M. Henri Coursier, General Consul of France in Montreal. Furthermore, the Vichy government sent to Quebec numerous emissaries, 'many protected by their monastic cloth.' French Canada hosts many French priests who come here with a propaganda mission, such as the director of the Collège Stanislas, Canon Méjecaze, who, last fall stayed at the Arch-bishop's Palace of Montreal after he had been the guest of the French Legation at Ottawa. One of the French bishops best known for his Vichy sympathies, Mgr. Beaupin, is in charge of recruiting and sending these spiritual ambassa-dors here."

"The Vichy regime broadcasts special daily programs for French Canada, from 10:00 to 11:15. Radio-Paris, under direct control of the Germans, has a Radio-Canada program which is presented as 'the message of France to New France,' which gives a tribune to many Canadian priests, or at any rate those who claim to be, interned in France, to praise the German authorities for the good care they receive."

Unbeknownst to Torrès, the Federal Communication Commission, Division of Foreign Broadcast Intelligence Service monitored Vichy shortwave broadcasts beamed to North America specifically addressed to French Canadi-ans. In confidential Special Report #18, dated August 19, 1942, they analyzed 13 programs which had been broad-cast between May and August 10, 1942. "It appears that half of the coded statements concerning French Canada are either overtly subversive with respect to French-Cana-dian loyalty to Canada (coded themes numbers 1 and 2: 'French-Canadians consider France as their Fatherland' and 'France considers French-Canadians as Frenchmen.') or are presumably intended to promote subversive atti-tudes (coded theme number 3: 'French-Canadians are being persecuted because of their French attitudes and actions.')[57] Interestingly enough, from January to May 1942, very few references to French Canada had been monitored while the period of mid-May to mid-June wit-nessed the apex of the subversive broadcasts. Could it be that the Vichy regime saw the outcome of the plebiscite of

27 April, 1942 as a Yes from French Canadians to the National Revolution of Marshal Pétain? Could it be that in an underhanded way the Vichy regime had helped the No side and became less discreet once victory was theirs?"

"Marshal, we are here. This is (the) rallying cry of all those of our tongue and of our race, independently of frontiers which divide us."[58]

Since the "Oeuvre des Trac"(sic) of Montreal has published a substantial booklet containing the Marshal's main messages, you have been able to measure what our leader expects from the Youth of France."[59]

The French-Canadian autonomist movement was a rebellion against Anglo-Saxon imperialism, witness the book of "Bostolaire Volue(?)" entitled *Separatism* and published in Montreal in 1937, that stated "We shall be condemned to death if we do not break once and for all with the deadening ideology of Anglo-Saxons."[60]

Full of Gallic mysticism, defined by Marshal Pétain in September 1940 as: "the French spirit which includes the spiritualism which our civilization has come to know," sharing "ties of blood, language and religion" with France, French Canadians were urged to join the Latin bloc with Spain and Latin America under the cultural hegemony of France.[61]

The Vichy regime was not the sole beneficiary of such propaganda: "Behind Vichy the Axis had a vested interest in exciting the population in Quebec to oppose Canadian "imperialism" in order to create important difficulties for the Ottawa government," claimed Torrès.

The rhetoric and the slogans heard from opponents of the plebiscite during the campaign never presented World War II as a defense of democracy or of Christianity, but as a conflict between imperialist powers, making opposition to conscription a rejection of imperialism. François-Albert Angers had written in the monthly *L'Action nationale* that French-Canadians wanted to live in peace and firmly refused to become entangled in quarrels between the great powers, whose pride and ambitions were a permanent cause of wars. Ottawa was guilty of putting the interest of the Allies above the ones of the motherland of French Canadians.

To realize that opposition to conscription is just an aspect of opposition to any participation of Canada in World War II, one has only to read the nationalist press of the time: *Le Devoir, La Boussole, l'Autorité, L'Union, L'Oeil, Le Droit*. In its December 31, 1941 issue, the daily *Le Devoir* doesn't express any wish to see the Allies win: instead it exhorts the warring parties to fraternally shake hands in order to relieve humanity from war. Torrès suggested it would be interesting to compare that issue with the issue of December 31, 1939 of the newspaper of Léon Degrelle, published in Brussels, the *Pays Réel*, whose publisher was wearing the German uniform in the Anti-Soviet Legion.

Mr. Pierre Viviers, editor of *l'Oeil*, Mr. Georges Pelletier, editor-in-chief of *Le Devoir*, and Mr. Omer Héroux, also of *Le Devoir, Mr. Dostaler O'Leary, Canadian editor of the French pro-Nazi newspaper Je suis Partout*, many priests and MPPs were members of the ultra-nationalistic Order of Jacques Cartier which published a virulently anti-British newspaper, *L'Émerillon* All these people frequently praised the Vichy regime on the radio.

L'Oeil and *Le Devoir* constantly exalted the "patriotism of Admiral Darlan" as well as the policy of "collaboration" with Germany for having stopped the war and for bringing a just and long-lasting peace. *L'Union,* on April 7, lavished praise on "the heroism and sublime words of Laval whose heart, revived with patriotism, is possessed by the love of France." Dostaler O'Leary, who was also president in Canada of a committee of *"Union culturelle des peuples d'Amérique"* and in charge, with Consul Henri Coursier, of curious *"journées pan-latines"* — also advocated a "dignified collaboration with the conqueror in order to save the name of France." Many French-Canadians, like the writer Eugène Achard, claimed that "in the end the armistice played against Hitler and in favour of France and its allies."

In Quebec City, at one of its meetings against conscription, the SSJB had leaflets signed The Iron Guard and entitled "Canadians! Lend Your Money!" distributed. That incident worried Torrès as much as it had Winslow.

Torrès believed it was highly significant that in a country where there was no "Jewish problem," a sudden and violent antisemitism arose, in spite of popes' encyclicals and of books written by eminent members of the clergy condemning racism in the name of universal catholicism. Following an anti-conscription meeting in Montreal, students showed their enthusiasm by breaking the windows of several Jewish-owned shops on one of the commercial streets of the city. The weekly anti-semitic publication *Chez Nous* had been founded and published Canadian-style articles straight out of Nuremberg's infamous *Der Stürmer*. It was banned, but the same propaganda in a subtler form "is disseminated through nationalist newspapers," wrote Torrès.

"One has to hope that such activities and propaganda will be stopped," emphasized Torrès. "The spiritual influence of the United States could and should powerfully contribute to that end by using press, lectures and, above all, radio. The author of this memorandum, for one, is ready to work with the competent authorities to prepare a rational plan to that effect," concluded Torrès.

A Circle of Friends

Winslow didn't hear from Roosevelt but from J. Edgar Hoover. Again, Hoover enlisted the help of the Assistant Secretary of State, Adolf A. Berle, to help the FBI conduct "an extensive and exceedingly discreet investigation into the activities, background and associations of one Gerard Joseph Oliver, 793 West Grand Boulevard, Detroit, Michigan. This individual is known to have corresponded with Kurt Frederick Ludwig, and there are some indications of his possible involvement in espionage activities, either in connection with the Ludwig group or independent of them."[62]

Oliver corresponded in the early part of 1941 with some individuals in Canada, "and a short time previous to that visited that country." Hoover requested information about them from the RCMP. The RCMP then turned to Winslow to get that information, since the individuals under suspicion lived in Quebec City. They were Charles de Koninck and Henry Medard Octave Putnam. The attention of Winslow soon focused on the former.

Mr. de Koninck was a professor of philosophy at Laval University and its future dean. A devout Catholic, he had wanted to become a Benedictine monk but his frail health had prevented him from doing so. He had applied for registration as an American citizen back on January 22, 1940 but the State Department had rejected his demand. When he wished to go to the U.S. in the autumn of 1941, he learned that no documents would be given to him since he remained under a presumption of expatriation. However, on Christmas Eve, using his Canadian passport, he received a border-crossing card.

During that process, he had given as a general reference his American students at Laval, and one Nathalie Lincoln was among them. For reasons Winslow does not mention in his reports, she was the subject of repeated inquiries by the police.[63]

On March 2, 1940, Miss Lincoln brought affidavits to the American consulate to be executed in connection with the immigration cases of two Austrians she wanted to assist in coming to Canada. They were a Dr. Otto Lederer and one Paul Lazarus. She said she did not know them but was acting upon the request of "The Committee for Catholic Refugees from Germany" (2559 West 14th Street, corner 8th Avenue, New York.) The suspicious Winslow noticed and pointed out that she had stated in the affidavits that both Dr. Otto Lederer and Paul Lazarus were her friends and that she knew them well. At first she insisted that the affidavits be nonetheless executed but moments later changed her mind without a word of explanation.[64] The day after, the ever-diligent Winslow informed the State Department that according to information received from British Intelligence service Dr. Otto Lederer was at one time connected with illicit arms traffic in Europe, but nothing was known about Paul Lazarus.[65]

He confirmed to the State Department that Miss Lincoln and the de Konincks were indeed friends, that she phoned and visited them often. She used to live at the Chateau Frontenac. She had left for New York City at the beginning of June 1942 and had requested that her mail be forwarded to her new address. However, in July Winslow had seen her twice in Quebec city.

While living in Quebec City, Miss Lincoln had befriended two Dominican priests, Father Florientine Guttierrez, a pupil of de Koninck, and Father Crescente

Gonzalez. Both these priests were under suspicion of espionage because of their ill-timed attraction to faraway and exotic places. Father Gonzalez had phoned the American consulate in the summer of 1941 to explain that he wanted to go to Iceland to cater to the religious needs of American troops stationed there. The obvious reply was that American priests already provided these services.[66] On November 19, 1941 the editor-in-chief of *The Nation* warned the students at the School of Social Sciences of Laval University that on a recent trip to Europe he: "had counted no less than 14 Axis bombers near Iceland which were much closer to Canadian harbours than British ports."[67] That kind of information might explain why the request of Father Gonzales was met with great suspicion.

During the fall (October 4, 1941), the Spanish Consulate General in Montreal had called to inquire if Fathers Guttierez and Gonzalez had received the transit visas they needed to reach French Indochina. As a result, Winslow warned the American consulate in Montreal about the activities of both priests.

Two other American friends of Professor Charles De Koninck were cause for concern to Winslow. Mgr. Francis C. Kelly, Bishop of Oklahoma and Reverend Pierre Eugène Conway(religious name Pierre Hyacinth), an American Dominican and a student of Professor De Koninck at the time: "had taken upon themselves the task of championing the cause of French Canadians"[68] as they understood it. Bishop Kelly's views that French Canadians wanted to be happy and that mandatory conscription would not help their legitimate pursuit of happiness were published in *l'Action Catholique*.[69] Winslow could not help wondering if these American friends of Professor de Koninck were motivated only by "their religious bias and racial preferences" or if they were "engaged in an effort to add fuel to a situation which might eventually cause trouble in the counsels of Allied Nations."[70]

After just two months in Quebec City, Father Conway had written a booklet entitled *French Canada's Life Vs Life's French Canada* which was an emotional rebuttal of an article on French Canada published in the October 19, 1942 issue of *Life* magazine. The School of Social Sciences of Laval University had published the booklet which the Provincial Tourist Bureau distributed free. On November 27, 1942,[71] Winslow invited Father Conway to register at the American consulate, this being merely a pretext to have a serious chat with the idealistic and misguided 27 year-old priest. Father Conway said that he had come to Quebec City to attend a course in philosophy at Laval University taught by Professor Charles de Koninck. Winslow reminded him that he was entitled to certain exemptions from expatriation under the Nationality Act of 1940, and that such exemptions were based, he believed: " (...) upon the supposition that members of the clergy residing abroad, would not enter into political affairs of other countries." He then admonished the young priest that: "it was not becoming of him as an American visitor to question the tolerance of Great Britain as regards French-Canadians (See p.6 of booklet) or otherwise take sides in Canada's extremely delicate racial problem."

After having forcefully expressed his opinion on the proper use of privileges granted to the "wearers of the cloth," Winslow asked Father Conway "if he would mind explaining the statement on page 22 to the effect that American and French-Canadian views on Vichy "are identical." Reverend Conway candidly asserted his conviction "that neither people were critical of Vichy but instead were very sympathetic." Upon which an ironic Winslow suggested that he seriously take up the task of "reading the

American newspapers." In the following days the American consulate cancelled Father Conway's passport.

On December 2, 1942[72] Professor de Koninck called at the consulate to renounce his American citizenship. He then insisted that his father's name was Louis and not Charles, notwithstanding that he had presented on February 9, 1940 a statement signed by his brother Andrew to the effect that their father Charles was naturalized.

Professor de Koninck stated that his father had lived "for a great many years" in a village near Amiens, France, where he worked as a building contractor. They had not spoken to each other for quite some years because the son had refused to join the father in the building trade. However, two years earlier, on January 22, 1940, Professor de Koninck had declared under oath that following his mother's death in Detroit in 1917, he had been brought up by Reverend Joseph Marx. In the opinion endorsed on the same form (no.213) American Vice-Consul Burke said de Koninck had recalled that his father who resided in Belgium had been interrogated at some length by the American consul in Ghent, Belgium, on September 30, 1930, when an application for a passport was made by Charles de Koninck. Winslow lost no time in informing de Koninck that his border-crossing card had been issued without the knowledge that he had close relatives in countries occupied by the enemy. Consequently, it had to be cancelled and authorization received from the department before a new visa could be issued.

Also according to Vice-Consul Burke, Charles de Koninck had expressed in 1940 his intention to obtain a certificate of derivative citizenship from the U.S. Department of Immigration and Naturalization in Detroit. He now claimed that he never obtained such a certificate. Back then, when he had applied for registration, Professor de Koninck had given the name of only one relative living in the U.S while now he could provide the name of three of them. The day before, Monsignor Roy, "reputed at one time to have been a strong Vichyite" had telephoned the consulate to inquire why a visa had not been granted to Professor de Koninck.[73]

Whatever happened next, Professor de Koninck lived happily ever after in Quebec City and Consul Winslow moved to his new posting in Tunisia.

Bibliography

Patricia Dirks, The Failure of l'Action libérale nationale, McGill-Queen's University Press, Montreal & Kingston, London, Buffalo, 1991

Jean-Louis Gagnon: Les Apostasies. Tome 1 et 2, Éditions La Presse, Montréal, 1985

Edited by Gregory S. Kealey and Reg Whitaker: RCMP Security Bulletins, The War Series, Part ll, 1942-1945, St. John's: Canadian Committee on Labour History, 1993.

Jacques Normand: Les nuits de Montréal, Montréal, Éditions La Presse, 1974

Jacques Normand: De Québec à Tizi-Ouzou, Montréal, Éditions Stanké, 1980

Archives
National Archives of the United States
Department of State Files, 1910-1944
Federal Communications Commission, Foreign Broadcasts Intelligence Service

National Archives of Canada
Paul Gouin Papers
French Canadian Nationalist Movement Communist Activities Within Quebec Province
National Archives of Quebec (Montreal)
    Paul Gouin Papers

National Archives of Quebec (Quebec)
Pierre Gravel Papers
Antoine Rivard Papers

Interviews

Raymond Chouinard a.k.a. Jacques Normand
Jean-Louis et Hélène Gagnon
Père Georges-Henri Lévesque, O.P.
S.T.

A Strange Sort of Hero:
French collaborators exiled in Quebec
after World War II

The Anglo-American landing on the beaches of Normandy on June 6, 1944, marked the beginning of the end for the collaborators, large or small, public or discrete, of the greater Nazi Europe and the National Revolution of the — by then almost 90 year-old — Marshal Pétain in France. Hardly two months later, on September 8, Pétain was taken to the Sigmaringen castle under German escort.

The idea of collaborating with the Nazi occupation forces, seriously compromised right from its initial enunciation in article 3 of the armistice agreement of June 1940, — which ordered French authorities to cooperate with the German military command — had nonetheless seen better days. Marshal Philippe Pétain was a World War I hero, a highly-decorated octogenerian called back to save a defeated nation. He bet on a short war which would inevitably culminate in the defeat of England and the definitive victory of the German Third Reich. For the forseeable future, in his analysis, Europe would be a Nazi playground.

Of all the occupied countries, France alone would undertake a national revolution in the wake of the German army to which it owed nothing but the opportunity to initiate it. The first order of business was to clean out all the undesirables who were, or so Pétain thought, associated with the hated Third Republic. From July to October

1940, the Vichy regime, named for the city where the new French government set up business, promulgated a series of exceptional laws aimed at Jews, Freemasons and Communists. During the week of August 23, 1940, the French Legion of Combatants was created[1]: by the end of 1941, it would count 1,500,000 members.

On October 24, 1940, Pétain met with the chancellor of the Third Reich, Adolf Hitler, at Montoire. At the head of a country reduced to two-fifths of its former size and divided into two zones — the northern, occupied zone and the so-called free or southern zone — by a demarcation line as impenetrable as a real border, Pétain perhaps thought that his position would permit him to obtain concessions from a dictator about whom the least one can say is that he was hardly ever disposed to concede anything.

The following day, newspapers splashed the photo of the historic handshake between Hitler and Pétain across their front pages. Six days later, on October 30, Pétain announced on Radio-Vichy that his regime would mark a break in history, it would be a "National Revolution" not constrained by any conditions, limits or span of time. The "National Revolution" had just entered the offical lexicon of French political vocabulary.

The National Revolution, with or without sincere collaboration with the German forces of occupation, stood on three ideological pillars: anti-Semitism, anti-Communism and anglophobia. As far as anti-Semitism went, the sinister train of raids, destitutions and summary executions began in 1941. On May 14 of that year, 1061 Jews were arrested in Paris by French police. The persecution accelerated quickly: on March 27, 1942, the first convoy of French Jews left for the death camps at Auschwitz, followed two months later — on May 29, 1942 — by the obligatory wearing of the yellow star by all Jews living in the occupied zone. Two months after that came the infamous round-ups of July 16 and 17, 1942 — the Winter Velodrome raid which would send 20,000 victims to Nazi extermination camps.

For the second pillar, anti-Communism, Germany took a leading role in the anti-Bolshevik crusade, as Pétain emphasized on July 7, 1941, at the ceremony of the creation of the Legion of French Volunteers Against Bolshevism. Pétain preferred to forget that hardly three weeks earlier, on June 22, Germany was still party to the Soviet-German non-aggression pact, and solemnly vowed to stand with Hitler in the struggle against Communism outside the borders of France.

Finally came anglophobia. The media and the politicians of the National Revolution relentlessly attacked perfidious Albion, that "Babylon of plutocracy and mother of parliamentary democracy."[2] This theme of an England worm-eaten by big capital and by democracy, with variations on it, each less imaginative than the last, would be hammered at by Vichy until the end of the war.

But the problem of the Resistance would soon raise its ugly head. The National Revolution, while still solidly anglophobic, anti-Semitic and anti-masonic, soon became anti-anything that opposed it. Special courts were quickly set up to judge resistants and members of the Maquis — the French Underground.

As the struggle against the internal enemy intensified, so did the number of organizations whose mandate was repression. In the free zone in the spring of 1941, Joseph Darnand founded the Legionnaire Security Service from the ranks of the French Legion of Combatants. The child had a military nature, unlike its political parent. Its volonteers were required to be ready to fight the internal enemy. Their solemn oath contained the following unambiguous words : "I swear to fight democracy, Jewish leprosy and Gaullist dissidence." The Security Service would soon have 30,000 members, of which from 12,000 to 15,000 were active. Special courts were established on August 1, 1941, whose purpose was to expeditiously punish all those who resisted the Revolution.

With the June 18, 1940 declaration by Charles de Gaulle from London, calling on Frenchmen to refuse to recognize the armistice and carry on the war, violent confrontations between partisans of a free France and supporters of sincere collaboration became more and more frequent. On many occasions, the Free French radio broadcasts from London attacked collaborators by their names. A warning soon reached the ears of all collaborators: you are the servants of the enemy and we will get you, we'll kill you like dogs. The underground Gaullist paper Bir-Hakeim published a list of collaborators, on which appeared, among others, the name of author Georges Simenon.

On November 11, 1942 the Anton operation took place, confirming what was already a virtual state of affairs: the Wermacht invaded the free zone and from then on occupied the entire territory of France.

On January 30, 1943, the Militia was created as a paramilitary organization of the Legonnaire Security Service. True to its origins, its aims were to combat terrorists and expose Jews. The Militia had about 30,000 adherents, about half of whom were active.[3] Created by Pierre Laval, it was placed under the command of Joseph Darnand.

On January 1, 1944 Darnand was named General Secretary for the Maintenance of Public Order. On January 27, 1944, pressured by the Germans who liked nothing more than having the locals do their dirty work, the Militia spread its activities to the whole of France. On March 20, 1944, the Militia, working with the Wermacht and the Gestapo, together attacked and overcame 400 resistants who had taken refuge on the Glières plateau in the Haute-Savoie region of the country. Shortly thereafter, they would repeat the exploit against the maquis in the Vercors region. On April 28, 1944, Pétain declared, "Whomsoever participates in the Resistance is guilty of compromising the future of France. This so-called liberation is the most deadly of mirages to which you may be tempted to succumb."

There were to be 2,500 summary executions of collaborators and other suspect individuals from the fall of 1943 until June 6, 1944.[4] After the Normandy landings, however, the civil war became generalized. On June 7, 1944, Darnand appealed to France in a radio address: "But in the struggle against anarchy and bolshevism, the ranks of the forces of order are open to all Frenchmen. As of tonight, I have mobilized the Franc-Garde of the French Militia. I call on all men to leave their places of work, to put their families in safe places, and to join their units in their appointed centres. French militia-members, stand and we shall save the country! (...)"

Darnand's call reaped a meagre harvest: the ranks of the Franc-Garde[5] would swell from less than a thousand in January 1944, to approximately 7,000 by the summer of the same year. In order to encourage ideological fervor which might be expected to flag during that summer when an Anglo-American invasion seemed imminent, the tidy sum of seventy thousand francs was offered in the Côte-d'Or region for denunciations of importance.[6] Commanded by the likes of Vaugelas, Dagostini and a certain Jacques Dugé de Bernonville,[7] the Franc-Garde undertook operations against the Resistance in the Massif Central, in Burgundy, in the Vercors and in the Alps. There were also the inevitable last-minute converts to the Resistance: the Allied cause became more popular as their victory seemed more and more inevitable.

On June 13, 1944, Darnand would see his power increased when Pierre Laval named him State Secretary for Internal Affairs. On August 6, 1944, Pétain — ceding to pressure from his entourage — sent a worried note to Laval: "For many months, reports have come to my attention concerning pernicious acts perpetrated by the Militia." Darnand replied sarcastically: "For the last four years I have received your compliments and congratulations. You encouraged me. And now, because the Americans are at the gates of Paris, you tell me that I will sully the history of France. You might have said so earlier." The war officially ended in Europe on May 8, 1945, one month after the German capitulation. According to historian Bertram Gordon, between 150,000 and 200,000 French men and women had belonged to one or another of the collaborationist movements. It is a surprisingly small figure, but large in comparison to the hardy 3,000 members of the Socialist Federations at the height of the Popular Front, in 1937.

Without necessarily resigning themselves to the coming defeat, many collaborators were now obliged to envisage the ultimate strategic retreat and flee the country. Some stubbornly refused, like Paul Touvier, Chief of the Second Bureau of the Rhône Militia and maniacal record-keeper. Considering himself innocent of any crimes, Touvier would not leave France except for very brief periods of time and even refused to seek refuge in the Province of Quebec, where he had been invited to reside after 1972.[8] Others succeeded in whitewashing themselves politically and had brilliant political or administrative careers in France, like François Mitterrand, the future socialist president, Maurice Papon, future prefect recently tried by a court in Lyon, and René Bousquet, future high civil servant.

Many active collaborators had to flee France, however, as their lives were in imminent peril. In the spring of 1944 they left for Germany or crossed furtively into Spain. They were taken in hand by the famous "rat line" which helped many war criminals and collaborators take refuge in South America. Others hid here and there, often in monasteries, waiting until they could find a way to escape punishment. A certain number would end up in Quebec. This was the case, among others, for Jacques Dugé de Bernonville, a hierarchical superior of Paul Touvier, who accepted the offer his subordinate would refuse almost thirty years later.[9] What follows are the stories of those whose traces we could find, as much as it proved possible to reconstitute them.

LIST OF CHARACTERS

Name: Georges Simenon.

Profession: Author.

Places of residence: 1940 to 1942 at Fontenay-le-Comte, in the Vendée region; 1942-1944: Saint-Mesmin, in the Vendée; autumn 1944: under house arrest at Sables-d'Olonne; spring 1945: the Hotel Claridge and at his apartment on the Place des Vosges in Paris.

Activities: Wrote for well-known collaborationist papers like *La Gerbe*, *Gringoire* and *Je suis partout*. Signed two contracts with the Continental Movie Company created by the Third Reich and financed by the German ministry of propaganda.

Judicial Dossier: The judicial police headquarters requests the Director of Foreigners and Passports to expel Georges Simenon from France.

Itinerary: London (end of September 1945), New York (October 5, 1945); Montreal (Autumn 1945).

★

Name: Paul Erwin Eberhard Reifenrath.

Profession: Journalist/Propagandist.

Aliases: Jean d'Alsace, Tonton, Leyzen, Chambord, Dumont, Paul-Éverard Richemont.

Political Affiliations: 1932 to 1934: Secretary-General of *Solidarité française* and editor of the paper of the name name; correspondent in Alsace-Lorraine for the ultra-nationalist paper *La Victoire* run by Gustave Hervé; 1934: collaborator of the weekly *Die Staatsreform* and of *l'Union paysanne*; principal figure in the anti-Semitic movement in Strasbourg; January 1, 1937: editor of *La Voix d'Alsace et de Lorraine*; author of: *Les Juifs en France mais surtout en Alsace*; founder of the weekly *La nouvelle voix d'Alsace*.

Means of escape: The Brothers of St. Gabriel

Itinerary: Arrived in Canada in the fall of 1947 or 1948; departed in 1951.

★

Name: Jacques Dugé de Bernonville.

Aliases: Jacques Benoît.

Political Affiliations: Belonged to the *Action française* Vannes section and was arrested there in 1926; chief of the

First Brigade of the Secret Revolutionary action Committee (C.S.A.R also known as *La Cagoule* - The Hood) in Paris; Rabat on October 18, 1941: named responsible for Jewish affairs by the Vichy Government; organized the Legionnaire Security Service in Rabat; Paris, 1942 — seconded to the Ministry of National Education; Chief officer of the permanent Franc-Garde of the French Militia; Paris, November 1942: Secretary of the African Phalanx; founder of the French Volunteer Corps; December 1, 1943: member of the Eighth Brandeburg Unit of the Waffen SS; January 1944: Commander of the Forces for the Maintenance of Order in Lyon; June 20-August 14, 1944: Military Governor of Lyon.

Judicial Dossier: Accused of collaboration with the enemy, of attacking state security, of arbitrary arrests, wilful arson, violence and theft. Condemned to death *in absentia* by the Court of Justice of Toulouse and by the Appeals Court of Toulouse.

Itinerary: Arrived in Canada on November 26, 1946.

*

Name: Dr. Georges-Benoît Montel.
Profession: Physician.
Alias: Gaston Ringeval.
Political Affiliations: Member of the Parti Populaire Français; Member of the Legionnaire Security Service; Member of the Militia; Assistant mayor of Annecy.
Places of residency: Annecy; Hidden at the Benedictine Abbey of St. Pierre de Solesmes
Judicial Dossier: On April 19, 1945, the Court of Justice of the Haute-Savoie condemned him to lifetime forced labour, with loss of citizenship and confiscation of property.

Itinerary: Arrived in New York in 1946; arrived in Montreal in September 1946.

*

Name: Dr. André-Charles Emmanuel Boussat.
Profession: Physician.
Alias: Alfred Bordes.
Political Affiliation: Militiaman in the Villeneuve-sur-Lot region.
Place of residency: Hidden at the Benedictine Abbey in Encalcat.
Judicial Dossier: Accused of collaboration with the enemy. Sentenced *in absentia* to lifetime forced labour, confiscation of property and loss of citizenship by the Court of the Lot-et-Garonne Département.

*

Name: Julien Labedan.
Profession: Interior Decorator.
Alias: Armand Bérard.
Places of residence: Saint-Gaudens; hidden at the Benedictine Abbey at Encalcat .
Political Affiliation: Member of the Militia; member of the Général Leclerc division.
Judicial Dossier: Sentenced to death.
Itinerary: Arrived in Canada in the summer of 1946.

*

Name: Jean-Louis Huc.
Profession: Water and forest warden.
Pseudonym: Jean Henry.

Places of residence: Saint-Gaudens; August 1945 - July 1946: hidden at the Encalcat abbey.

Political Affiliations: Member of the French Legion of Volunteers against Bolshevism; member of the Legionnaire Security Service; member of the Militia.

Judicial Dossier: Sentenced to 5 years of national disgrace.

Itinerary: Left France on July 13, 1946, arrived in Canada on July 30, 1946.

★

Name: Dr. Michel-Lucien Seigneur.
Profession: Physician.
Alias: Vincent Desgarets.
Places of residence: Verrière in the Vienne region; hidden at the Château d'Ars-sur-Formans.

Political Affiliations: member of the Cross of Fire; member of the Parti populaire français; member of the Legionnaire Security Service; member of the Militia and deputy chief of the Militia in Vienne; March 1944 - intern at the School for Militia Chiefs at Uriage.

Judicial Dossier: On March 28, 1945, the Court of Justice of Poitiers sentenced him to death *in absentia*.

★

Name: Roger Pau.
Places of residence: Creuse; hidden at the Château d'Ars-sur-Formans.

★

Name: Victor Keyserling.
Profession: Journalist.

Places of residence: Paris (1940-1944); Bordeaux (July 1944); Paris.

Activities 1940-1947: member of the Kurt Eggers SS, the only professional corporation of Nazi war correspondents; employed by the German Embassy in France; editor, translator and war correspondent for Radio-Paris; 1946-1947: correspondent of the British United Press' Montreal office, run by his cousin, Robert Keyserling.

Judicial Dossier: Indicted for attacking the exterior security of the State, detained 16 months, file subsequently closed.

Method of escape: An officer in the American army helped him cross into Spain.

Itinerary: Spain-Portugal-Canada; arrived on October 16, 1947 with a non-immigrant visa good for 6 months.

Departure: Under threat of deportation, left Canada on November 11, 1949.

*

Name: Gabriel Dorget.

Profession: Insurance salesman.

Aliases: Berger Dupuis, Gabriel-Olivier Dorget.

Political Affiliation: Member of the Cross of Fire before World War II, then of the French Social Party.

Places of residence: Pre-war: Paris; 1940 to 1942: caretaker of an estate at Herqueville in Normandie, belonging to French automobile magnate Louis Renault; 1942 to 1944: owner of a watermill near Eymet, in the Dordogne region.

Judicial Dossier: Sentenced *in absentia* to 20 years at hard labour by a court in Périgueux, the administrative capital of the Dordogne Département.

Escape route: Benedictine monks of the rue de la Source in Paris. Father Roméo Thibodeau.

Itinerary: Paris-Belgium-England; departed London on May 1, 1947, arrived on May 6 in Gander, Newfoundland.

★

Name: Dr. Masquin.
Profession: Physician.
Place of residence: St. Didier (near Carpentras, in Provence).
Itinerary: Spain-Montreal; legally entered Canada.

★

Name: M. Jacquet.
Alias: M. Gros.
Place of residence: Vienne, in the Dauphiné region.

★

Name Robert J. Garry.
Profession: Administrator in the Civil Service of French Indochina.
Activities: Close collaborator of Admiral Decoux.
Itinerary: Indochina-France; arrived in Canada in 1947.
Contact: Robert Rumilly, through Admiral Decoux

★

We have divided this account into three parts. The first recounts the movements of a number of Frenchmen accused of collaborating with the occupation forces of the Third Reich during World War II who sought refuge in Quebec. This part begins with the tribulations of Georges Simenon because they are typical of those of many of these fugitives. Simenon's pre-war political proclivities were right-wing extremist and they continued during the war, notwithstanding the writer's after-the-fact denials. Forced to flee France in a hurry, Simenon obtained a Mission Order from the French Government thanks to the intervention of Honorez de Konink, an adventurer who miraculously appeared and swore on his ancestors' graves that he witnessed Simenon's heroic resistance to the Nazi invaders. Simenon subsequently met with Georges Vanier, the Canadian Ambassador to France, and obtained the required Canadian visa. He led a quiet life with his family in Quebec, at the Esterel domain of Sainte-Marguerite-du-Lac-Masson, just north of Montreal. The only serious problems that troubled the family's idyllic Canadian existence concerned Simenon's unbridled passion for his future second wife, Denyse Ouimet, prior to his having taken formal leave of his first spouse. At a convenient time, Simenon left Canada and set up shop for several years in the United States.

Many other Frenchmen who threw their lot in with the Vichy regime had stories similar to Simenon's. They fled France using the same or similar esacape routes, arrived in Canada without publicity and became the darlings of the chic set in Montreal and Quebec City. Hope sprang eternal.

The second part relates the public struggle undertaken by many of the exiles in order to remain in Canada after their past became known. Unlike the well-oiled and cloaked system which helped them reach this country, the public hue and cry that followed their discovery brought, for many of them, a deportation order, and not the permanent residency visa promised by their influential French Canadian pro-Vichy friends. But some fugitives were never exposed, nor ever troubled, and this in itself raises some interesting questions.

The third and final part tells the astonishing story of a third-rate French Nazi propagandist, who, exiled in Quebec after the war, became a close adviser to Premier Maurice Duplessis.

1. The exiled collaborators

Inspector Maigret in America

As was the case for most of the Nazi collaborators who were quietly brought to Quebec after World War II, Georges Simenon showed extremist right-wing political sympathies well before the conflict erupted. During the 1930's he published articles in both right-wing and left-wing papers, but his preference was clearly for the right wing of the political spectrum, sometimes eagerly extremist. His ill-paid collaboration with the tony royalist monthly the *Courrier royal* stopped one month before the Popular Front won the 1936 French elections. The Count of Paris was determined that this publication avoid the violent and vindictive tone of Charles Maurras' *Action française.* Better to promote the quiet return to the monarchy, he said, in order to redeem France. This was too much for Simenon: if he could not take broad aim at liberalism, capitalism and democracy at the very time when the Left was about to take power in the country, he might just as well leave the publication and slam the door behind him. His sentiments on these questions would not diminish with time. To the contrary: his love for the people, he would declare in 1938, made him despise democracy.

From 1940 to 1942, Simenon lived in the Vendée region, more precisely at Fontenay-le-Comte, with his wife Tigy, his son Marc and Boule, their cook. All was well in the best of all occupied worlds, except, naturally, for the little frustrations that came from living in a country that was cut in half: no travel was possible without an *Ausweis*, the pass issued by the occupation authorities, good for only one trip, and non-renewable under normal circumstances. But Simenon would not flinch in his optimism: in 1941, he would write to his mother that he had every confidence in the German offensive and hoped to see the English quickly defeated.

Simenon would sign two contracts with the Kontinental film company, created by the Third Reich and financed by the German Ministry of Propaganda. The second contract, signed by him on March 19, 1942 gave the company exclusive use of the Inspector Maigret character. Simenon signed underneath Article 9 of the contract which stated:

"I declare and certify that I am French and of Aryan origin and undertake to bring you the documentary proof upon your request." Subsequently, according to his biographer Pierre Assouline, Simenon would feel remorse, but of an unusual kind, and, taking his pen in hand, he struck out the word "French", leaving only "of Aryan origin."[10] It was a gesture that spoke louder than words. And in case he could be thought to have been unaware of the nature of Kontinental Films, he would have been put right by the large bust of Reichsführer Adolf Hitler, which dominated the entrance to the company's prestigious offices at 104, avenue des Champs-Elysées.

His contacts with the cream of the crop of Paris collaborators began to bear fruit. His old pal Jean Luchaire, a beacon for the Parisian pro-Nazi literary world

and editor of *Nouveaux Temps,* had Simenon appointed to
the jury for the Nouvelle France literary award. Other
well-known collaborators sat with him on that jury: Abel
Bonnard, Abel Hermant and Alphonse de Châteaubriant.
Luchaire was even able to remedy one of Simenon's most
vexing frustrations, in obtaining a rare and much-sought
after permanent *Ausweis* with which he could travel freely
between the free and the occupied zones of France.
Simenon wrote for well-known collaborationist papers
such as *La Gerbe, Gringoire* and *Je suis partout*. He also kept
company with the "in" crowd of Franco-German clients
of the famous and ultra-chic Paris whorehouses like the
Sphinx and the One-Two-Two. Things were going at such
a brisk clip that he was even able to offer his wife a mink
coat.

Then, the first serious problem arose: Simenon got a
taste of his own medecine and was denounced as a Jew,
either by the French resistance in Vendée, or by his neigh-
bours in Fontenay-le-Comte who (it is improbable that we
will ever know for sure the source of the denunciation)
resented him carousing around when the enemy occupied
three-fifth of the country. This noted anti-Semite would
then have to prove to the satisfaction of the General Commissariat for Jewish Affairs that he was not a Jew, and that
his true family name was not Simon (a derivative of Shi-
mon), instead of Simenon. And so this Simenon, who not
so long ago had denounced the Rothschilds and the specu-
lators on the Paris stock market, who had pointed his
finger at Ixovtich, Zetivief and other Jews working in the
film industry, who had refused to help Jewish refugies
fleeing Belgium because, according to him, they were not
really Belgian, the author of *The Jewish Menace* and creator
of endless ugly literary characters to whom he gave typi-
cally Jewish surnames, this man of so many lofty moral

qualitities was ordered to prove his Aryan racial purity. The General Commissariat demanded his proof of non-Jewish origin as required by Article 1 of the law of June 2, which called for the certificates of baptism of three of his grandparents. If those were not available, he would have to produce his own certificate of baptism dated prior to June 25, 1940, and if he was married, the same proof was required of his wife.[11]

This posed quite a problem for Simenon, inasmuch as he was unable to get to his native Belgium because of the war. As an alternative, he boldly offered to drop his pants before the Commissioner and prove that he was uncircumcised! The offer was politely declined. Still, since he could not locate the required documents, Simenon once more called for help from his old friend Luchaire, president of the National Press Corporation and close acquaintance of Otto Abetz, German Ambassador in Paris. Luchaire gave him a letter of reference to which Simenon appended his own hand-written note addressed to the chief of police for Jewish questions in Paris. These letters have never been found — Assouline suggests this might be for the best — but they did resolve the problem inasmuch as Simenon soon received a letter from the Commissariat for Jewish Affairs, informing him that there was every reason to believe that Simenon's claims of Aryan origins were true.[12]

Shortly after this incident, in November 1942, Simenon moved his family to Saint-Mesmin, also in the Vendée region. They would remain there until 1944. In November 1943 and again in January 1944, the Gaullist monthly Bir-Hakeim included his name in a blacklist of collaborators and threatened him with proper punishment as soon as France was free. In the fall of 1944, he was under house arrest at the Hotel Roches Noires in Sables-d'Olonne, while an investigation into his activities in the Vendée was proceeding. Aided by his attorney, Maître Garçon, and by the Belgian Ambassador to France, Simenon was cleared of all accusations of criminal activities.

Simenon then arrived in Paris in the spring of 1945, living first at the Hotel Claridge and then at his apartment in the Place des Vosges. He had decided to leave the country, he would later confide to publisher Marcel Dumoncel, because he could not put up with the climate of denunciation that he judged 'truly revolting.' But there is no evidence whatever that the climate of denunciation that ate away at the French social fabric during the previous few years of Nazi occupation ever disturbed his peace of mind,[13] according to his biographer, Pierre Assouline.

In order to emigrate, Simenon first had to obtain an exit visa. This required that he prove that he had not collaborated with the Germans. The Belgian Embassy in Paris, always ready to lend a helping hand, obtained an authorization for Simenon, dated March 25, 1945, and endorsed by the French Ministry of Foreign Affairs, which allowed him to travel. Still, this authorization was by itself insufficient to leave. Then a shadowy figure emerged to help, the kind of person that seems to flourish in times of a general stampede. His name: Honorez de Koninck, well-spoken adventurer who claimed to be a Chargé de mission of the Belgian Embassy and a former commander of a Franco-Belgian resistance network. Despite the fact that he hardly knew Simenon, he vouched for the latter's conduct during the war, going so far as to tell Marcel Pagnol, influential president of the Society of Authors that on numerous occasions he called on the good offices of Simenon for particularly delicate missions, and that on each occasion, Simenon completely acquiesced to his requests, without hesitation and in full knowledge of the risks involved.[14] Overwhelmed with emotion, the panicked Simenon gave Honorez de Koninck his power of attorney in Paris, an act he would later have cause to bitterly regret, as it became clear that de Koninck's honesty was cut of the same cloth as his truthfulness.

Simenon cast his eye on Canada as his destination of choice when he learned that the Canadian Embassy was not particularly stingy in issuing visas. He undertook to discreetly approach his prey (strangely, this is not mentioned in any of his biographies); results soon followed. On June 4, 1945, the day after a meeting between Simenon and Canadian Ambassador Georges Vanier, the Canadian publisher Bernard Valiquette wrote to Vanier on behalf of the famous author. Simenon had considerable income, wrote Valiquette, and wished to purchase a permanent residence in Canada and to invest his capital there.[15] The following day, Simeon himself wrote to Georges Vanier to express his strong desire to go to Canada in the near future, and requested the honour of a short audience with Vanier.[16] The next day, Simenon received a favorable response to his request and a meeting was set for Tuesday, June 12, 1945, at 4 p.m., "if that was convenient, of course."[17]

At that time, priority on berths on America-bound ships was given to soldiers returning to their country, but a French Government Mission Order could also serve to obtain one of the rare spots, and to that end, the Belgian Embassy and Honorez de Koninck again and again pressured the Ministry of the Provisional Government of the French Republic, which on August 24, 1945, finally acceded to their demand and issued Mission Order 5498 in the name of Georges Simenon. Object of the mission: the development of contacts with newspapers and publishers in Quebec. Departure: as soon as possible. Date of return: when the mission was completed.[18]

Time was of the essence, in more ways than one. Six days later, on August 30, the Directorate of the judicial police asked the Chief of Foreigners and Passports to expel Georges Simenon from France. The expulsion order arrived too late: Simenon was already in London, staying at the tony Savoy Hotel with Tigy and Marc only, as Boule had not succeeded in getting away. One month later, the family boarded a Swedish freighter belonging to the Cunard Line, bound for the United States. They landed twelve days later in New York, on October 5, 1945. A certain Justin O'Brien was waiting on the docks to welcome them to America. Mr. O'Brien, a recently-demobilized professor of French literature at Columbia and Harvard was formerly in charge of the French section of the wartime predecessor of the CIA, the Office of Strategic Studies, and had known Simenon in pre-war Paris. O'Brien introduced Simenon into New York literary circles, but it is not known whether other, non-literary interests linked the ex-intelligence operator and the collaborationist author.

Simenon soon left New York and set up residence north of Montreal in l'Estérel, the domain belonging to the legendary and mysterious Baron Empain who was, like Simenon, Belgian. Simenon would live there for six months, during which time he made frequent trips to New York. Then he packed up and moved into a villa in St-Andrew's-by-the-sea in New Brunswick, where his family — which now included his recent French-Canadian mistress-soon-to-become-second-wife, Denyse Ouimet — would reside for six months before leaving for more permanent quarters in the United States.

We know very little about Simenon's activities in Canada. He did not like to discuss those years, and when he spoke about the war-time period, he judiciously embellished events with serviceable lies. For example, he often recounted how he had refused to sell the German translation rights to his books after Hitler took power, forgetting the small detail that this had nothing whatsoever to do with politics, and everything to do with money (he wanted to sign a general contract for all his works, and not, as the Germans wanted, for one book at a time). There was also the telling incident recounted in the Assouline biography of Simenon:

"Denounced to the Germans, I had to take my family and seek refuge in the countryside, for nearly two weeks... A blond woman arrived with a German officer to interrogate me, and only the presence of mind of Boule saved us." All of which was perfectly true, except that it wasn't a German officer, but members of the French Resistance that were after him.[19]

In *Intimate Memoirs*, published in 1981, Simenon repeats over and over the anthem of his guilty conscience: "I knew so little... the war, about which we knew just about nothing." Still, he seemed to have known enough to leave France in a flurry at the conclusion of a war whose existence he hardly seemed to have noticed!

The flight

At the same time as Simenon and his pal Honorez de Koninck set siege to the Belgian and Canadian Embassies to obtain the necessary exit papers, there was a dramatic rise in the population of two French monasteries. Admiral Gabriel Auphan, Secretary of the Navy and and a confidant of Pétain, arrived in a great rush at the Saint-Pierre-de-Solesmes monastery; in addition to the traditional hospitality, the monks extended the concept of Christian charity to the point of giving the refugee a new name, Vidal. Dom Guy-Marie Oury, who was candidate at the monastery in 1948, later laughed this off, claiming that everyone in France had a phony name in 1944-1945.[20] The Prior of the Abbey, Dom Germain Cozien, also eagerly welcomed Dr. Georges-Benoît Montel, who became Gaston Ringeval, thus borrowing the name of an already-consecrated Benedictine Father. Dr. Montel, who was an important surgeon in Annecy, the capital of the Haute-Savoie district, knew Dom Germain Cozien from when he treated him for a broken leg. Montel was a ferocious anti-Communist who had run for mayor before the war, been defeated by the outgoing head of the Municipal Council, and blamed the Communists for his defeat.

He would join the ranks of the most important collaborationist political movement, Jacques Doriot's Parti populaire français, and the Cercles populaires français as well. He also became, in short order, an influential member of the Legionnaire Security Service and an important local leader of the Militia, making numerous speeches stigmatizing the Resistance and the allies, and calling for violent reprisals against them. Montel became assistant mayor of Annecy just at the moment when the whole region collapsed into civil war; there would be 279 summary executions of militia members by the Resistance, and 433 executions of Resistance members by the Militia in the area.[21] From London, the Free French radio denounced him with the by-now traditional formula: "Don't bother waiting around for us to arrive." In fact, he barely escaped death on November 23, 1943, when resistance fighters invaded his home, determined to rid the area once and for all of this undesirable. But Montel was not there.

Instead, he was to be found at the Convent of the Visitation
in Annecy where the good Sisters consented to letting him
hide in the bell-tower. From there, he somehow reached
Paris and met with Dom Cozien who offered to hide him
at the Saint-Pierre-de-Solesmes Abbey. He would remain
there for one whole year, ensconced in one of the better
rooms, just next to the room of a young colonel of the
Vichy army. On April 19, 1945, the Court of Justice of the
Haute-Savoie sentenced him to a lifetime of forced labour,
and stripped him of his citizenship, as well as ordering the
confiscation of his property for his wartime activities.

At about the same time, not far from Annecy, in the
Haute-Garonne region, 200 kilometers from Toulouse, yet
another Benedictine monastery was abuzz with im-
promptu vocations. Dr. André-Charles Emmanuel Boussat, a militia member from the Villeneuve-sur-Lot
region,[22] Julien Labedan and Jean-Louis Huc were all
hidden with the complicity of the Prior, Dom Bernard de
Chabannes. Labedan andt Huc both came from the same
hamlet of Saint-Gaudens. Later on in life, Huc would
proudly mention in his resumé, under "Honorary Titles,"
that he had been a Member of the Legion of French
Volonteers against Bolshevism, of the Legionnaire Security Service, and finally, of the Militia. The people of
Saint-Gaudens had cause to remember him with far less
nostalgia than they had for Julien Labedan. Unlike Labedan, who was a loudmouth and a hothead yet with sufficient flair to see a change in the wind and join General
Leclerc' army in the spring of 1944, Huc actively denounced his fellow Frenchmen to the Germans.[23]

But as it was not possible to permanently reside at
these monasteries without actually becoming a monk, in
1946 a network patched together by Dom Cozien and Dr.
Montel succeeded in spiriting the latter out of France.

Montel now held papers in the name of Gaston Ringeval. Thanks to the intervention of an influent friend, he was able to obtain the indispensable French Government Mission Order and leave Bordeaux ten days later, bound for New York on a Liberty Ship.

The same scenario was played out at the Abbey of Encalcat. There, Dr. André-Charles Emmanuel Boussat became Dr. Alfred Bordes, Julien Labedan took the name of Armand Bérard, and Jean-Louis Huc became Jean Henry. All received false Mission Orders. It is also possible that agents of the French Government itself actively facilitated the departure of many militiamen. An RCMP report states that "Three of the latest arrivals had French passports with consecutive numbers and all were issued by the same Préfecture de Police bureau."[24] Just like Georges Simenon, these people went to the Canadian Embassy in Paris in order to obtain an entry visa for Canada.[25] No one can say for sure exactly what transpired, but we do have some indication of the nature of the discussions that took place between the fugitives and the Canadian Ambassador, Georges Vanier. The biographies of both Georges and Pauline Vanier, his wife, recount in practically identical terms what took place, except for one astonishing detail: Pauline Vanier's biography attributes to herself the role that her husband's biographer, Robert Speaight claims to have been played by... Georges Vanier![26] The two versions dovetail on the following: Georges Vanier — or his wife — submitted to their friend Pierre-Henri Teitgen the names of dozens of Frenchmen accused of having collaborated with the Nazis and who urgently wanted to enter Canada.[27] Teitgen, who in addition to being a friend was y "Garde des Sceaux" or Keeper of the Seals of the Republic, would investigate the charges against the would-be emigrants and make recommendations. The embassy would then accelerate the procedures for issuing the desired visas for the inocent, advise those guilty of minor offenses to hand themselves over to the authorities since they risked only a three-month sentence, and suggested to those guilty of major crimes to hide out for an indeterminate period of time.

Pauline Vanier states that they only made one serious mistake, and that was in the case of Jacques Dugé de Bernonville. Mrs. Vanier had met with Bernonville's wife, who assured her of her husband's complete innocence. Pierre-Henri Teitgen informed the Vaniers that his inquiries corroborated Mrs. Bernonville's story, and Bernonville thus arrived in Canada with the full assent of the embassy. The Vaniers would subsequently regret their error, for when the truth about Bernonville came to light several years later, a front-page political scandal ensued that remained in full view of the Canadian public for a number of years.

Jacques Dugé de Bernonville had been particularly active at the end of the war in the region of Lyon, which was the second largest city in France, and also the known heart of the resistance movement to German forces. In other words, the civil war in that area had been especially bloody. In January 1944, the commander of the Forces for the Maintenance of Order in Lyon was none other than the selfsame Jacques Dugé de Bernonville. From June 20 to August 14 of the same year, he was also the regional military governor. An article in the *Je suis partout* newspaper had boasted of his merits shown in the attack on members of the Resistance on the Glières plateau, and on July 6, 1944, he received the Minister of the Interior's Order of the Nation Award, signed by Prime Minister Pierre Laval himself. It borders on the incredible that the activities of such a man could remain undiscovered by

Pierre-Henri Teitgen's investigation. That Teitgen knew the truth about Bernonville but hid it from his close friend Georges Vanier is an equally astonishing possibility.

There is more to this tale. Another small group of fugitives and their families were in hiding also, this time in a Château at the edge of the small town of Ars-sur-Formans, whose chief claim to international fame was the fact that one of its priests, Jean-Marie Vianney, had been made a saint known as the Curé d'Ars.

Michel-Lucien Seigneur and Roger Pau belonged to this group. Seigneur was a physician who, between the years of 1939 and 1944, practiced in Verrière, a town in the Vienne region. His political action began prior to that time, however: both he and his wife Geneviève had been a part of the right-wing extremist Cross of Fire movement run by Colonel La Rocque. In a 1984 conversation with the author, Madame Seigneur confirmed that during the war, the couple joined Doriot's Parti populaire français, and that they subsequently became followers of Darnand.[28]

Dr. Michel-Lucien Seigneur was at first a member of the Legion of Combatants; he later joined the Security Service and the Militia while remaining in the Parti populaire français. If the report of the Poitiers Appeals Court is to be believed, Michel-Lucien Seigneur was not active in the field of propaganda but very attentive to enforcing respect for the symbols of the National Revolution. In August 1942, he brought to the attention of the Departmental Head of the Security Service a party organized by some local girls for war prisoners, from which Pétain's portrait was obstinately banned, and at which the Vichy hymn, "Marshal, Here We Stand!" was not sung.[29] In March 1944, Seigneur was to be found at the School for Militia Leaders in the town of Uriage. Records found there called him an "excellent candidate from all points of view, among the top students of his class, completely in his element." The performance would lead to a promotion, and he was named Volunteer Assistant Chief of the Vienne Militia. The Poitiers Appeals Court noted that he accomplished his tasks with exemplary zeal. On March 28, 1945, the Court of Justice of Poitiers sentenced him to death *in absentia*.

Dr. Seigneur hid out for about six months at the Château near Ars-sur-Formans, along with his wife and his five children. The owners of the château, who were called Des Garets, gave them shelter and food, and pieced together an escape route to Canada by loaning them the surnames and first names of some of their own family members. These false identities were authenticated by passports obtained from the Order of Malta, according to a member of the Des Garets family who was ten at the time the events took place. He explained that Seigneur was unable to ask the prefecture for passports since he had been condemned by the courts, and went on to confirm that his family (the Des Garets) had personal connections to Ambassador Vanier.[30] The terms of the agreement between the Des Garets and the fugitives could not have been clearer: the name was loaned on a short-term basis. In fact, as soon as the Seigneurs reached Canada, the Desgarets surname was dropped.[31] In the interim, Michel-Lucien Seigneur was now Vincent Desgarets.[32] His wife obtained a passport and a visa using the name of one of the Desgarets daughters, and all the other members of the fugitive band at the Château d'Ars followed suit, including Roger Pau and his wife, Germaine.

In a highly unusual move, Michel-Lucien Seigneur was given a student visa under his false name, which stipulated that Vincent Desgarets was going to Canada to study at Stanislas College in Montreal. But Seigneur was a 42 year-old doctor, which would have made him a curious recruit for Stanislas which was in fact a well-known high school. The fact that none of the embassy personnel noticed this contradiction, or that no customs officer or civil servant in the entire administrative chain which assured Michel-Lucien Seigneur's coming to Canada blocked his entry because of a patently absurd visa, is surprising, to say the least. It might have looked suspicious, for example, in the eyes of embassy staff, that an entire Des Garets family was leaving France in such a rush, given the exceptionally trying times: berths on transatlantic ships were rare and expensive, administrative formalities for leaving France were quite complicated, and so on. In the summer of 1984, the late Mrs. Geneviève Seigneur remembered a conversation she had with General Georges Vanier before her departure from France, that ended with him telling her, "Nothing that we have discussed here can ever be repeated. We must both agree on that." She added, "He did more than just close his eyes to our false identities. He showed me how to get along in the United States." Julien Labedan, interviewed at the same time, confirmed Mrs. Seigneur' version of events, which shows that Canadian Ambassador Georges Vanier was not duped by the faked passports; to the contrary, he was consciously helping the fugitives to escape justice.

None of the members of this band of fugitives from the Château d'Ars would ever be threatened with deportation from Canada, unlike those who arrived from hiding in the Benedictine monasteries of St-Pierre-de-Solesmes and Encalcat. "They were protected by powerful people," according to the late Yvette Germain who welcomed them in Montreal.[33] Mrs. Germain arranged for Roger Pau and Michel Seigneur to meet a young lawyer, Maurice Riel, now a Liberal Senator, who would help these exiles to establish themselves in Canada on a permanent basis.[34]

The Arrival

Dr. Georges-Benoît Montel had no particular problems finding his feet in the Unites States. What we know of his time there comes from his (unpublished) memoirs, entitled *Memoirs of a Free Man*. As soon as he reached New York safely, he called his friends from Philadelphia, the Whites. Mrs. White, the daughter of an important industrialist, had been a frequent guest of the Montels in Annecy. But Montel was unable to reach her by phone, and so he turned to another good friend that he had met in Lyon, Mr. Stanley, the wealthy New England manufacturer who was president of the company that made Yale locks. Montel's tribulations were at an end, and he was able to recover nicely on an island Stanley owned in the Adirondacks. A visitor at the Stanley estate who worked at the FBI, encouraged Montel to go to Argentina, where he would more easily be able to establish himself than in the United States, where, says Montel in his autobiography, "My status would be a bit difficult to regularize."

Mrs. White had in the meantime returned home, and Montel stayed as her guest in a sumptuous villa complete with chauffeur and limousine at his beck and call. One day, the Father Abbot of Solesmes, Dom Germain Cozien, in Canada on a triennial visit to the Benectine monasteries at Saint-Benoît-du-Lac and Sainte-Marie-des-Deux-Montagnes, asked some friends of the Whites if they might know of the wherabouts of the good doctor. Having contacted Montel, Dom Germain Cozien invited him to come live in Quebec, where he would be welcome, and where he would surely find a good position. The rector of the Univerity, moreover, guaranteed it. And so it was that in September 1946, Montel arrived in Montreal, still using the name Gaston Ringeval.

Jean-Louis Huc, alias Jean Henry, left France on July 13, 1946, after having spent 11 months in hiding. He arrived in Montreal on July 30. Dr. Charles Emmanuel Boussat (alias Dr. Alfred Bordes) and Julien Labedan (alias Armand Bérard) arrived in the summer of 1946 too, having preceded Huc by several weeks.

The Marshal's morning exercises

A curious rearrangement of players took place around this time, unbeknownst to most of the protagonists. Just when this little cohort of collaborators were planning their visit to Montreal, some of Marshal Pétain's devoted Québécois followers visited him in exile at Île d'Yeu, off the coast of France, where he would remain until his death. In the summer of 1946, Maurice Vincent, from Quebec City, Member of the Legion of Former Combatants of France and an employee of the Anglo-Canadian Pulp and Paper Company, made his second trip to Île d'Yeu. He recounted the trip to Robert Rumilly, former Camelot du Roy in France, then translator in the Canadian Public Service, a man who aspired to writing the Marshal's biography. Maurice Vincent immediately told Madame Pétain of the idea: "Madame Pétain urged me to contact Attorney Isorni, who can supply everything you may require to write the biography (...) I have also brought you back a Frankish battle-axe as a gift."[35]

Three days later, Maurice Vincent took a different, conspiratorial tone in a second letter.[36] "I think it better not to mention the name of Mrs. Pétain in discussions about what we might publish, in order to avoid a closer

surveillance of our activities and perhaps cut ourself off
from useful contacts." Mrs. Pétain also asked that they
write to her using her maiden name to avoid arousing
suspicion. Vincent continued with his account of his trip
to Île d'Yeu: "I was so moved to hear about our dear, great
Marshal that I cried like a baby. Mrs. Pétain lives in a bare,
tiny room, smaller than the one she occupied previously,
with space for only one chair. While we spoke, she sat on
the bed and offered me the chair. How shameful it is for
we Frenchmen to see a Marshall of France so shoddily
treated. She seemed so poor that I allowed myself to ask if
we could help her materially." The news about Philippe
Pétain, though, is of a nature to lift the spirits of his last
faithful defenders: "he is in perfect health, looks wonder-
ful and his face is a beautiful rosy pink. He does his
exercises each morning." Maurice Vincent showed exemplary diligence in remedying the vicissitudes that beleaguered the aging detainee, sending him a parcel with some
soap and shaving cream.

   Not that it was so easy to get close to Pétain. Only
Madame la Maréchale was allowed to hand him parcels,
but she could only see her husband in the presence of two
witnesses. No matter for the entreprising Maurice Vincent, who succeeded in corrupting a well-placed guard:
"Apart from Madame la Maréchale who was charming, I
met and purchased the services of a member of the penitentiary service who was allowed to see the Marshal without witnesses. This man is very highly-placed, and at my
disposal to exchange messages with the Marshal. He already gave him my card and told him of our activities and
other interesting news: d'Argenlieu's reception, the
French flag at the Kerhulu restaurant, the magazine *La
Droite,* etc. Utmost discretion is called for as far as this
person we bribed to approach Pétain: he made me promise

never to divulge his identity, even to close friends. None of this must ever be discussed outside of our little group."

Salon heros

On September 22, 1946, Professor Jean Houpert, Secretary of the Faculty of Letters of the Université de Montréal was enjoying an elegant dinner party at the home of his colleague Arthur Léveillé, who was Dean of the Faculty of Sciences and head of the mathematics department. Dom Cozien of the Solesmes abbey was visiting Quebec and attended too, happy to break bread with one of the men whose escape from France and flight to Canada he had facilitated, Dr. Georges-Benoît Montel, alias Gaston Ringeval. Another elegant dinner guest that evening was Dr. André-Charles Emmanuel Boussat, still going by the name of Dr. Alfred Bordes.

Dom Albert Jamet, Chaplain of the Sainte-Marie-des-Deux-Montagnes monastery, was also among the select list of invitees that evening. A worldy Benedictine monk, small, plump and vivacious, he was the darling of the French-Canadian middle class in Montreal, and the private counsellor of M$^{gr.}$ Georges Courchesne, Bishop of Rimouski. Of French origin, like Jean Houpert, and a strong supporter of Pétain, Dom Jamet had crossed swords with one of the emissaries of the Free French in the Province of Quebec, Admiral Thierry d'Argenlieu in his civilian incarnation, a Carmelite brother whose religious name was Louis de la Trinité. Jamet wrote a long attack on Argenlieu that *Le Devoir* published in its April 15, 1941 edition.

Jean Houpert and Dom Jamet were great friends: Jamet came to lunch each week at Houpert's Elmwood street residence in Outremont. In addition to a fervent commitment to catholicism, the men shared a past in the *Action française* movement, and both professed a clear, strong and untiring support for Marshal Pétain.

That dinner party at Mr. Léveillé's house marked the start of a long friendship between Dr. Montel and Jean Houpert, a friendship which would also ricochet through the rest of the small band of fugitive militiamen who transited through the monasteries of Saint-Pierre-de-Solesmes and Encalcat before escaping to Canada. Jean Houpert wrote in his (unpublished) memoirs: "On Sunday, November 3, 1946, Dr. Montel came to lunch at our home with Father Lemoine and two other refugees who were using false passports (...), Dr Boussat from Pau, using the name Bordes, and Julien Labedan, from Saint-Gaudens, who called himself simply 'Julien the interior decorator.' " On December 3, Houpert noted in his diary: "Dr. Ringeval came to live with us." It was a visit that would last six months. From December 22, another entry: "I had the four musketeers for dinner." These weekly dinner that brought together Montel, Boussat, Huc and Labedan would go on for another six months.

Mrs. Alfred Thibaudeau and her husband belonged to the upper crust of the French-Canadian bourgeoisie and any Frenchman of note who passed through Montreal would inevitably be invited to the Thibaudeau's well-appointed Westmount home. Dom Albert Jamet was a frequent guest at these elegant receptions, and it was at one such event that Jean Houpert had the occasion to meet Victor Keyserling. Keyserling had arrived in Canada via Portugal on October 16, 1947, on a non-immigrant visa valid for six months.[37] His father, Count Archibald de Keyserling had been an officer in the Imperial Russian navy.

During the war Keyserling first worked at the German embassy in Paris and then became an editor, translator and war correspondent for Radio-Paris, the Nazi occupation forces official radio. In 1943, he made a series of reports from Rome and Normandy, and in July 1944, withdrew to Bordeaux with the rest of the Radio-Paris staff. He was arrested in Bordeaux after Liberation, charged with attacks on the Foreign Security of the State, detained 16 months and released after his case was closed.[38]

Keyserling then went back to Paris and worked for a year for British United Press where he was employed as a correspondent of the Montreal office which was run by his cousin, Robert Keyserling. He claimed that French police, irritated by his anti-Communist views, had tried to kidnap him and hand him over to the Soviet embassy which wanted to repatriate him as a Latvian to his now illegally-annexed country of origin. He fled to Spain with the help of an American officer, he later explained, and eventually came to Canada.

The Houpert's dinner table in Outremont became one of the places where French illegal refugees and properly-documented exiles could mingle. People like Dr. Masquin, from Saint-Didier (near Carpentras), who was brought over by Dr. Montel in the fall of 1949. Dr. Masquin first took refuge in Spain and apparently came to Canada quite legally. He worked in the Gaspé from 1949 to 1951 before returning to France to face a relatively mild sentence, the loss of his citizenship. Or like Mr. Jacquet, from Vienne in the Dauphiné region, who called himself Mr. Gros. And author Michel Mohrt, who published intermittently during the war in *Je suis partout*, was a French fascist fellow-traveller[39] and an unconditional admirer of Henri de Montherlant, and who also lived in Montreal. He

had been invited by Mr. Pierre Péladeau of the Variétés
publishing house, to become the literary editor of the
house (he kept that job for only six months). Péladeau had
met Mohrt in Paris when the latter was a literary adviser
to Paris publisher Robert Laffont. Mohrt left Montreal in
January 1947 for the United States, where he would remain for two years. Mohrt related his time in Montreal in
"L'Ancien régime," the last part of a novel — more of a
piece of non-fiction actually — entitled *Mon royaume pour
un cheval.*[40]

Others supped with the Houperts, like Gabriel Dorget, known more recently in France under the name of
Berger Dupuis and who, like so many others, belonged to
a right-wing extremist movement before the war. While
living in Paris, Dorget joined the Cross of Fire and quickly
was promoted to the rank of trustee of a unit that was
similar to a cell in the Communist Party. Dorget subsequently joined the ranks of the Parti Social français,
which was a creation of the Cross of Fire. From 1940 to
1942, Gabriel Dorget worked as warden of a domain situated at Herqueville, in Normandy, which belonged to the
legendary French car manufacturer, Louis Renault, a man
Dorget knew for quite some time. Renault, a long-time
adversary of the non-white, non Christian part of French
society had his Paris factories bombed by the RAF in
March 1942. After he was found guilty of collaboration
with the enemy, his company was nationalized by the
post-war government of France.

From 1942 to 1944, Gabriel Dorget lived with his
family at a small water-mill he bought, located six kilome-
tres from Eymet in the Dordogne region. After he was the
target of an assassination attempt when local Communists
discovered his membership in the Parti Social français, he
returned to Paris in November, 1944, and lived there until

March, 1947 under the name of Berger Dupuis. Sentenced in absentia to 20 years of hard labour by a court in Périgueux, the administrative capital of the Dordogne, sought by the police, Dorget went to the Benedictine Monastery on the Rue de la Source in Paris — "I suppose I thought that, as men of the cloth, they would help people in trouble"[41] — and met Father Roméo Thibaudeau who helped him somehow to get to Canada. He first left Paris for Belgium, then headed for London where he was able to change the name on his brother Jules-Olivier's passport for Gabriel-Olivier Dorget. He departed London by plane on May 1, 1947 and arrived in Gander, Newfoundland on May 6. From there, he came directly to Montreal, where he remained quietly with his family, and was never bothered by immigration authorities.

Having left France with the complicity of some admirable French-Canadian members of some of the best-loved religious orders in the Province of Quebec[42] — according to Robert Rumilly who unfortunately never identified them by name — Jacques Bernonville destroyed his false papers upon his arrival in New York, and quickly wrote to his Canadian protectors to ask them to find him work. They were as good as gold and as fast as mercury, and Jacques Dugé de Bernonville was able to enter Canada on November 26, 1946 using the name Jacques Benoît. He headed straight for Quebec City, where he was hired at the Provincial Liquor Commission, in the central accounting department. Jacques Benoît/Bernonville's immediate destination and the speed with which he found employment leads us to believe that the Canadian friends he contacted from New York lived in Quebec City. In any case, in his newly-adopted place of residence, Bernonville soon met Father Simon Arsenault, director of the Scholasticate of the Fathers of St. Vincent-de-Paul and former editor of the magazine *La Droite*. The two had known each other in pre-war Paris, where, according to Arsenault, they both were "interested in the same charities."[43] It is not known which charities Jacques Dugé de Bernonville favored with his largesse, but we know that he did belong to a clandestine right-wing extremist movement during these years, the Comité Secret d'Action Révolutionnaire (C.S.A.R.), known as La Cagoule (The Hood), which in 1936 attempted to overthrow the French government.

Besides, the nationalist circles of Quebec City welcomed Jacques Bernonville with open arms even if they didn't already know him. He hung out with the Frédéric and Noël Dorion brothers, as well as with René Chaloult and Philippe Hamel. They would regularly meet for a tasty meal at Joseph Kerhulu's restaurant and Bernonville, like Maurice Vincent, boarded at the Old Homestead. On January 1, 1947, Bernonville left Quebec City, and moved downriver to Saint-Pacôme de Kamouraska where he soon joined the staff of the sales department of the Power Lumber Company.

Everything's swell (popular tune)

January 1, 1947 was celebrated gaily at the home of Jean Houpert. "Had the Bordes, Huc and Montel to dinner. Everyone was very happy," Houpert noted in his diary. In fact, they all had good reason to look to the future with optimism. Their wives and children had joined them in Canada, or were en route, and they had received assurances from highly-placed political figures that permanent resident visas would soon be issued in their names. Senator Jean-Marie Dessurault, an influential Liberal organizer in the Quebec City region had agreed to intercede with Minister of Justice and future Prime Minister of Canada Louis

Saint-Laurent and with the Minister of Mines and Resources in their favour. In Julien Labedan's case, for example, it was at the insistence of Father Lemaître, former
principal of Stanislas College that Dessurault took matters
in hand in 1947 and obtained an immediate extension of
stay, valid for one year.[44]

With steady employment and good connections in
hand, there seemed to be plenty of light at the end of the
exiles' tunnel. Dr. Montel, for example, became a professor
at Laval University on May 1, 1947, in addition to con-
tinuing the practice of medicine in Dr. Gilbert's clinic in
nearby Charny. Only the fate of his wife and children still
in hiding in Lyon worried him, he would write to Robert
Rumilly on March 16, 1947. Now that he had the kind of
job that would favorably impress Canadian immigration
authorities, he took steps to have his family join him in
his new country.

In May 1947 Jean Houpert hosted another party, to
celebrate Dr. Montel's departure for Quebec City and the
arrival of Jacques Benoît/ Bernonville in Montreal. Houpert had not known Bernonville for long: "On March 4,"
he wrote in his diary, "had Rumilly and Commander
Benoît (32 wounds) over." It didn't take long for other
Outremont doors to open to Jacques Benoît, a turn of
events which irritated his wife, because no matter how
doubtful was their claim to nobility, she attached less
importance to its use in public than she did to personal
security.

In Quebec City, Dr. Montel was not left to his own
devices either. Far from it: the same handful of notables
that welcomed Jacques Benoît/Dugé de Bernonville upon
his arrival now had Montel over to their well-appointed
residences for pleasant evenings between the right kind of
people. An important lawyer, to use Montel's own phrase,

presented him to the Premier of the province, Maurice
Duplessis, who offered him these reassuring words: "My
dear man, you will not be bothered here. We never believed
Marshal Pétain to be a traitor."[45] Duplessis even invited
Montel to a session of the provincial parliament, where,
Montel comments laconically in his Memoirs, his authority was considerable. Noël Dorion became friends with Dr.
Montel and introduced him to some of the most important
families in the provincial capital: "Without being immod-
est, I see that everyone here is impassionned by my stories."[46]

Of course, some details of these stories were better
left unspoken. Julien Labedan and Jean-Louis Huc kept
the lid on their past in the Militia and their participation
in anti-Resistance operations when they were questioned
by Canadian Immigration.[47] Jean-Louis Huc could count
on the support of Mgr. Gerlier, Archbishop of Lyon who
was travelling in Canada in 1947 and who had coined the
following maxim: "Pétain is France, and France is
Pétain." Gerlier recommended Huc to the Secretary of
State for External Affairs, Louis Saint-Laurent. The ma-
neuvre was successful, because in August 1947, Huc met
with Saint-Laurent who, in Huc's presence, instructed the
Chief of Immigration to promptly settle his case. Even
better, Saint-Laurent agreed to have the case of Huc's
family — who had arrived earlier in the month on a
thirty-day visa — added to his file, rather than beginnning
a new dossier with all the problems that might entail. Huc
could also give as a personal reference his very good friend
and Deputy Provincial Minister of Lands and Forests,
Avila Bédard, who he had met in Nancy in 1924, at the
centenary celebration of the School of Forestry. And Huc
now had a good job at the Howard Smith Paper Mill.

In fact, all of the French collaborators mentioned here so far had steady employment, except for Jacques Benoît/Bernonville. If there was no shortage of politicians, intellectuals and professionals seeking his company, it was a different story for business people, who carefully kept their distance. Rumilly complained about the problems he had finding "someone with our mentality, our ideas, a pure soul to hire de Bernonville." Illegally in Canada and with false papers, Jacques Benoît/Bernonville would have a succession of temporary jobs for most of 1947: clerk in the sales department of Power Lumber Company's St. James street office, manager of the Chalet-Café restaurant on Park Avenue, and manager of a bus and taxi service in Montreal. Benoît/Bernonville appealed for help to Robert Rumilly who considered passing around the collection plate to help him out.[48] It wasn't until December 1947 that steady work came his way; Albert Pinel, an employer of French origins who shared Bernonville's political convictions, hired him as sales director for the Franco-Canadian Milk Products Company at the respectable salary of $300.00 a month plus a small share of profits. Benoît/Bernonville lived during this period at the home of a friend and colleague of Jean Houpert, Jean-Paul Vinay, at 6239 Deacon Road in Montreal.[49]

For the others, 1947 was spent waiting for permanent residency visas. Their material conditions were good however: the Bernonville and Montel children stayed throughout the summer at the Knowlton residence of the Marquis de Cardaillac. The bucolic interlude did not change much however, and Montel still found himself without a visa as summer turned into fall. The rector of Laval University, Mgr. Ferdinand Vandry, then sent a letter to Louis Saint-Laurent, by now Minister of External Affairs, begging him to help Dr. Montel, "whose only crime was to have believed that Marshal Pétain would save France and, to have been a municipal councillor of Annecy during the Occupation. The dearest wish of Montel was now to live in peace under the protection of British freedoms."[50]

Vandry's letter fell on deaf ears. Louis Saint-Laurent, who professed ignorance of Montel's case responded caustically that to have supported Pétain was at the very least an error of judgement, and that the doctor's professional usefulness was really the only justification for allowing him to remain in Canada. The letter ends with this stinging remark: "I would be astonished if his past displayed much enthusiasm for these same British rights and freedoms."[51]

Montel's troubles did nothing to encourage any optimism on Bernonville's part as to his own chances of gaining landed immigrant status in Canada. At the very end of the year, he thought it wise to sound out the immigration authorities on their eventual reaction to a formal request for permanent residency for himself and his family. On December 29, 1947, he submitted a very informal request to the Chief of Immigration in Ottawa, and "upon having received assurances from him that I would be granted the visa, I will officially present myself this week."[52]

In his file, Bernonville mentioned having as an officer, carried out many missions for Marshal Pétain. He also stated having been named by Pétain, in 1944, Regional Chief of Public Order and Military Governor of Lyon. On August 20, 1944, declares Bernonville, Pétain, knowing he was going to be taken to Germany, relieved Bernonville of his post. The Secretary of Pétain's cabinet offered Bernonville a passport for Switzerland, which he claimed he refused. He was then "chased by the Communists" and for the next two years was obliged to hide in various convents and monasteries. Since the immigration authorities suggested he produce letters of recommendation from noteworthy Canadians in support of his request for landed immigrancy, he attached documents praising him from Alfred Plourde, prefect of Kamouraska, Frédéric Dorion, Independent Member from Charlevoix-Saguenay in the House of Commons, Antoine Lamarre,[53] and Jean Bruchesi,[54] Undersecretary of the Province de Quebec. Bernonville was so confident of the outcome of his request that he rented a five-room flat at 5551 Côte-des-Neiges, at $93.50 a month, and purchased $1,200.00 worth of furniture, paying half of the bill in cash.

2. The Struggle

Nothing is going right (another well-known refrain)

The new year had hardly begun before things began to unravel. On February 13, 1948, instead of the much-hoped for permanent visa, Dr. Georges Benoît-Montel received a deportation order: he had to leave Canada within sixty days. The public servants of the Department of Mines, Natural Resources and Immigration were unimpressed by the representations made by Senator Dessurault and by the letters offered in his support. Disappointed, Dessurault wrote to Louis Saint-Laurent to remind him of his promises to Montel, and to underline the fact that many other powerful people, including Senator Gouin, were interested in this case. "You will no doubt recall that Dr. Montel was the protégé of His Eminence Cardinal Villeneuve, and also of General Vanier, Canadian Ambassador in Paris."[55] Over the next few months, Julien Labedan,

Jean-Louis Huc, and Dr. André Boussat each received a similar expulsion order.

At that point the fight really began. René Chaloult, Philippe Hamel, Frédéric and Noël Dorion, and Robert Rumilly, who had remained fairly discrete up until then, now turned this business into a crusade, inciting anyone with any influence at all in Ottawa to press the government to rescind the deportation order against Dr. Montel. Their main target was Louis Saint-Laurent, the most influential French-Canadian in the federal government. But as they would soon discover, "He is not as pliant as other politicians."[56] In Montreal, the university establishment did not require much convincing to jump into the fray: Canon A. Sideleau, dean of the Faculty of Letters at the Université de Montréal, sounded the attack on February 26, 1948, and was quickly followed into battle by the Rector of the same institution, M[gr.] Olivier Maurault. In their letters to Saint-Laurent, now Minister of Justice again, Sideleau and Maurault insisted that Laval University needed the services of Dr. Montel. They claimed that he had been condemned to death in France by a Communist tribunal, and that his deportation would be the equivalent of a death sentence. In Quebec City, the Laval University Senate approved the request for landed immigrant status for Montel.[57] M[gr.] Maurice Roy, Archbishop of Quebec, gave assurances that he would intervene with Louis Saint-Laurent to block the deportation order against Montel.[58] M[gr.] Philippe-Servule Desranleau, Bishop of Sherbrooke, did not remain on the sidelines either. Egged on by Jean Houpert and M[gr.] Émile Chartier, M[gr.] Desranleau begged Saint-Laurent to rescind the deportation order against this poor man who was being pursued by French Communists.[59]

René Chaloult and Robert Rumilly, who normally would only frequent the pure and the faithful and who rarely let slip an opportunity to rail against the trusts, corrupt democracy and parliamentary fat cats, now unhesitatingly lowered themselves to the the level inhabited by the practitioners of that good old remedy, spreading around bribes. Dr. Gilbert, of the Charny medical clinic where Dr. Montel worked, came up with $5,000.00 to help his friends sharpen the convictions of useful intermediaries.[60] Reinvigorated by the smell of money, Rumilly lost no time in writing to René Chaloult two days later: "Can you confirm that five thousand dollars will be at my disposal? I can't say in writing what use I will make of this sum, but I believe it will be of immense help." The next day, exhibiting a rare exuberance, Rumilly cried victory: "I have it. Last night I made an important contact, a very-well received approach. I have my hand on the prize and I won't let go. Greetings and brotherhood. I enclose an important postscript."[61] The following day brought even better news: "For the time being, the money is not needed. When I wrote to you last night I thought to use it to obtain the influence of someone. That person has come over to our cause without asking for payment."[62] Disinterested Good Samaritans apparently still existed in this vale of tears.

A somewhat more timorous Dr. Montel preferred that René Chaloult and Robert Rumilly not interfere with M[gr.] Vandry's efforts to help. Montel's reserve brought the mayor of Montreal to their side. Camilien Houde, who was as or more indignant about the matter than his wife, burned with the desire to begin a blistering campaign in favor of Dr. Montel alongside René Chaloult and Maurice Duplessis.[63]

The winter dragged on with the shilly-shallying of M$^{gr.}$ Vandry, the growing fears of Dr. Montel and his wife's depression, with René Chaloult and Robert Rumilly angrily chomping at the bit. In mid-March, Georges-Benoît Montel received good news from Senator Dessurault. But a month later, one week from his official deportation date, with no tangible news to encourage him, Dr. Montel was weighing whether or not to accept M$^{gr.}$ Vandry's offer of safe haven on the grounds of the Quebec Seminary.

Louis Saint-Laurent kept wavering, and asked for more information about Montel's wartime activities. The RCMP told him that Montel had collaborated in every way imaginable with the Germans and that he had denounced his compatriots, while Georges Vanier transmitted the opinion of French Minister of Justice and Keeper of the Seals Pierre-Henri Teitgen, which was that, inasmuch as Dr. Montel's crimes were essentially of a political nature, his government would probably not ask for extradition. Still, because of the violent propaganda campaign he conducted against the Allies during the war, it was not his view that Montel was a proper choice to be teaching at a Canadian university.[64]

A political wasp's nest and a diplomatic minuet

French authorities acceded to Canada's requests for information, but with considerable reticence. True, Montel's brother was a member of the French National Assembly, a fact which did not escape the attention of a certain D.W. Munro, who at Vanier's request initiated numerous contacts with the Government of France to obtain the facts concerning the exiled militiamen in Quebec. But it appears that there was more than simple nepotism at work. For example, during the winter of 1949, the CCF Member of Parliament for Winnipeg North, Alistair Stewart, caused quite a stir in the House by his questions about the presence in Canada of Montel, Boussat, Huc, Labedan, Seigneur, and de Bernonville. He demanded the government make public what it knew of these men's past. In response to official requests for more information by the Government of Canada in order to satisfy the opposition's legitimate concerns, the French continued their dilatory maneuvres. Dr. Michel-Lucien Seigneur, for example, had no politician for a brother, but only a distant relative, the Bishop of Tournai, M$^{gr.}$ Walrasens, who was his wife Geneviève's godfather.[65]

On February 24, 1949, the Secretary of State for External Affairs wrote to the Canadian Ambassador in Paris: "Reference was made in the House yesterday to the case of Seigneur. The Prime Minister is very anxious to have authenticated documents covering the charges against Seigneur, as well as judgements against him, which can be made public should circumstances require the Government to do so. The documents which you forwarded on February 1, 1949, regarding this person have been received, but authenticated documents are still required."[66]

On February 26, D.W. Munro reported to Georges Vanier, who transmitted the information in turn to External Affairs: "As to the eventual use to which these documents are to be put, I was given to understand that their publication would not be welcome. They are, after all, French documents, and if they are to be published, I feel that the French prefer to do it themselves. If, on the other hand, they are to be used in the course of legal proceedings against Seigneur — in which case they become public documents only secondarily — I gathered that French objection would be less."[67]

Munro went on to explain that the French Justice Ministry was a prizewinner at lethargy, taking up to a week to send documents over to the Foreign Affairs Department which was accustomed to acting with more speed. He concluded that the Justice Ministry quite obviously did not appreciate the numerous requests made by the Government of Canada, fearing embarrassing revelations which would light up past fires of hatred. "I have been left the impression that the French do not want to rewash their dirty linen in public. The original trials were probably painful, particularly to those conscientious French who stopped to reflect that there were in their midst, persons capable of selling fellow compatriots over the Rhine. These conscientious Frenchmen probably now feel that, with the presence in their midst of other persons capable of selling their country over the Elbe, the present problems eclipse the past."[68]

Nor was France the only government hesitant to make certain documents public. A legal adviser to the American Secretary of State, E.R. Hopkins, expressed his fears in a note — classified 'secret' — dated February 26, 1949. All of the protests against the upcoming deportation of the Vichy exiles used the same language, hardly convincing proof of their spontaneity, and received a standard response from the office of the Prime Minister. Moreover, "(...) if letters which the Prime Minister sent marked 'personal,' and the incoming letters to which he replied personnaly are not included, I fear that very few of the documents tabled will be in favour of the Frenchmen concerned."[69] This suggests that Louis Saint-Laurent entertained private correspondance in which he expressed more favorable opinions to the exiles that his high civil servants in the Department of Immigration wanted to deport. Shortly thereafter, the French Foreign Affairs Department softened its position and decided that the texts of accusations, proofs and judgements concerning Vichy collaborators were in public domain. The Government of Canada could thus use them as it wished, with, however, some restrictions: in no event could these documents be cited verbatim or submitted in extenso to the House. Information contained in the documents could be mentioned in general declaration, but without revealing the documents' origins.[70]

On March 14, J.W. Pickersgill, Special Assistant to the Right Honourable W.L. Mackenzie King, wrote in a secret memorandum to the Prime Minister that they could submit summaries of the documents to the House when Stewart's motion was tabled. However, he went on, it would be difficult to justify this action without the explicit consent of the French. He concluded by suggesting that Stewart be shown the judgements and informed of the situation.[71] In the end, the documents were not submitted to the House and in fact, Bernonville's complete file was never made public either.

The French government showed no particular desire to extradite Bernonville in any case. For example, while the Deputy Minister of Mines and Resources Hugh Keenleyside declared before Judge Cousineau that French authorities had informed the Government of Canada of their desire to see Count Bernonville returned to France,[72] he was contradicted by the interim Prime minister, C.D. Howe, who issued a press release stating that at no time since the cessation of hostilities had the French Government presented a request for the Count's extradition.[73] Two years later, the Canadian Embassy in Paris informed the Government of Canada that the Ministry of Foreign Affairs responded to an official question about its intentions in the Bernonville case with a stern "no comment."

"Nevertheless," the embassy added, "I think it is fair to interpret the note as an assurance that Bernonville will have a fair trial, and an implied expression of hope that he will be returned."[74] Still, there would never be an official request for the extradition of Bernonville. On the eve of Bernonville's forced departure from Canada, he received a note from Louis Saint-Laurent which reminded him that France was not the only country in the world, and that many destinations on the planet were open to the fugitive. It is easy to conclude that France was not overly-anxious to have Bernonville within its borders. In the end, Jacques Dugé de Bernonville chose to go to Brazil, but the saga did not end right away.

In September 1955, the Supreme Court of Brazil granted Bernonville a *habeas corpus* which prevented him from being deported to France. The official reason was that the French embassy in Rio never sent the court Bernonville's war crimes file.[75] This was a dramatic turn of events, inasmuch as only six months earlier, the same court had unanimously rejected Bernonville's request for *habeas corpus*. The court mentioned in the same judgement that the Government of Brazil did not seek to deport Bernonville for his political crimes, but for crimes of common law, in the commitment of which he had shown such cruelty, said the judges, that the Germans themselves had asked that he be replaced. The first judgement of the Brazilian Supreme Court was, however, never executed, because several days before it was proclaimed, Bernonville disappeared from his residence in Sao Paulo where he lived using the names Jacques Benoît and Maurice Delegrize, and hid from the authorities until the proclamation of the second, more favorable judgement.

Some stay, some go

Similar events took place in the chronicle of Dr. Montel's stay in Canada. On April 15, 1948, Rumilly spoke with Chief of Immigration A.L. Joliffe, who assured him that Montel need not worry about the expulsion order against him, because "we have re-opened his file, and a decision will shortly be made."[76] As of April 22, Saint-Laurent was informed about Montel's past exploits as a member of the Parti populaire français and of the Legionnaire Security Service; he also knew that the good doctor was a hated man in his native Haute-Savoie, and that the Government of France was quite firm in its decision to keep him far away from its territory. While he was mulling over the desperate and futile idea of taking refuge in the Quebec Seminary, Montel learned on May 8 of the suspension of the deportation order. To Philippe Hamel, Louis Saint-Laurent justified his decision to intervene in Montel's favour by weighing the usefulness there was of keeping him in Canada, as against the weight of the sentence awaiting him in France. Still, he added a categorical conclusion to his note: "As a government, it is absolutely unthinkable for us to take the position that the Pétainistes were in the right during the war."[77] For his part, Senator Jean-Marie Dessurault claimed victory for his efforts in this decision, while recognizing that they only bore fruit thanks to the constant and precious compassion of the Very Honorable Louis Saint-Laurent.[78]

The federal cabinet would soon know the reaction of certain high civil servants in the Department of Mines, Natural Ressources and Immigration to this decision. Deputy Minister Hugh Keenleyside, in particular, did not mince his words, informing his Minister that, if Nazi collaborators were given the right to remain in Canada, he would have to go back on his decision to deport to Germany five Jewish immigrants who had entered Canada with false passports. The Jewish refugees had a much better claim to clemency than would ever have the likes of Labedan, Boussat and especially Montel, said Keenleyside. As for Bernonville, wrote the same Deputy Minister, "no attenuating circumstances existed to excuse the behaviour of this man who remains a traitor to his country and possibly the murderer of the Canadian citizen whose passport he used to leave France. Bernonville was condemned by a regular Court of Justice on October 8, 1947, well after the end of the war." With the Minister's accord, Keenleyside proposed having Bernonville arrested the next day, and on September 4, Bernonville found himself behind bars, with the story on the front page of *La Presse*.

Just as one chapter in the Nazi collaborators in exile in Quebec was ending, another began. In a letter dated September 2, 1948, the Sollicitor-General of Canada, Joseph Jean, promised Robert Rumilly that a favorable decision would soon be taken in the cases of Montel, Huc and Labedan but that he was quite pessimistic about the situation of Bernonville. He was as good as his word, for on September 13 or 22, 1948, the federal government approved a secret Order-in-Council — no. 4233 — which allowed these men to remain in Canada as political refugees. Against the advice of the civil servants at Immigration, the cabinet ruled in favor of the former militiamen.[79] Acting Prime Minister C.D. Howe and James Angus MacKinnon, the Minister in charge of immigration, defended the government's decision by saying that these Frenchmen had suffered overly-hasty trials in post-war France and that a rigorous investigation by Canadian Immigration Services had judged them apt to remain in

Canada. Robert Rumilly was gleeful at what the government had conceded.[80] But in a private letter to Philippe Hamel, Louis Saint-Laurent stated that Bernonville would not be the beneficiary of a similar Order-in-Council. "The Canadian Ambassador in France and his legal counsel had given assurances," Hamel in turn wrote to Rumilly, "that if the Count is extradited, he would have a new trial at which he could demonstrate his innocence, if such were the case, according to Saint-Laurent, who added that 'the accusations against Bernonville are too serious for us to ignore.' "[81]

Possibly in order to resolve once and for all the problem of French illegals in Canada, Ottawa decided to modify the rules of immigration and give French immigrants the same privileges accorded to British immigrants, i.e. the right to come to Canada without either a passport or a visa.[82] This measure would avoid the necessity of deporting certain other French immigrants for possession of false identification papers, which was the main charge pending against Dr. Montel and the others of his band. In short, in order not to have to deal with the criminals, "let's abolish the crime." In taking this step the federal government also acceded to an old demand of Quebec nationalists, the same crowd that was defending the exiled collaborators in Quebec, and who saw in the preferential treatment received by British immigrants an unjustified privilege whose purpose was to reduce French Canadian to demographic insignificance, if it wasn't to eradicate them, pure and simple.

The Communists, the Jews and the "Emigration" (sic)

If Montel, Labedan and company saw their cause triumph, Victor Keyserling, for his part, was not as fortunate. The

Department of Immigration rejected his request for permanent residency, and the RCMP asked its foreign service to investigate him. The information gathered — that Keyserling had been a member of the only organization of Nazi war correspondents, the SS Kurt Eggers — supported the rejection of his request at the end of 1948. Keyserling did not deny the information.[83] He explained it by saying that he had joined the staff of the German Embassy in France and of Radio-Paris only to avoid forced conscription, as a Latvian, into the German army.[84] His reporting from Rome in 1943 was only an innocent recreation and his dispatches from Normandy in 1944 an unsuccesful attempt to cross over into American-held territory. But a second RCMP report — dated July 5, 1949 — confirmed the first. "Under secret cover the RCMP informed us that they have now received definite information concerning Victor Keyserling's activities on the Continent, which indicates that he is NOT CLEARED FOR SECURITY PURPOSES."

Miss Madeleine Thibaudeau, of the illustrious Westmount family mentioned earlier, protested the fate of her protégé with a vehemence that showed her ignorance of the facts all the more clearly: "This very grave affair," she wrote, "can become the scandal of the Emigration [sic] which has been a long time coming." She claimed that the Communists, under the cover of beings DPs — Displaced Persons — entered Canada with no problems, "and let's not forget that the Jews also come in far too easily, and I could give you an earful about them."[85] If Louis Saint-Laurent and the Liberal Party of Canada wanted to show the least bit of recognition to the Thibaudeau family for services rendered, they would grant this favor.[86]

Miss Thibaudeau's caustic remarks and the recommendations of Senator Léon-Mercier Gouin were met with understanding from Jules Léger, Secretary to Prime Minister Louis Saint-Laurent. Léger moreover remarked to Saint-Laurent that Mr. Keyserling was living in great turmoil during the occupation of France, and this confusion was reflected in his immigration file.[87] Jules Léger received Keyserling at his office and listened to him in an understanding, elegant and humane manner.[88] Saint-Laurent maintained that as far as he was concerned, there was nothing to be done for Victor Keyserling if a legal obstacle to his definitive admission to Canada existed in that he had, at least technically speaking, belonged to the German Armed Forces during the war.[89] Jules Léger consequently remained resolutely prudent: "The problem of Keyserling's extradition is a very complicated one: despite the interest I have taken in this case, there remain certain shady areas of his life that are difficult to define."[90] Hoping to change the course of events, Robert Rumilly then put pressure on the Sollicitor-General, Joseph Jean, but got nowhere. He suggested that Keyserling hire Édouard Masson as his attorney, because he was Maurice Duplessis' principal organizer in Montreal.[91] But Masson refused the case without even knowing who or what was involved.[92] Rumilly read into this refusal a sign that Duplessis, initially favorable to Keyserling, was now distancing himself from these matters.[93]

Rumilly next advised Keyserling to contact Bona Arsenault, the Liberal Member for Bonaventure in the Federal Parliament. Keyserling met Arsenault on a cold March evening at a Liberal Party banquet held at the Windsor Hotel on Peel Street, in central Montreal. He gave Arsenault a copy of the attestation from the French Ministry of Information which exonerated him of accusations of collaboration. In relating this event to Rumilly, he said: "I don't know what you could have told M.

Arsenault, but he was extremely friendly, and the light of your kindness shone over our short meeting."[94] And what was this "kindness" that Rumilly offered to Arseanult that made him so eager to be of help to Keyserling? Just the threat of making him lose his seat in the next elections if Keyserling and Bernonville were deported.[95]

Keyserling, despite having a permanent job that allowed him to live in Westmount (at 6 Park Place), denied having the means to fight the decision in court and chose to avoid a Bernonville-style scandal. He left Canada on November 11, 1949, bound for Haiti.

Important Names and Bags of Money

The mobilisation around Dr. Montel and Victor Keyserling would be small potatoes compared to the hue and cry that surrounded the case of Jacques Dugé de Bernonville. It began with a bang: two days after he was arrested, on September 6, 1948, a Committee for the Defense of Political Refugees was formed in Quebec City under the leadership of Philippe Hamel. A similar Committee was set up in Montreal on September 9, with lawyer, King's Counsel and former Bloc populaire candidate Paul Massé in charge. Roger Lacoste, another lawyer and King's Counsel, was Secretary of the Committee while Dr. J.A. Chevrier was treasurer.

Five days after Bernonville's incarceration, a petition in his favor already had 6,000 signatures.[96] The same day however, Bernonville's appeal of the deportation order was denied, and he was given sixty days to leave the country. But all hope was not yet lost, as he appealed to a higher authority, and at the end of September, he and his wife were freed on $5,000 bail, ostensibly paid by one Georges Fréchette, of 3860 Sherbrooke Street East in Montreal.

The RCMP believed that the real source of the bail money was businessman Jacques Fichet, who together with Jean Bonnel were constantly helping Bernonville financially.[97] In fact, Messrs. Fichet, d'Allemagne and Bonnel took financial responsibility for the entire Bernonville family in a hearing at Immigration Court.[98]

Jacques Dugé de Bernonville repeated *ad nauseam* to whoever would listen that he was only a poor pariah, with no means of earning a living. True, he often changed jobs. A few months after having requested landed immigrancy, he left his $300-a-month plus a percentage of the profits job at the Franco-Canadian Milk Products Company and took employment at a company controlled by Paul Massé, that sold home products, food and pharmaceuticals. By mid-November 1948 he was having great difficulty settling current household bills but didn't dare raise the question with Camilien Houde who, he wrote, "helped me considerably to compensate for lost revenue while I was held by Immigration."[99] On April 12, 1949, he confided to Philippe Hamel that sales were not going well and that he had met with some well-known Montreal businessmen who might be able to help him.[100] By May 1951 he had been hired by the head office of the Union Commercial Insurance Company.[101]

Bernonville seemed to have a knack for squirming out of trouble. A profusion of lawyers, and not just anybodies either, took up his appeal. Emery Beaulieu, K.C. and one of the legal eagles of the National Union Party, Bernard Bourdon, Liberal Party of Canada organizer in his spare time, Jacques Perrault, brother-in-law of André Laurendeau, Roger Ouimet and Jacques Sénécal all helped, as did Attorney Bourdon, who for one, however, demanded a retainer.[102] Attorney Ouimet took the case on a *pro bono* basis, and as far as the others went, the facts are not known.

Catherine, Bernonville's youngest daughter, attended the tony Montreal private school, Collège Marie-de-France. Chantal, the eldest, studied at Université de Montreal where a law student, Jean-Marc Léger, courted her. When the time finally came to leave, Madame Bernonville and her daughters had the means to return to France. Father Simon Arsenault donated freely to Bernonville, and the Fathers of St. Vincent-de-Paul in Paris, encouraged by Arsenault, engaged in discrete financial transactions whose aim was to exchange francs for dollars out of the view of French currency-control authorities. The method was simple. A certain sum in French francs would be deposited into a Paris account in the name of Louis Auboire, attorney for the St. Vincent-de-Paul order, at 3 Square Léon Guillot, Paris XV. Joseph Kerhulu would then buy these francs by sending a cheque for the Canadian dollar equivalent.[103]

The Comittee for the Defense of Political Refugees was not out of funds either. In addition to what was maybe left of the $5,000 that Dr. Gilbert placed at Chaloult and Rumilly's disposal for the defense of Dr. Montel, there were several thousand dollars promised by the provincial Minister of Colonisation and National Union organizer Jos-D. Bégin to René Chaloult in the name of Premier Duplessis. Was this sum paid as promised to Robert Rumilly? Probably, since René Chaloult asked Rumilly to inform him if the funds were not received, and there is no trace of a follow-up request in the papers of Chaloult or Rumilly.[104] Montreal mayor Camilien Houde and restaurant owner Joseph Kerhulu each gave $400 to the fund.[105] Alfred Plourde, a Kamouraska businessman, donated $100.[106] M[gr.] Félix-Antoine Savard kicked in the munificent amount of $3 and protested against "the invasion of the country by Protestant immigrants, the abandonment of the countryside in favour of the cities, industrialization which profited only foreigners, and the spinelessness of our policies."[107] But some donors had a change of heart. In 1951, someone retracted his pledge of $500 in favor of Bernonville after learning of the serious nature of the charges against him.

On November 19, 1948, Robert Rumilly gave a speech entitled 'The Truth about the Resistance and the Purges in France" under the auspices of the Young Chamber of Commerce at the Cercle universitaire in Montreal. At the head table with him was Montreal Mayor Camilien Houde, the president of the Young Chamber, Jean-Paul Ste-Marie, and their respective spouses. The president of the Laurentian Youth of Quebec, and the Société Saint-Jean-Baptiste of Quebec, organized a similar event on November 29, 1948 at the Palais Montcalm in Quebec City.[108] The francophone press dutifully reported the speeches given there and showed a constant sympathy for Bernonville. The sole exception was the liberal paper, *Le Canada*. By contrast, *Le Devoir* warmed to Bernonville and his cause, worrying, for example, that he and his family were unable to attend mass during their detention by immigration authorities in Montreal, and saw in this nothing less than an oppressive attack on religious freedom.[109] *Le Devoir* agreed moreover to Robert Rumilly's demands that it stir up the waters in favor of Bernonville[110] and Rumilly recommended André Laurendeau as a certain supporter of the Union of French Civilian Victims which defended collaborators who had received various sentences.

Father Lemaître, former director of Stanislas College, also made every effort to help Bernonville and used

whatever influence he presumed he had to pressure Louis
Saint-Laurent. On November 8, 1948, Bernonville forwarded to Philippe Hamel the letters from two Benedect-
ine monks and asked him to deliver them to Abbot Henri
LeMaître, at the St. Jean-Eudes Externat, 801 12th Street,
Quebec, "as he has promised me to give them personally
to Saint-Laurent as rapidly as possible."[111] Then, several
days later, in sharing with Hamel the secret of his past
membership in the French terrorist organization The
Hood, he included three additional documents to be sent
to Father Lemaître "who must only show them to Saint-
Laurent." Bernonville demanded that documents I and II
be kept secret, especially from Canadian newspapers, "in
order," he added with a straight face, "not to feed the
ongoing polemic."[112]

On April 17, 1950, Paul Massé forwarded to his Member of Parliament a list of more than 150 prestigious
names, all requesting the federal government to show
humanity towards a political refugee and maintain Canada's good name by allowing Bernonville to remain in the
country.[113] M[gr.] Olivier Maurault, Édouard Montpetit and
Maximilien Caron, respectively Rector, Secretary of the
Université de Montréal and Vice-Dean of the Faculty of
Law, all signed the petition, as did the Deans of various
other faculties: R. P. Forest, Dean of the Faculty of philosophy; Dr. Georges Baril, Dean of the Faculty of sciences; Jean-Paul Vinay, Director of the department of
linguistics. Other supporters of the exiled war criminal
included Dr. J.-A. Rouleau, professor at the Université de
Montreal and Chief Physician of the Notre-Dame Hospi-
tal; Victor Barbeau and Marie-Claire Daveluy, both of the
Académie canadienne-française; Dr. Camille Laurin, psy-
chiatrist and future Cabinet Minister in the first Parti
québécois government; Charles-Étienne Gravel, Presi-

dent of the Banque Canadienne-nationale; L. Geoffrion, banker; Jacques Rousseau, Director of the Montreal Botanical Gardens; Arthur Tremblay, President of the Société Saint-Jean-Baptiste; Léo Guindon, President of the National Alliance of Catholic Teachers; Rosaire Morin, President of the Laurentian Youth Movement; and Maxime Raymond, former federal leader of the Bloc populaire.

An overwhelmed-with-gratitude Bernonville thanked Paul Massé in a letter *Le Devoir* published on May 2, 1950. In the letter, Bernonville underlines the fact that "the community of ideas and traditions that I feel so alive between Canadians and myself is now even stronger."[114] In the same vein Bernonville had two years earlier warmly congratulated René Chaloult on the adoption of the fleur-de-lis as Quebec's flag: "You are the real keeper of that marvellous French and Catholic tradition, which awes those who visit your beautiful land where Providence has destined me to live (...) Your faith has convinced the doubters."[115]

As of December 15, 1950, 543 representations had been made to the federal government in favor of Count Bernonville, including 13 petitions with a total of 2,007 signatures. Among the signatories were the Chicoutimi Board of Trade;[116] M[gr.] Georges Courchesne;[117] M[gr.] Alphonse-Marie Parent;[118] M[gr.] Valois in the name of M[gr.] Joseph Charbonneau, Bishop of Montreal;[119] Alfred Plourde, Mayor of Mont-Carmel;[120] the Mayor of Three-Rivers, J.A. Mongrain;[121] the Progressive-Conservative MP Henri Courtemanche and the Liberal Jean-François Pouliot; M[gr.] Alexandre Vachon, Archbishop of Ottawa;[122] Adhémar Raynault, former Mayor of Montreal;[123] provincial Treasurer Onésime Gagnon, "who always welcomed me"[124] Bernonville wrote one day, sent a telegram in support of the latter.[125] Only three organizations and twelve individuals (unnamed) opposed giving Bernonville residency.

The Credo

Why were all these people up in arms? Why should ex-militiamen from Vichy France be allowed to emigrate to Canada? It certainly was not by chance that the champions of the exiles' cause were the former stalwarts of the Bloc populaire canadien: this struggle was just the continuation of their starry-eyed tryst with the National Revolution of Marshal Pétain, Mussolini's Italy and Salazar's Portugal. In the words of André Laurendeau, their actions were in lockstep with their pressing demands for a national socialist regime for the province of Quebec. In defending Jacques Dugé de Bernonville, they were simply defending their own militant activities during World War II. This explanation for all the hoo-ha is much more reasonable than the inspired platitudes of the Cousineau judgement on the right of asylum in a Christian land.

High on their agenda was to absolve the Third Reich from having started the war, for it would then follow that the partisans of Nazism in France and elsewhere were less guilty. André Laurendeau and Philippe Hamel shared the same premises as to the origin of the war: if only Poland had been more reasonable — read pliant — to Germany's demands, nothing like this mess would have had to happen, come on! According to Laurendeau: "The Polish government has grave responsibilities to bear in the origin of the Second Great War. Its intransigence, probably encouraged by Great Britain, brought on Hitler's armed coup."[126]

Dr. Philippe Hamel affirmed that an intractible Polond shot itself in the foot when it refused to acquiesce to Nazi Germany's reasonable demands and we saw what that brought on. Poland's allies, hardly more enclined to compromise, refused to consider Hitler's generous peace offers, Hamel went on. In 1939, Hitler quite reasonably was willing to accept a simple corridor to Danzig and the restitution of the German character of that city. Again, according to Philippe Hamel, the same Adolf Hitler in July 1940 offered an honorable compromise to a weakened England. [127] But no! cried an indignant Hamel. The imperialists and western economic dictatorships sank the magnanimous Hitlerian efforts to save peace. Realizing that some poor soul might jump to the wrong conclusions, Hamel added that he was in no way defending the evil theories of nazism[128] nor playing defense attorney for Hitler.[129] Jacques Bernonville applauded the publication of Dr. Hamel's pamphlet and distributed it zealously.[130]

As true descendants of Pétain's National Revolution, Bernonville's amen chorus didn't miss a trick, taking aim at Freemasons, Jews and Communists: "Hugh Keenleyside was a Mason — a fact confirmed by the Canadian *Who's Who* of 1936-1937 — and a fanatic who hated French-Canadians," cried an indignant René Chaloult in the Provincial Legislative Assembly. He continued his flight of oratory, harpooning the Jews and the Communists as he went on. "If Jacques de Bernonville had been called Bernovitch, if he had hunted down the noble Marshal of France, if he had been a Communist or an anticlerical fanatic, well then, all our Keenleysides and company would have embraced him tenderly and naturalized him Canadian."[131] On February 24, 1949, using the immunity of his seat as an independent Member of the federal Parliament, Frédéric Dorion proclaimed his conviction that had it been Communist Jews and not French Catholics come to our shores, there would have been nary an eyebrow raised.[132] The Jesuit *École sociale populaire* published this last tirade as a booklet entitled "The Bernonville Case." Robert Rumilly often repeated similar convictions. In a letter he wrote to Victor Keyserling he summed up his views about the protagonists in the case: "Still and all, I must tell you this. One one side there is World Jewry, Freemasonry, Communism, the Christian Democrats, the Socialists, the hateful bureaucracy, the Liberal government, the Tory fanatism and the opportunism of the self-righteous. Against all that, a grand total of myself, alone, with a few friends that I have manage to assemble."[133] Here and there, a few new enemies pop up on his list: "The Crypto-communists, the Jewish element and English fanatics seek their deportation."[134]

André Laurendeau also saw the hand of English-Canadian fanaticism in the French political refugees scandal. These men were not, he maintained, Nazi collaborators, but civil servants in the Pétain regime, a legitimate government that had been recognized by Canada. The opposition to these exiles' establishing themselves in Canada, so firmly entrenched in English-Canadian newspapers and in the upper ranks of the Canadian immigration service, smacked of fanaticism and anti-French bias, according to Laurendeau. Some newspapers, such as *The Ottawa Citizen*, pushed the outrage as far as pronouncing a summary judgement against the entire Vichy regime, he went on to say.[135]

As the years passed, and with them the Axis powers, no lessening of the fervour for the regimes and ideologies of the far right surfaced among the well-known members of the French-Canadian elites that gave so much support to Bernonville and his friends. In 1951, a "highly placed official Montreal personality" — a description that aptly fit the city's mayor — confided to an astonished French journalist: "Here in Quebec, we are of the far right. We don't want to wage war on any country with a similarly-oriented government, even one as bad as Hitler's. England dragged us into two wars against our will."[136] Anatole Vanier lamented to Saint-Laurent that if Spain had only given political asylum to Pierre Laval, who had been President of the State Council in the Vichy government, a "political assassination" could have been avoided.[137] Young André Payette, future star journalist at Radio-Canada, learned his lessons well, and wrote later on that same year that "Bernonville had wanted, like Pétain, to work for the survival of the French people, and that is why there was a price on his head."[138] Noted author Claude-Henri Grignon, for his part, decried with every ounce of his energy the trial that Bernonville would have submitted to if he returned to France, a trial before judges who were his political enemies, the same kind of judges that lynched Charles Maurras, "that glorious French journalist, because they knew he could prove his innocence."[139]

Judge Cousineau, selected to hear the Bernonville case, did not only declare illegal the composition of the Immigration Board that wanted to deport the former military governor of Lyon, nor only refuse to accept the medical diagnosis that reported Bernonville and one of his daughters infected with tuberculosis. He decided that Count Bernonville, against whom this phalanx of evil bureaucrats were aligned, deserved "(...) our highest esteem."[140] Why? Because he was descended from a noble family and had a glorious military career. His conduct during World War II was impeccable because... the accused said so himself: "His testimony clearly indicates that he always conducted himself irreproachably."[141] What is more, how can one doubt his word when he himself claimed that he was a political refugee? "It is thus evident that the plaintiff Bernonville was a political pariah when he entered Canada. To see that one has only to refer to his own testimony."[142] It was an astonishing assessment, coming from a judge!

Judge Cousineau justified Bernonville's presence in Canada by invoking the right of asylum in civilized, Christian countries, a right that went back to the religious immunity in place at the beginning of Christianity.[143] Things had changed since those ancient times, Cousineau deplored, but the religious immunity which had since disappeared from the civil code, still obtained under canonic law. Gérard Filion, editor in chief of *Le Devoir*, went further: "If Canada refuses the right of safe haven to people who are being hunted down because of their political opinions, it would be proof that neither civilisation nor Christian charity have made any progress since the last war."[144]

REALPOLITIK

On September 1, 1949, Jules Léger sent a memo to the Prime Minister in which he informed him of the recommendations of Senator Élie Beauregard concerning the Bernonville affair: "Any new investigation opened by the immigration department on this matter would be ill-appreciated by a not inconsequential part of Quebec's population that is presently favorable to the government. Such an inquiry would allow Camilien Houde to make considerable political hay in the House of Commons or during the by-elections that would soon take place on the island of Montreal. Political interests would suggest a strategy of holding off with any inquiry for at least two months, or even better, of pressuring the French Government to open its own hearings, and claiming the return of one of its own citizens in the name of certain principles of international law."[145]

Gérard Filion, of *Le Devoir*, who saw in the Bernonville affair nothing less than a sinister plot to stop French immigration to Canada, openly used electoral blackmail in his defense of the exiled band of former militiamen. According to Filion, the leader of the conservatives, George Drew had decided to use his newspapers, *The Globe and Mail* and *The Gazette*, to stir things up about the presence of loyal followers of Pétain in Quebec, not only to embarrass the Liberals, but also to stick it to the French-Canadians. He suggested that Drew remember the unwritten law of Canadian politics according to which political parties had no interest in displeasing the French-Canadians.[146] But political blackmail would not save Bernonville from having to leave Canada.

In an affidavit submitted on May 19, 1950, Robert Rumilly swore to all the gods that on September 23, 1948, Mr. Joseph Jean, Sollicitor-General of Canada and Liberal organizer for the island of Montreal, had demanded that Rumilly and his friends René Chaloult, Philippe Hamel and Camilien Houde, stop their attacks on the government for its treatment of Bernonville. In exchange for this pre-electoral biting of the lips, Count Bernonville would receive a permanent residency visa. As a matter of fact, Rumilly did meet in mid-November 1948 with Jean, who promised him — in the absence of witnesses — a satisfactory settling of the Bernonville case.[147] But Louis Saint-Laurent still refused to meet Bernonville,[148] any promises that were made were without effect,[149] and on February 17, 1950 the Immigration Board unanimously decided to order the Count's expulsion.

Urbi and Orbi

The hue and cry surrounding the Bernonville affair and the cases of the others in the band of French exiles in Quebec echoed through the American, French and even Spanish media. The Spanish national radio service, for example, sang praises to Camilien Houde, calling him "An honest and devout Canadian who prevented one of the most magnificent heroes injured in the service of his country, Jacques de Bernonville, from being delivered over to his enemies."[150] The same radio service would quote at length from Philippe Hamel's brochure, *The French political refugees and the strange advice of the ambassador.* Nothing more was needed to incite one Pierre Héricourt, exiled in Spain under a French death sentence, to write to Philippe Hamel asking for the address of "my old friend Jacques de Bernonville who will also, I believe, be happy to have my current address."[151]

After he recommended to anyone still listening the reading of the *Letter to François Mauriac* by Maurice Bardèche, especially for the words "We are ashamed to be Frenchmen, and we did not feel this shame during the Occupation," Philippe Hamel replied with all due haste to the request for information he received from the brother-in-law of Robert Brasillach, a veteran reporter at *Je suis partout* who was being tried in Paris as a result of his book entitled *The Nuremberg Trial.* "I will have no difficulty at all in giving him powerful ammunition. I am sending him this very day official information on the atrocities committed by the Allies in Germany."[152]

Maurice Bardèche was not alone in seeking support in Quebec. Another unconditional partisan of French fascism, Henry Coston, looked to the Montreal Mayor

Camilien Houde for help. Houde had become over the years a kind of society patron for fascist collaborators in prison or exile.[153] In 1949, Coston found himself in the penitentiary at St. Martin-de-Ré in France, serving out a life term of hard labour along with other notables of the Vichy collaboration: Henri Béraud, Bernard Faÿ and Jacques Benoist-Méchin. Although he was in poor health, Coston was in good spirits because, wrote the prison social worker to Houde, "he knows that you are doing much to achieve a prompt amnesty for the victims of the purges."[154] Camilien Houde found the letter touching and sent Madame Coston a few francs to help her provide some food and candy to her husband, while he at the same time admonished her to keep out a little for herself.[155]

As if it was really necessary, a second correspondent at the same jail — this time a social worker *and* pharmacist — sent Houde a plea for Henry Coston. Coston's service record was impressive. The letter recalled that Henry Coston had been editor of *La libre parole* for nine years (this infamous anti-Semitic paper, "Free Speech" had been founded by Édouard Drumont) which had many subscribers in "your" province before the war. During the war, Coston was mandated by the Pétain government to take care of "masonic" questions. Finally, the letter requests Houde to inform Mr. Coston of the fate of Adrien Arcand (founder of Quebec's fascist party) and his close associates, Messrs. Lapointe and Ménard.[156]

But why stop at sending gifts of candy to Nazi propagandists rotting away in prison, when you could invite former Vichy personalities to come to Quebec for pro-Pétain speeches in support of the exiled executants of Vichy policies?[157] To that end (which never arrived), Philippe Hamel approached Attorney Tixier-Vignancourt, famous for his eloquence in the courtroom, and a

lesser Minister of the Vichy regime. The meeting took
place in May, 1950. Tixier-Vignancourt had already been
found sufficiently compromised by his association with
the previous government to have been declared ineligible
to run in the 1945 legislative elections in France. Rumilly,
for his part, invited a Colonel Rémy to speak in Quebec.
A former resistance member who had called for clemency
for pro-Pétain Frenchmen "of good faith," Rémy worried
a Robert Rumilly who was terribly anxious to avoid having
French-Canadian public opinion caught between two different views of this thorny issue. With disdainful cyni-
cism, Rumilly explained the problem to Rémy: "Our
public opinion which can be chracterized by the term
'traditionalist,' worships Marshal Pétain. It is obviously
less able than French public opinion to understand the
nuances of the situation in France. Equating de Gaulle and
Pétain would throw it for a loop."[158] But even Rémy's
mitigated opinion of de Gaulle was too much for Philippe
Hamel, and he firmly opposed Rémy's coming to speak in
Quebec.[159]

Given these strong convictions, the most visible defenders of Jacques de Bernonville could not help but be
favorably impressed by the letters of recommendation sent
in his defense by so celebrated a collaborator as Abel
Bonnard, former Minister of Education under Pétain.
Bonnard had sought refuge at the end of the war in the
shattered remnants of the thousand-year Reich, along
with the last stalwarts of Nazism. From his haven in
Franco's Madrid, where he had successfully fled after the
capitulation of Germany, he wrote to the Canadian Government that he had known de Bernonville well between
1942 and 1944 and that the latter was "a soldier, a gentle-
man and a knight."[160]

Like many other Nazi sympathisers exiled in Quebec, Bernonville had belonged, before the war, to an extremist right-wing clandestine movement, *La Cagoule* (The Hood), which aimed to defend the War Ministry in the event of a Communist uprising.[161] But Philippe Hamel and René Chaloult were not particularly concerned by the nature of the letters of support piling up in the Bernonville file: even the warning about Bernonville given by the very-Pétainist French Commander Quivault could not shake Philippe Hamel's support for the Count. Quivault informed Hamel that Bernonville, "acting loyally in the exercise of his functions, had in turn taken German money." Philippe Hamel, either by omission or commission, carefully kept this warning a secret until March 1951. When these facts were revealed to his close associates René Chaloult and Robert Rumilly, neither one even blinked.[162] But Noël Dorion, upon hearing the news, showed extreme caution and refused, along with Wheeler Dupont, then President of the Saint-Jean Baptiste Society, to allow his name to appear on the letterhead of the Committee for the defense of political refugees.

What worried Philippe Hamel more than the nature of the accusations against Bernonville — "No one will ever convince me that you did anything but heroically serve your country" — was the obligation to reply after the fact. He pleaded with Bernonville: "Please, give us the means to refute the accusations that you were paid by the Germans and belonged to the German militia. We have to be able to provide the explanations right away, not weeks or months after the accusations are made."[163]

The Jacques Dugé de Bernonville file

In a letter to Louis Saint-Laurent written six years after
the end of hostilities, Bernonville gave his simple answer
to why he would not be able to refute the charges against
him if he was called to defend himself in a French court.
"How could the required witnesses come forward, since
most were dead, imprisoned, in hiding or in exile?" It was,
of course, a rhetorical question. "Abel Bonnard, for example, and my one-time superior officer, General Bridoux,
former Minister of National Defense from 1942 to 1944,
are both under sentence of death and in exile in Spain.
How could they appear for me in France?"[164] A difficult
nut to crack, to be sure... But it was not only that witnesses
were unavailable for duty in France. Even in Canada,
Bernonville was unable to fully reply to the accusations
against him nor explain away his conduct,[165] any more
than he could give the "names of my superiors who gave
the orders I merely carried out."[166] When giving his version of his wartime activities to his own lawyer, Bernard
Bourdon, Bernonville was very evasive about the events of
1943. He simply stated that he left Lyon at the end of 1942
and went back to live in Paris, with no particular mission
to carry out, nothing at all official, just some things dealing
with youth, military inspections, work camps. Like many
officers, he claimed, he awaited further orders. "Being an
unemployed officer, I took it upon myself to organize my
life without an official mission, just like in the civilian
world, the same as it was for a large number of military
men who had nothing to do because of the Occupation. In
1944 though, I did receive a few mission orders (...)."[167] If
attorney Bourdon was not curious enough to ask Jacques
Dugé de Bernonville about his "unofficial" activities in

1943, it does not mean that he had nothing to answer for. What were these activities, exactly? To answer that question, we looked at the records of the Paris judicial police, which provide some questions and some answers.

1. The content of Bernonville's Paris judicial police file. These records were first published in Montreal in the *Petit Journal* newspaper, prior to André Laurendeau and *Le Devoir* endorsing Bernonville.[168] They indicate that Bernonville was accused of collaborating with the enemy, breach of state security, arbitrary confinement, arson, violence and theft. If found, the records state, the subject is to be incarcerated in a secure place, and the Paris DST is to be immediately advised by telephone (number Anjou 24/20) and telegram using the following code: "The individual whose file is S-45/922 had been located. UNDER NO CIRCUMSTANCES MENTION HIS NAME. French police are seeking him, not to try him, but to execute the death sentence for treason pronounced against him by the Toulouse Court of Justice."

2. The file contains the citation of the Order of the Nation in Bernonville's favor, issued by the Minister of the Interior and signed by Pierre Laval on July 6, 1944. The award calls Bernonville a "unit chief of the permanent Franc-Garde of the French militia, (...) a particularly energetic officer. In numerous operations for the maintenance of law and order that he participated in, in the Haute-Savoie, the Vercors and the Saône-et-Loire regions, he showed a calm and collected courage (...)." This document was made public in the House of Commons in December 1949 by Alistair Stewart.

**3. A copy of an article by Claude Maubourguet publish-
ed in the April 7, 1944 edition of *Je suis partout.***
Maubourguet had just been posted to the 2nd unit of the
Franc-Garde of which Bernonville was commander-in-
chief. "Tireless, he conducts patrols, visits guard positions, rushes from one end to the other of his sector in his
old jalopy-turned half-track and self-propelled machine
gun. Commander Bernonville often repeated these words:
'Aim sure but fire with no hatred because these are our
brothers.' "

**4. The reports of the investigation by the Ministry of the
Interior, Central Head Office of National Security,
dated August 8, 1945.** They confirm that Bernonville
travelled with an S.R.A. (German espionage service) convoy on August 24, 1944, from Lyon to Klimbach, in the
Alsace district, where he stayed for 15 days. Many sworn
statements suggest, oddly enough, that Bernonville was
having an affair with the mistress of Colonel Dernsbach,
chief of the S.R.A. for the South of France. Her name was
Charlotte, and, in a classical scenario, she was Dernsbach's
secretary. According to Bernonville's former secretary,
Louis-Paul Mace, the real reason for Bernonville going to
Klimbach was to be with Charlotte. But he was unable to
remain in Germany, and had himself parachuted back into
France, in October 1944, near the forest of Rambouillet.

**5. Ministry of the Interior, Report of Judicial Police
Inspector Henri Rontard to the Chief Commissioner,
Head of the 13th Brigade in Rennes, dated August 3,
1946.**
Jacques Dugé de Bernonville was Section Head of the
Action française movement in Vannes. He was appre-
hended there in 1926 by the Service of the 13th Mobile

Brigade for distributing royalist propaganda. Bernonville subsequently became the chief of the First brigade of the Secret Revolutionary Action Committee (also known as The Hood) in Paris where he was arrested on January 27, 1938. The authorities released him on August 13, 1939, without formal charges. In October 1940, Bernonville became regional director of the Centre for Information and Study in Lyon. Once this organization was dissolved, he went to Morocco, where he was Chief of Mission for Jewish questions. Back in Paris in 1942, he became Chief of Mission at the Ministry of National Education. In 1944, he directed operations targeting the maquis in the Glières Plateau in Haute-Savoie and in the Vercors region (in the Drôme département), afterwards becoming Chief of the maintenance of order for the Côte d'Or, Aine and Saône-et-Loire départements.

One Jacques de Vannes from Cambourg stated that Bernonville was a recruiter for the Legion of French Volunteers and for the Militia. He affirmed having been himself recruited by Bernonville into an organization whose aim was to fight the maquis and the Resistance in Bretagne, the *Selschutz*.

Bernonville was also apparently one of the chiefs of a clandestine organization called *L'Équipe*, (The Team) which was directly armed and financed by Germany to combat Communism and the Resistance. He used the name Jacques Boissière, having had an identity card in that name issued by the Saint-Romain d'Urse (Loire) city hall.

According to the central police archives of Casablanca, Bernonville enjoyed very close relations with the head of the Militia, Joseph Darnand. But he left Morocco for Paris in September 1942, and became there the General Secretary of the African Phalanx whose offices were on the

Place Malesherbes. Bernonville next founded the Volunteer Corps, located on the rue de Grenelle.

6. Court of justice of the Haute-Garonne, details of facts known to the Commissioner of the Government dated May 12, 1947.

Jacques Dugé de Bernonville moved to Rabat on October 18, 1941. There, he was a Chargé de Mission for Jewish questions on behalf of the Vichy government. He also organized the Legionnaire Security Service in Rabat, whose activities were felt throughout the country. He then returned to Paris to found the French Volunteer Corps. (Here we have a glimpse of Bernonville's 1943 activities about which he remained so discrete.) "Back in North Africa in 1943 with the rank of Commander, he was selected for sabotage missions and espionage run by Intendent KESSLER using the Waffen S.S., members of the P.P.F. (Parti populaire français) and the Militia.

7. Verdict maintaining the death sentence by the Toulouse Appeals Court, October 8, 1947.

"Insofar as the documents in the procedure judged normal and the whole of the evidence shows, it has been proven that DUGE DE BERNONVILLE is guilty of wartime collaboration in France and in North Africa, and notably in Paris, Lyon and Rabat from 1940 to 1944 where no prescription applies, with a foreign power, namely Germany and its agents, in order to assist the designs of that power against France; by entering into a relationship with agents of the S.D., by organizing a French Volunteer Corps and the African Phalanx, by performing sabotage missions in North Africa and by handing over to the Germans two French citizens detained in a jail-house; (...)

The Court, after due deliberation in conformity with the Law Referring to the demands of the Commissioner of the Government and by applying the above-cited texts; SENTENCES the adult DUGE DE BERNONVILLE to death.

8. RCMP report of August 3, 1948.[169]

"I venture to suggest therefore, that, because of his particularly black war record, consideration be given to having him deported to France, so that the French authorities may deal with him as they see fit," wrote the author of the report.

9. January 22, 1949 Report of the Commissioner of the Government to the Court of Justice of Toulouse.

According to this report, "The methods used by Dugé de BERNONVILLE and his accomplices created such a climate of terror in the local population (of Saône-et-Loire) that the German Commander himself ordered the withdrawal of the forces under the control of Dugé de Bernonville.[170] In May and June 1944, Bernonville proceeded with massive arrests and himself oversaw and took part in many interrogations where burnings and beatings of prisoners took place, resulting in permanent damage to the detainees. In addition, many prisoners were handed over to the Germans for summary execution. These arrests and torture are confirmed by incontrovertible witnesses.

The same documents supply details of earlier accusations:

On April 16, 1944, Bernonville's troops — 250 strong — attacked 90 members of the Maquis in the Vercors region. The battle went on all night long and in the morning DUGÉ de BERNONVILLE personally supervised the mopping-up operation and vigorously used extreme measures against the population of surrounding villages. This repressive action went on until April 24. For example, accompanied by his adjutant Dr. Dagostini, Bernonville set fire to many farms and houses and made numerous arrests, which resulted in three patriots being odiously tortured before being executed.

10. German language receipt for payment.

This is an identification card dated June 18, 1944, issued to Bernonville at his Paris address, with the following information:

ZAHLUNGEN (Payment)
Varschuss Am B1 Unterhalt (Subsistance) Ab
4.000 19/2/44 5 N.Z. 5023 19/1/44
24/2/44

Jean Bruchesi confronted Bernonville with the testimony of a high civil servant in the Immigration Department who assured him that his service was in possession of a document which proved that Bernonville had joined the ranks of the German Army. Bernonville did not deny that such a document existed, but scoffed at its meaning, claiming it was a two-week interim document valid from December 15 to December 30, covering an espionage mission in which he was to locate an SS group near Paris, determine its size, discover if possible the nature of the new armaments about which the Germans had begun to talk, and evaluate the morale of this group.[171]

11. A photo of de Bernonville approved by German censors.

The photo identifies him as Secretary of the African Phalanx.

12. Membership card number 605 in the 8th Branden-burg unit of the Waffen SS.

This reveals that Bernonville joined the Waffen SS on December 1, 1943. It is the second piece of information of the Count's 1943 activities and another reason why he chose to remain silent about that year.

13. A Waffen SS document dated February 23, 1944 authorizing the payment of a pension to Bernonville's family.

Mrs. Bernonville's name is crossed out with the mention that she is not to be informed of her husband's status as a volunteer in the Waffen S.S.

14. A Waffen SS volunteer's identification card, dates March 15, 1944.

15. Copies of 13 German-language documents.

A Canadian immigration officer scribbled on the letter addressed to the translation service: "Documents placed (illegible). They would be on the Nazi files in Paris."[172] The nature of these other German documents is not known, at present.

An article written by McKenzie Porter that appeared in *Maclean's* magazine in 1951 and which was based on documents in the reporter's possession since 1949, confirmed and completed most of the information in the Bernonville file.[173] It states that under orders from Abel Bonnard, Bernonville organized the Legion of Combatants. On October 13, 1941, he embarked with his wife and four children at Marseille on the Lamoricière, heading for Algiers, where, according to his visa, authorized by Abel Bonnard, he would be in charge of the General Commissariat of the Vichy Government for Jewish affairs. Bernonville took up residence in Casablanca where he organized the Legionnaire Security Service.

According to MacKenzie Porter, on July 19, 1942, Bernonville informed Dr. Menetrel, private secretary to Pétain that, unable to contain himself in North Africa, he wished to return to France and join the Tricolour Legion, made up of French volunteers who wanted to fight the Soviets under German command, because, as he put it, "this legion has a lot in common with the Security Service." His request was granted.

In 1943, sensing a German defeat, Bernonville joined the ranks of a strange organization called the Corps of French Volunteers, which aimed to first eliminate the Resistance and then take on the Germans in order to be able to present its members as heroes to the victorious Allies. After that, what could follow but the happy restoration of the monarchy in France? The Germans, understanding poorly and incompletely this plan, approved the constitution of the Corps under the command of Sturmbanführer S.S. Best with Bernonville named as liaison. This bizarre enterprise only lasted for fifteen days, until Joseph Darnand caught wind of it and accused Bernonville of defeatism and treason. Darnand called for the members of the Corps to join the Waffen SS. Rushing to get back into Darnand's good graces, Bernonville made an example of himself and became, as previously mentioned, number 605 in the Brandenburg unit of the Waffen SS.

In a sworn statement produced when he was arrested in Germany, *Maclean's* also reported, Louis Mace declared that after his flight from Lyon with Colonel Dernbach, Bernonville volunteered for espionage and sabotage missions behind Allied lines, and received the required training at Wissenbourg in Alsace. He was then parachuted into

Chartres on September 20, 1944, along with three men, a radio transmitter and three million francs, worth about thirty thousand dollars in 1951 terms. From that time on, his whereabouts, and the whereabouts of those funds are unknown; he, of course, later turned up in Canada.

It is understandable from the preceding that the often-repeated affirmations of Dugé de Bernonville of only having done what was necessary for the Vichy Government did not convince the Canadian Minister of Immigration nor Louis Saint-Laurent. Pierre Asselin, private secretary to Prime Minister Saint-Laurent, wrote Bernonville that the documents in his dossier amply justified the Minister's decision to maintain the deportation order. In addition, he went on, "If everything in the file is shown to be factual, no Canadian government could justify a favorable extraordinary exception in your case."[174] Asselin suggested to Bernonville that he should seek refuge elsewhere than France. Otherwise, the courts would decide his fate, not a good outcome for him since his appeals had already been been rejected twice.

A dupes' game

The years passed and the documents piled up in Bernonville's file, but his defenders refused to abandon the game. Bona Arsenault, for example, worked the back rooms in favour of Bernonville, but had no more success there than he had when defending Victor Keyserling. In a moment of giddy self-deception, Arsenault reassured Rumilly in December 1950 that he had communicated with Saint-Laurent and with Minister Harris and "The replies I received gave me great encouragement. I sent the letter I received from Mr. Harris directly to Bernonville."[175] Arsenault's enthusiasm would not stop Harris from issuing a new deportation order against Bernonville, who then had just sixty days to leave the country. Arsenault, member for Bonaventure in the House, would not accept defeat though and increased his activities on behalf of the Count, some of which turned out exceptionally fruitful and which convinced him that Bernonville would never be deported. "I am in any case proposing a law on the right to asylum for political refugees in order that Mr. de Bernonville can take advantage of it. (...) But I learned yesterday that this law, if passed, could not apply in Bernonville's case."[176] He told Rumilly that his draft law was prepared right in the offices of the Minister of Immigration who gave it his full approval. Bona Arsenault added that Mr. Harris showed great sympathy for Bernonville and desperately wanted to help him. This aroused Rumilly to comment: "What prodigious hypocrisy!"[177]

Bernonville assured Jean Bruchesi that in a meeting with Immigration Minister Harris in September 1951, "Harris honorably refused to act as a judge, did not demand to know the names of my superiors, and took me at my word."[178]

Exile and death

Jacques Dugé de Bernonville left Canada on August 17, 1951, for Rio de Janeiro, with a Brazilian permanent residency visa in his pocket. He preferred to take a circuitous, longer route, rather than a direct Pan Am flight through New York, so as to avoid U.S. immigration authorities, a prudent precaution under the circumstances. According to Robert Rumilly, a French group including the Count of Paris had invested money in Brazil and could, through its influence, offer Bernonville a job. Bernonville confirmed this account to Jean Bruchesi: "Devoted friends, including the Count of Paris, organized my coming to Brazil. I spoke of you to the Prince who asked me to transmit his most warm and friendly memories to 'Dear Jean.' And so, thanks to him, I was able to contact several persons who were highly sympathetic to me and I feel a little less lost."[179] One of those he contacted to find work was a friend of Robert Rumilly, a man named Robert Soliva.

Eventually threatened with deportation by the Government of Brazil, Bernonville disappeared from his official residence in Sao Paulo and began using the alias that had served him so well in the past, Jacques Benoît, and occasionally a second alias, Maurice Delegrize. Brazil's efforts to deport him ultimately failed though, because while in May 1955 the Federal Supreme Court of Brazil refused to grant him *habeas corpus*, four months later, on September 30, it granted his request on a technicality. Bernonville's last known place of work was the Economic Institute of Rio, a semi-official organization.

Jacques Dugé de Bernonville apparently never again set foot in his native France. In 1968 he was covered by the twenty-year prescription on his crimes, but all the subsidiary penalties remained, including the forfeiture of his disability and service military pensions, the seizure of his property, deprivation of civil rights and the interdiction of living in certain administrative areas of France and in the big cities of the country.[180] He lived in Brazil from from 1951 to 1972, and met his family in Spain once a year for a time.[181] This gave him the opportunity of seeing his brother in arms and companion in misfortune, Christian du Jonchay,[182] which tends to confirm that just like du Jonchay, Bernonville had belonged to the African Phalanx.[183] Annual family reunions also took place in the Black Forest region of Germany[184] and in the Tyrolian Alps.[185]

Bernonville died at the hand of an assassin in his Rio de Janeiro working-class neighbourhood apartment on April 27, 1972 at the age of 71, strangled with his own neck-tie by the son of his housekeeper who claimed to have been possessed by voodoo. Dirceu Aives, a reporter with the Brazil daily newspaper *Diario Da Noite*, gave no credence at all to this explanation. He recalled that the feet and hands of the victim were carefully bound, which suggested that the assassin was in full possession of his mental faculties and was not a novice at this kind of operation. The reporter also suspected that there was an accomplice to the murder and wondered if the hand of Klaus Barbie, one of Bernonville's old 'acquaintances' from Lyon, was not at work in the murder. Barbie was then living in exile in Bolivia under the name of Klaus Altmann. According to this version of events, Barbie, the former Gestapo Colonel and Chief of Section IV of the Sipo-SD in Lyon feared what Bernonville might inadvertently reveal in the Memoirs he was writing at the time of his death.

3. Mr. Richemont and the Prime Minister

Paul Reifenrath

While Montel, then Bernonville occupied centre stage in the affair of the exiled French militiamen in Quebec, another character arrived quietly in Montreal in 1947 or 1948, and quickly became an adviser to Quebec Premier Maurice Duplessis. Paul Erwin Eberhard Reifenrath, also called Jean d'Alsace, was born in Sarralbe in the Moselle region on July 2, 1905. He was a former officer in the French army, who, after resigning his commission, became a journalist in Paris.[186] Well, 'propagandist' would better describe his real activities, because from 1932 to 1934, Reifenrath was the General Secretary of Solidarité française, a pro-Nazi movement founded by Jean Renaud and François Coty; he edited the newspaper of the same name. He subsequently distanced himself from Solidarité française and became the Alsace-Lorraine correspondent for Gustave Hervé's paper, *La Victoire*. Hervé was a former nationalist and pacifist who had become an ultra-nationalist. Reifenrath had ambitions for himself in the Alsatian right-wing movement but his plans always seemed to come up short: he worked for the weekly *Die Staatsreform* in 1934 and at Joseph Bliger's *Union paysanne* but in both cases, was quickly removed from the fast track. Nonetheless, he did succeed at one thing: he became the leading figure in the Strasbourg anti-Semitic movement.

On January 1, 1937, Paul Reifenrath succeeded Oscar de Férenzy as editor in chief of *La Voix d'Alsace et de Lorraine* and gave this weekly a violent anti-Semitic bent, but was soon (again!) removed from his position. During this period he published a pamphlet with the provocative title, *The Jews in France but especially in Alsace*.[187] The Jews are described in this brochure as parasites and Reifenrath, an industrious if unimaginative Nazi scribe, denounced Communism as a Jewish enterprise, and Jewish-American high finance as the "mother of Bolshevism."[188]

Reifenrath also founded a weekly entitled *La nouvelle voix d'Alsace*, devoted to the struggle against the Judeo-Masonic and revolutionary peril. This newspaper lasted from February 18, 1937 to December, 1938. In the building where the paper had offices, 9 rue du Fossé des Treize in Strasbourg, was also to be found a bookstore specializing in anti-Semitic and anti-Masonic literature. A police report indicated that Reifenrath was financed by a working group of Lower-Rhine industrialists during his years in Strasbourg.[189]

Reifenrath's wartime activities remain obscure, but if the past can serve as a template for the future, he probably pursued his struggle against the "Reds, the Kikes and the Masons." Occupied France would have offered him no end of possibilities to exercise his particular talents.

Paul-Éverard Richemont

Judged and sentenced for his political activities, Reifenrath reached Canada in the fall of 1947 or 1948 using the name Leyzen, thanks to the help of the St. Gabriel Brothers.[190] Jean Bonnel and a delegation from that Order welcomed him upon his arrival and for six months he resided at Bonnel's home on Bernard Street in Outremont. He still called himself Leyzen but many referred to him with familiarity, as "Tonton," or uncle. The one name he never pronounced was that of Reifenrath.

Tonton, alias Leyzen, lived for a time on Chambord Street in east-end Montreal, and used the name Chambord. He even managed to convince Adrien Arcand, head of the Canadian Nazi movement, that he was the Count of Paris, heir to the French throne. Bonnel hastened to disabuse Arcand about Tonton's identity. By 1950, Reifenrath's fortunes had taken a dramatic turn for the better, and he now lived in Westmount, at 4839 Westmount Avenue more precisely, and calling himself Paul-Éverard Richemont. His new family name was seemingly inspired by the little French town of Richemont, situated not far from the Maginot line. Geography always seems to play such an important role in the choice of aliases!

In any case, it was to the Westmount address that Maurice Duplessis wrote him a note on June 1, 1950, wishing him a safe trip to Rome. Some months earlier, in November 1949, Jean Bruchesi, Under-Secretary of the Province of Quebec, had received a letter from his good friend, the Count of Paris (the real one, this time). The heir to the throne of France was looking for news of the professional activities and the past of Mr. Richemont, who had visited him in Portugal some days earlier. At the foot of the letter were hastily scratched a few words: "Journalist, Alsace, very cultured, wife and children, very well connected, studied the Law, army officer."[191] Jean Bruchesi remembered having this note: "One week earlier I received a letter from the Count of Paris who had been visited by a Belgian refugee just arrived from Canada, who claimed to be on very good terms with the political masters of Quebec, and en route for Rome, on a delicate mission to the Vatican authorities on behalf of the 'Chief.' The Prince asked me if I knew this individual, about whom, and for good reason, no one had spoken to me. That's when I called one of the city's priests who might have been 'au courant.' The next day, or perhaps it was on the following evening as chance would have it, I came face to face with the very same priest, who was leaving a meeting with the Premier."[192]

What miracles had transpired between the arrival of a homeless and destitute Paul Erwin Eberhard Reifenrath in Canada and his moving to the most exclusive enclave in the province? The answer to this question throws some new light on events from recent Quebec history that are as famous as they are poorly-understood, such as the Silicosis Scandal and Asbestos Strike.

The Silicosis Scandal

In March, 1948 *Relations* magazine published an article written by the Franco-Americain journalist Burton Ledoux entitled "Silicose, from St. Rémi d'Amherst to the Ungava." In it, Ledoux accused the silica mining companies in St. Rémi d'Amherst of criminal negligence in exposing miners to unsafe working conditions. Particularly targeted was the Timmins family of Canada, minority shareholders with seats on the boards of directors of Hollinger Consolidated Gold Mines and Noranda Mines Limited. Noranda Mines controlled Canada China Clay and Silica Ltd., which ran the mining operations at St. Rémi-d'Amherst.[193] Since the exploitation of the immense iron ore deposits in the Ungava peninsula had just been handed to Hollinger Consolidated Gold Mines, and if industrial hygiene was not better respected there that at St. Rémi d'Amherst, we risked "multiplying beyond belief the ravages of silicosis, with its cortege of physical, social and moral ruin,"[194] wrote Father Jean d'Auteuil Richard, the magazine's director, in an editorial.

The companies reacted quickly and went far beyond what the intrepid editorial team of the little magazine had ever anticipated. Through Alphonse Raymond, administrator of Canada China Clay & Silica Ltd. and Noranda Mines Ltd., and chief conduit between Premier Duplessis and Canadian and U.S. financiers, N.A Timmins Junior of Hollinger Consolidated Gold Mines Ltd. and R.A Timmins, of N.A. Timmins Corporation Limited demanded that *Relations* publish a retraction —which they piously called a 'rectification' —of the Ledoux article, failing which there would be legal action for libel and defamation. Father d'Auteuil Richard explained these reactions by the companies' fears of the article affecting the negotiations of loans they needed to float on the U.S. financial markets to finance the development of the Ungava mines.

Naturally, Father d'Auteuil Richard rejected this demand. He would allow the mining companies to reply to the article in the next issue of the magazine and, as was customary, Burton Ledoux would then have the last word. Alphonse Raymond and the Timmins family, though, were intractable: either *Relations* published the retraction, signed by the magazine's editor in chief, or they would find themselves in court. Jesuit Father Arthur Dubois, Provincial Police Chaplain and confidant of Maurice Duplessis, made tireless efforts to convince the magazine, published by the Company of Jesus, to give in, and eventually succeeded, because in July 1948, under the signature of Father Adélard Dugré, *Relations* printed its regrets and withdrew the principal accusations contained in Burton Ledoux' article and professed firm optimism concerning the prospects for industrial hygiene in the Ungava mines.[195] Things would not end with that, however. On January 12, 1949, *Le Devoir* took up the cause and published a second article by Ledoux: "Asbestosis in East Broughton. A village of 3,000 souls suffocates in dust."

The Asbestos Strike

In the second week of February 1949, the asbestos miners struck the Thetford Mines Asbestos Corporation. The strike would last until June of that same year.[196] As it was in the silicosis scandal, the improvement of health conditions on the job was the centerpiece of the strike, the fundamental demand of the miners.

But the workers also wanted to have a say in the management of the mines, and this demand was in no way acceptable to the owners. In 1947, to Duplessis' dismay, the principle of workers rights to participate in company management won the support of the Religious Commission of Social Studies of Quebec. Two years later, the same Commission published their report, *The participation of workers in the life of their company*. A response was not long in coming. Father Arthur Dubois, a tireless scribe devoted to Maurice Duplessis and to the struggle for healthy ideas, came up with a doctrinaire analysis refuting the report. He saw in it the pernicious influence of the social literature of France, that unhappy country suffering under the yoke of a neutralist government and torn by class struggle. Which was not the case, maintained Dubois, of the Catholic government in the Province of Quebec, where harmony between employers and workers must be preserved at all costs. In a hurry to settle his scores, Father Dubois denounced the abuse of confidence, the notorious incompetence and the absence of maturity on the part of the authors of the report. The confrontation between Duplessis and the Commission, like the one that opposed him to *Relations*, displayed a clear ideological character.

It is thus hardly surprising that the Premier and the Johns-Manville Company, owner of one of the mines, reacted to the strike by engaging in a province-wide and international crusade that gave no quarter.[197] Duplessis saw in the strike the prelude to a revolution against established order, and expressed these fears clearly to the Apostolic Nuncio, the Pope's ambassador to Canada: "Credible information in our possession and which for obvious reasons cannot be made public, indicates clearly that the matter at hand is not simply a fundamentally illegal strike, but an anarchist revolution against the Law, the Courts, and legitimately constituted authority."[198]

Paul Reifenrath, as luck would have it, knew quite a bit about ideological crusading, having spent many years of his life in France railing against democracy, Communism, and their puppets, the Jews and the Masons. The asbestos strike gave him an unforeseen opportunity to win the confidence of Maurice Duplessis and to use his propagandist's talents.

Reifenrath, alias Paul-Éverard Richemont, joined forces with the Professional Association of Industrialists run by Eugène Gibeau, with the help of moral adviser and association founder, Jesuit Father Émile Bouvier. They led the crusade against the "foreign agents of revolution who were trying to weaken established order which the very Catholic Government of Quebec had the responsibility of maintaining."[199] The Association took the side of the Canadian Johns-Manville Company throughout the conflict and tried to conscript other major employers to the cause. An urgent meeting of employers was thus called at the Windsor Hotel in Montreal on April 11, 1949, to discuss the terrible threat to private property in the province that the strike represented.[200] No fewer than 300 worried employers showed up at the meeting. But how had Richemont connected with Gibeau and the Association? We don't know for certain, but his past work as a paid agitator for Rhine industrialists could not but help his introduction to Quebec's business milieu.

The Custos Report

In December 1949 a confidential report, simply signed "Custos," was circulating in Quebec. It was published by the Confederation of Christian Workers of Canada (defined as a union of militant Catholics) and was meant for the exclusive attention of members of the clergy.[201] There was, in reality, no such group. The name was apparently chosen for its resemblance to that of the Confederation of Catholic Workers of Canada, with which the asbestos strikers were affiliated. The report takes aim at Subversion (with a capital "S") — which it defined as the combination of subversive and occult forces whose final aim is the destruction of the Church — which it said had taken control of the Catholic unions. Subversive Christian movements like The Furrow, New World and Progressive Catholics had arisen in France, and their ideas were now spreading through the Province of Quebec.

In the preface to his report, "Custos" quoted the great specialist on secret societies and ardent propagator of the infamous Tzarist Secret Police propaganda piece, the *Protocols of the Elders of Zion*, Mgr. Jouin. Jouin quoted a directive supposedly given in Basel, Switzerland, by a high official in the Bnai B'rith: "We must maintain the spirit of revolt among the working classes, and send them to the barricades, but we must also ensure their demands are never met, because we require their full dissatisfaction in order to destroy Christian society and bring on anarchy." (Mgr. E. Jouin, in *The Faithful of the Anti-Church*, RISS publishers, Paris 1921, page 122.)[202]

Custos also attacked, in passing, those Catholic leaders who were so complacent towards certain Jewish and Protestant capitalists and towards the Socialist or socialist-inclined governments of other Canadian provinces.[203] Custos ended by claiming that the Canadian media, rampant with Subversion, had refused to publish the article distributed by the Vatican's Fides Press Agency concerning the Jewish abominations in the Holy Land, which also stigmatized Zionism as a worse evil than Nazism and the precursor in the Middle East of Communism, which would never tolerate any form of expression of the doctrine of Christ on its territory. (*Documentation catholique*, May 25, 1949.)[204]

Between the Preface and the Conclusion of the Custos Report was the proof that "The active participation of the Comintern in the Asbestos Strike could no longer be the least bit in doubt."[205] The pamphlet relied on endless quotes from *Le Devoir*, which was called Subversion's main voice in Quebec, as well as a pamhplet produced by the Quebec Provincial Police, which was denounced by M[gr.] Desranleau in a public letter on August 22, 1949 for its vulgarity and its lying accusations against the parish priest of St. Aimé d'Asbestos, Father Camirand.[206] The QPP pamphlet went into endless accounts of the suffering endured by its forces during the Asbestos strike. The icing on the cake was an article in the Report, reprinted from a June 21, 1949 letter to the *Montréal-Matin* daily newspaper (controlled by Duplessis' National Union Party) signed by a worker who called himself by the patently-invented name ON. LEZAURA (We're gonna get 'em). Presented straight-faced as a real individual ON. LEZAURA denounced the unwanted influence of the Red Terror on the voting of miners during the strike.

Inasmuch as the true identity of the author or authors if the Custos Report, published by a non-existing organization and signed with an alias, was not known, some suspected the author to be the Jesuit Father Émile Bouvier, head of Industrial Relations at the Université de Montreal and close collaborator of Premier Duplessis. Bouvier never denied the rumors. The most credible hypothesis is that there were more than one author, because we can identify the literary style of Father Dubois, the ludicrous ideas of Richemont concerning the Subversion, Jews and the Comintern, and significant excerpts from Father Bouvier's book, *Employers and Workers*.[207]

They're all so sleazy, it makes us queasy...
(General Charles de Gaulle)

The tone taken by the bosses' supporters in the asbestos conflict was conspiratorial, but this was not surprising, as Duplessis and his consorts remained convinced that they were facing an international plot against established order. The correspondence we will quote occurred many months after the end of the strike. It shows that Quebec City and the Canadian Johns-Manville Company considered the resolution of the strike to be a defeat.

On October 11, 1949, on a letterhead of Trans World Commerce Limited/ Le Commerce Mondial Limitée, "L" wrote to Maurice Duplessis outlining the reasons calling for a greater propaganda effort.[208] Conrad Black attributes the letter in question to Father Cyrille Labrecque, because of the "L". But Black jumped to this easy conclusion too quickly, for several reasons. First of all, it would be surprising (but not impossible) that a man of the cloth would write such a letter on corporate stationery. But even more convincing is the fact that Father Labrecque was in Canada during the months of October and November 1949, at the very time this mysterious "L" was definitely in Rome. So we can say categorically that Father Cyrille Labrecque was not the signatory of the letter.[209] But there was a chronology that fit the schedule of a different person, Richemont, who sent a report to Duplessis from Rome on October 19, 1949, one week after "L" had left Montreal for... Rome. And "L", of course, could also stand for Richemont's alias Leyzen or the "LEZAURA" referred to above. And surprise, surprise, we find "L" writing the following: "In re-reading my report, I have found numerous imperfections. I am having it recopied and you will soon receive a revised and corrected version." He could very well be referring to the Custos Report, which began circulating in December of the same year.

M$^{gr.}$ Courchesne and "L" agreed, according to "L's" letter of October 11, 1949, that the motive behind the apparent passivity in dealing with the social issues at hand was a lack of documentation which handicapped their attempts to keep the controversy with the left-wing Catholics alive. In order to remedy the situation, "L" created on a crash basis, an information and documentation service that M$^{gr.}$ Courchesne joined, following Eugène Gibeau, M$^{gr.}$ M. (Morin), Dr. "V," and "L" who made up the original nucleus.

But as it happened, M$^{gr.}$ Laurent Morin was the general vicar of the Montreal archdiocese, and a long-time close collaborator of M$^{gr.}$ Joseph Charbonneau, whose days as Archbishop of Montreal were numbered, unbeknownst to him. Paul-Éverard Richemont knew both M$^{gr.}$ Charbonneau and M$^{gr.}$ Morin, a fact which alarmed one of Charbonneau's old friends, Father Édouard Gouin of the St. Sulpice order, then living in the French city of Nantes. Abbot Gouin had long lived in Canada and was in fact there in 1948, to lead prayers at an ecclesiastical retreat in Montreal. He crossed swords with Robert Rumilly when he wrote a letter to *Le Devoir* denouncing the lucubrations of the latter's speech entitled "The truth about the resistance and the purges in France." Father Gouin ridiculed the claim Rumilly made that 6,000 priests and 30,000 civilians had been executed after the war because of their political opinions, that the Resistance had initiated orgies of violence throughout the French provinces and that France had become one immense penitentiary.[210]

In the fall of 1949, using a trusted friend as intermediary, Gouin warned his old friend Joseph Charbonneau about the activities of a former Nazi collaborator, condemned to death after the French Liberation, who belonged to an international anti-Communist organization, and who called himself Richemont, or sometimes Dumont. This individual had been recommended by the St. Gabriel Fathers to the good offices of M$^{gr.}$ Charbonneau, who had welcomed him and assisted him upon his arrrival in Canada. According to Father Gouin, the impostor Richemont/Dumont was writing a report critical of the Archbishop at the request of Premier Duplessis and was on the verge of leaving for Rome to submit it to the Vatican. Gouin recalled that his emissary urged Charbonneau to immediately leave for Rome to defend himself; when the Archbishop declined, the emissary offered to go in his stead.

Thus informed, M$^{gr.}$ Charbonneau, aware or suspicious of the originator of this blow,[211] confronted Dumont/Richemont with the latter's betrayal. He then demanded that M$^{gr.}$ Morin explain his relations with this unsavoury character. Morin, for his part, informed Dumont/Richemont of Father Gouin's Vatican contact and of Gouin's steps taken with Charbonneau.

Between the intrigues of Dumont/Richemont at the Montreal archdiocese and at the Vatican, and the forced resignation of M$^{gr.}$ Joseph Charbonneau on January 30, 1950, there was a line that Abbot Gouin refused to cross. The affair was a complex one, affirmed Gouin. The rancour of Duplessis and the treason of Dumont/Richemont certainly played a part in the demotion of the Montreal Archbishop, but not a central role. "The Archbishop's fate was more or less sealed and his demotion planned in Rome for close to two years," he wrote.[212] When Richemont went to Rome in 1949, his memoir attacking the Archbishop of Montreal in hand, Charbonneau's disgrace had already been decided. In his *Mémoires*, M$^{gr.}$ Alex Carter attributed Charbonneau's resignation to the concerted efforts of his powerful enemies in the Quebec clergy to remove him from office. They had prepared a negative dossier about him, and had pushed it, at whatever cost, through the Vatican power labyrinth, until they finally succeeded in having the man sacked. The Duplessis intervention, wrote Carter, only confirmed to the Vatican the correctness of its decision, since the church authorities could not blandly reject the representations made by the Premier of the very Catholic Province of Quebec.[213]

M$^{gr.}$ Alex Carter did reflect on the many strange events surrounding Charbonneau's forced departure. Within the archdiocese itself, in the days following M$^{gr.}$ Charbonneau's departure for Victoria, B.C., some of his former colleagues gave the impression they felt indirectly responsible for his fate, as if they had been used as pawns in a game of chess.[214] A priest at Montreal's Stanislas College told Father Carter confidentially that one of his students broke down in tears in front of him and confessed to having stolen a letter from the Archbishop of Montreal which had been left on the priest's desk. When he questioned the student about his motives for the act, the latter replied that he had been promised that his school fees would be taken care of if he could get hold of the letter and deliver it to the Vatican Delegation to Canada.[215]

The Pope and the World Jewish Conspiracy

We recall that on October 11, 1949, "L" informed Duplessis of his imminent and agreed-upon departure for Rome, the following day. The information and documentation service that he had created now extended his sphere of activities to include the Vatican. Richemont explained to

Duplessis that he had to deliver a report on Canada's social problems to the Holy Father. An enthusiastic M$^{gr.}$ Courchesne, informed of the plan, promptly proposed a joint presentation of the document and joined Richemont in Rome in mid-November. As soon as he arrived, Richemont went right to work, diligently gaining support for Duplessis among the Cardinals. The Pope would then "cease to be the exclusive prey of left-wing Catholics and would listen to Richemont's version of the Canadian social problem." There was no mention, even surreptitiously, of Archbishop Charbonneau. The report on the social question to which Richemont referred is much more likely to have been the Custos Report than a direct attack on Joseph Charbonneau.

On October 19, 1949, Richemont, having moved into a comfortable Roman villa, sent Premier Duplessis a first report on the Vatican's views about contemporary social problems. Alas, alas Richemont whined, the partisans of pernicious Neo-Modern ideas censor the news reaching the Holy Father, because they control the Curia, the Offices and the Holy of Holies, the Secretariat of State. The Pope "even though he is concerned about developments in the world political situation, understands the Jewish plot for a world government and means to work against against the neomodernist tendencies by encouraging instead the development of Catholic action and the establishment of corporations uniting Capital and Labor in harmonious cooperation."

The Vatican only knew about the situation in Canada, said Richemont, what it learned from the Anglo-Protestant, Masonic or Jewish agencies, which all held baneful prejudices against the Government of Quebec. A Vatican informant assured him that when the Ungava mineral deposits would begin to be worked, a new propaganda campaign would emerge, aiming to prove that Duplessis had sold out to American anti-social and anti-Catholic capitalists. Richemont ended on an alarmist note: "These kinds of ideas are helping to form the opinions of the men in the Vatican, and nothing, absolutely nothing, is around to contradict them."

Given this news, it made sense to Duplessis that his government had enjoyed such bad press outside of the province during the Asbestos Strike, and that the Pope, through his emissary to Canada, M$^{gr.}$ Ildebrando Antoniutti, had harassed the Premier with requests for pardons of the strikers who were before the courts. The Holy Year, which commenced on December 24, 1949, was one of forgiveness and indulgence, Antoniutti reminded Duplessis. "This could be a highly-Christian occasion for interceding on behalf of the Asbestos workers who are on trial. If your government could, at the appropriate moment, accede to the Holy Father's wishes in this instance, please be assured, Prime Minister, that your actions would give him great joy."[216] Insensitive to this plea, Duplessis replied that his government had shown itself magnanimous towards the delinquant miners and that this weak attitude had only served to make things worse. "And," he went on, "this is not just an illegal strike, but an anarchist revolution against duly constituted authority."[217] The Papal Nuncio would not give up so easily, however: "The diocese priests involved in the dispute helped the strikers and their families. Could not the Premier show the same spirit of charity, and at the same time demonstrate to the general population the harmonious accord which resolved this work conflict? Is it fair to make the strikers alone shoulder the responsability for the violents acts which marked this conflict? Did not the Premier accord such importance to this Holy Year that he sent two of his Ministers, Antonio

Barrette and Albiny Paquette, to the symbolic ceremony of Universal Forgiveness that marked the opening of the Holy Year in Rome?"[218] But Duplessis would not budge. And at the start of this Holy Year whose theme was Forgiveness, in which M[gr.] Charbonneau learned from M[gr.] Antoniutti that the Pope now demanded his resignation, Messrs. Barrette and Paquette also asked the Pope to remove the Dean of the Faculty of Social Sciences of Laval University, Father Georges-Henri Lévesque, and his official condemnation by the Holy See.

The Premier's personal and confidential ambassador to the Vatican

Paul-Everard Richemont was by now working harder than ever in the Vatican corridors of power, and his influence was at a zenith. In March 1950, Duplessis verbally offered him a two-year post as "Personal and confidential ambassador to the Vatican, with the rank of Minister." Richemont, now more than ever locked in a struggle to the death with the forces of Subversion, required an intermediary between himself and Duplessis for this delicate and dangerous mission: this go-between was Father Cyrille Labrecque.[219] But Richemont had other important contacts in the Quebec clergy: M[gr.] Courchesne, M[gr.] Laurent Morin, Father Pierre Gravel (a long-time friend of Duplessis) and Father Arthur Dubois.[220] During the same period, Father Édouard Gouin complained to his Montreal correspondent that Richemont seemed in a position of strength and had won over powerful allies at the Vatican, where he was close to at least three Cardinals.[221] Richemont boasted, in fact, of having obtained a special audience for Canadian Johns Manville President Lewis H. Brown in mid-May 1950, with the Pope and many Cardinals.[222]

When not engaged in the struggle against international Subversion, Richemont used his time to improve Duplessis' image at the Vatican. On May 4, 1950, Father Roméo Bélair, on behalf of the Vatican Secretariat of State, signed him a short note to the effect that Maurice Duplessis was known as an excellent Catholic, very devoted to the Pope, and a constant defender of the interests of the Church.[223]

Whenever Richemont was in Montreal, he diligently fulfilled his role as faithful scribe. Along with Father Dubois, he wrote the Government's reply to the article on the Asbestos Strike published by *Civiltà Catolica* on December 3, 1949, which was reprinted in *La Documentation catholique* on May 7, 1950.[224] Entitled "The actions of the clergy and the Catholic hierarchy during the Asbestos Strike," the *Civiltà Catolica* article was a fierce attack on the position of the Duplessis Government and the mining companies in the Silicosis Scandal and during the Asbestos Strike. *Civiltà Catolica* abundantly quoted the Burton Ledoux articles from *Relations* and *Le Devoir*. It vigorously applauded the collections organized by many bishops to come to the assistance of the Abestos miners. The article also gave benediction to the incendiary sermon given by Mgr. Joseph Charbonneau at the Mothers' Day Mass, where the Archbishop denounced the will of the provincial government and Johns-Manville to crush the working class, and announced the obligation of the Catholic Church to come to their defense.

Richemont took his shuttle role very seriously. On May 29, 1950, he requested an urgent meeting with the Premier. Some of his acolytes in the province's clergy, including Father Labrecque, Father Gagnon — Rector of Laval University — and the ubiquitous Father Dubois were alarmed by the presence in Rome of certain unnamed visitors, and wanted Richemont to leave immediately for the Vatican to ward off their pernicious influence. Duplessis was strongly convinced by this argument and his response shows us what he counted on Richemont for. He sent Richemont a copy of a letter that M$^{gr.}$ Douville, Bishop of Saint-Hyacinthe, had sent him upon returning from Rome on July 24, 1946. In it, Douville informed the Premier that he had met with the Papal Secretary of State, M$^{gr.}$ Montini (who would later become Pope Paul Vl) to discuss the province's law on religious education. M$^{gr.}$ Montini had expressed great satisfaction at the news and assured Douville that he would not fail to inform the Pope of the matter. "I believed it to be my duty to speak of this great victory, one of our greatest victories in fact, in the field of religious education in our land and I congratulate you again with all my heart,"[225] wrote Douville to Premier Duplessis.

The year 1950 would give another victory to the enemies of Duplessis. The Quebec Espiscopate published its now-famous *Collective letter on the problems of the working class in Quebec*, which was the logical follow-up to another document, *The participation of workers in the life of the enterprise* (1949) which had provoked Duplessis' ire and given rise to the furious retort by Father Dubois that we have already mentioned. The *Collective letter* had global repercussions, as it was translated into English, Italian, Spanish, Portugese and Dutch, and approved and promoted by Pius XII's Secretariat of State. Of course, all that did not prevent the contents of the letter from being denounced by the ultra-conservative elements in the church in Quebec and elsewhere.[226] It should surprise no one that Richemont's clerical allies had cause for concern; they probably attributed the "Letter's" approval by M$^{gr.}$ Montini to the presence in Rome of the unnamed enemies of Duplessis.

According to Father Gouin, Richemont, whom he suspected to be the agent of Duplessis, was in Rome during the fall of 1950, conspiring against the Canadian Episcopate in general and against the new Archbishop of Montreal, Paul-Émile Léger, in particular.[227]

One year later, in September, the first issue of the *Custos Bulletin* appeared, edited by Richemont. On the masthead was written: Confidential; Strictly limited circulation; Variable-frequency periodical.

The Bulletin's press run was 125 copies. Richemont wrote essentially for the Pope and the Cardinals of the Curia. He requested subscribers communicate to him any and all pertinent information they believed should appear in the Bulletin's pages. Highly confidential information, he added, instead of being published, would be communicated directly to the Cardinal for whom it was intended, by means of a personal letter.[228]

The pages of Richemont's *Custos Bulletin* were chock full of worn-out, cliché-ridden stories about the Communist-Jewish-Freemason conspiracy for world domination. For example, Richemont thought it wise to inform his readers that the Argentinian bishop, M[gr.] d'Andrea blessed the marriage of the daughter of a Freemason named Babin to another notorious Mason.[229] An unsettling piece of news, as should be obvious to any alert Roman Catholic. And what about the Catholic Mayor Impelleteri of New York, who went to Israel at the invitation of Ben-Gurion, passing through Rome on the way but refusing a private audience with the Pope for fear of angering his Jewish and Masonic friends. Worse, one can read in the Bulletin, Mayor Impelleteri had the audacity to name a Jew, Jacob Grumet, as Fire Chief of New York, rather than a Catholic as tradition required. Grumet was a "known anti-Catho-

lic" and active in the B'nai Brith Jewish Masonic movement and in the "infamous" Anti-Defamation League.[230]

Still, according to Richemont, all was not lost. In this
world seething with delinquency, a small ray of light came
from prestigious personnages, such as, no less, Juan Perón
and Maurice Duplessis, who headed governments which
incarnated hope for the future, valiantly fighting the good
fight against the forces of evil. In Argentina, the Perón
government struggled to instill a Catholic spirit in that
country's youth, and to save it from the poisonous North
American Judeo-Protestant influence in spite of some
subversive infiltration (...).[231] The only Catholic government in North America, in the Province of Quebec, led a
similar struggle under the guidance of a model Premier
Maurice Duplessis, a man of the quality of Franco and
Salazar, a man fighting a trench war with subversive infil-
trators who were eating away at the province's Catholic
trade unions. In reality, these "agitators" were progressive,
modern or Christian-democratic priests and union leaders
espousing Marxism, who led the Catholic unions to "zeal-
ous excesses of language and to revolutionary demands
that easily rivaled those of the traditional Communist
trade movement."[232] In short, the Duplessis Government
had no hostility towards the true, well-established unions
of Quebec. To the contrary, every effort was being made to
help them grow, and demonstrate that in the Catholic
"Belle Province," harmony reigned supreme between employers and workers as long as professional agitators
avoided disrupting the social peace.[233] Richemont/Custos
blasted, in passing, M[gr.] Desranleau for his frequent attacks on capitalism, and M[gr.] Charles-Omer Garant, aux-
iliary Bishop of Quebec, who is described as an advanced
modernist, almost a copy of Father Boulier, a man Garant
much admired.[234]

The *Custos Bulletin* ended with an excerpt from a letter by a Quebec priest which deplored the infiltration of Subversion into the Quebec Seminaries: "And as our Grand Seminaries no longer dare to teach about the forces of subversion such as Freemasonry, the Synagogue, modernism and its contemporary forms, Catholic progressivism and Christain socialism which is to be found in a milder form in Christian Democracy, our young chaplains fall into the trap set for them by the concentrated forces of the anti-Christ. We require a new Council of Trent."[235]

We do not know if other Custos Bulletins were ever issued. The year 1951 saw Richemont's star rapidly waning in the Vatican, and indeed, in the office of the Premier of Quebec. At the beginning of the year, Father Gouin informed his Montreal correspondent that Richemont had been unmasked as an affiliated Member of the Temple, an international secret society based in Switzerland, an offshoot of what had been called during the Restoration "La Sapinière" (the Pine Grove), devoted to enrolling the ecclesiastical authorities into its backward and undemocratic vision of Roman Catholicism and to denouncing any priests who stood in its way.[236] Richemont's influence was reduced even more by this news.

Whether it was because of his abating influence or not, Richemont no longer satisfactorily fulfilled his role as Maurice Duplessis' Personal and confidential Ambassador to the Vatican, and payments to him grew less and less frequent. Seriously concerned, Richemont questioned Father Labrecque about the delays in the payments for his services, and was told that Labrecque, through a misunderstanding, had failed to inform the Premier of the various phases of Richemont's activities. Malevolence did the rest of the job. Other people claimed for themselves the results of his work in Rome, tarnishing his reputation with Duplessis. Father Labrecque assured him, however, in a letter dated June 19, 1951, that the Premier had every intention of honoring the terms of the contract until its expiration.

Richemont wrote to Duplessis and urged him to respect the terms of the agreement they had concluded in the presence of Gérald Martineau, the financier of the National Union Party, by paying the $3,200 still owed to him. The need was all the more urgent, pleaded Richemont, because his wife was ill and he had suffered serious financial losses in his struggle against Subversion. Soon after having written this letter, Paul Erwin Eberhard Reifenrath, alias Tonton, alias Leyzen, alias Chambord, alias Dumont, alias Paul-Éverard Richemont, left Canada and Italy for good, thus ending the astonishing saga of an obscure Nazi propagandist who had the most brilliant, if short-lived episode of his career in the Province of Quebec. He took his family to South America, and settled in Peru, where he died during the 1970s. His elderly wife was living with one of her daughters in England when last heard from, several years ago, while the other Reifenrath children lived in Belgium and Spain.

If all of the exiled French collaborators in Quebec did not enjoy the meteoric rise in society experienced by Paul-Éverard Richemont, they nonetheless benefited from considerable support. Perhaps this can be explained by the fact that in the minds of these people and their supporters, World War II had not really taken place. Or, more exactly, it was but an epiphenomenon in the ongoing struggle against the forces of Evil, represented by the constellation of Communists, Bolshevists, English-Canadian fanatics, Jews, Masons and other vague but powerful enemies. This can also explain the anti-Semitism in their ideology, despite their knowledge of the Nazi death camps and of the genocide of the European Jews. And not forgetting that all the violence was the fault of England and Poland, as Philippe Hamel and André Laurendeau so opportunely recalled, making the poor Nazi collaborators mere victims of circumstance.

The Padlock Law, so dear to the heart of Maurice Duplessis and unanimously adopted by the provincial Legislative Assembly, stemmed from the 1930s, well before the advent of what we call the Cold War. For the extreme right here and elsewhere, the defeat of the Axis forces in 1945 was not the end of the struggle. In that sense, lending a helping hand to fascism's most valorous elements seeking refuge in Quebec seemed to be in the natural order of things.

Its phantasmagoria intact, and its devotion to Pétain and his National Revolution as fervent as ever, the French-Canadian intelligentsia elevated to the rank of war heroes the rag-tag band of French Nazi collaborators exiled in Quebec. This commitment is its lasting ideological testament in that it reveals its durable and profound convictions towards the conflicts that shook the planet in the first half of the twentieth century.

Bibliography

Pierre Assouline: *Simenon*, Paris, Paris, Julliard, Laurédit Inc., 1992

Fenton Bresler: *The Mystery of Georges Simenon*, Heinemann Quixote Press, London 1983

Conrad Black: *Maurice Duplessis, 1944-1959, Le pouvoir*, Montreal, Les éditions de l'homme, 1977.

Jean Bruchesi: *Souvenirs à vaincre, Tome 1*, Montreal, Hurtubise HMH, 1974

Alex Carter: *A Canadian Bishop's Memoirs*, Tomiko Publications, North Bay, 1994

Deborah Cowley and George Cowley: *One Woman's Journey. A Portrait of Pauline Vanier*, Novalis, St. Paul University, Ottawa, 1992

Rapport Custos ou Recueil de documents sur la grève de l'amiante, 1949. Organized by the Confederation of Catholic Workers of Canada, Volume 1

Commission Deschênes: *Rapport de la Commission d'enquête sur les criminels de guerre*, Ottawa, Supply and Services Canada, 1986

Abbé Gérard Dion: *La grève de l'amiante*, Memoirs of the Royal Society of Canada, Fourth Series, vol. XVll, 1979

Pierre-Marie Dioudonnat: *Je suis partout 1930-1944. Les Maurassiens devant la tentation fasciste*, Paris, La Table Ronde, 1973

Pierre-Marie Dioudonnat: *Les 700 Rédacteurs de Je Suis Partout*, Paris, Sedepols, 1993.

Stanley Erskin: *Simenon: A Critical Biography*, McFarland and Company Inc., 1987.

Bertram M. Gordon: *Collaborationism in France during the Second World War*, Cornell University Press, Ithaca and London, 1980

Philippe Hamel: *Les responsables de la Deuxième Grande Guerre*, 1948

Jean Houpert: *Mémoires*. Unpublished document

Renaude Lapointe: *L'histoire bouleversante de M$^{gr.}$ Charbonneau*, Montreal, Les Éditions du Jour, 1962

André Laurendeau: "Les Russes ont-ils toujours tort?" in *L'Action nationale: Pour gagner la paix*, May 1949

Yves Lavertu: *The Benronville Affair*, Montreal, Robert Davies Publishing, 1996.

Herbert R. Lottman: *The Purge*, William Morrow and Company, Inc., New York, 1986

Michel Mohrt: *Mon royaume pour un cheval*, Paris, Albin Michel, 1949

Georges-Benoît Montel: *Souvenirs et commentaires d'un homme libre*, Unpublished.

Vera Murray: *À la recherche des crimes de Julien Labedan*, Television report produced for The Fifth Estate, summer, 1984.

Pascal Ory: *Les collaborateurs 1940-1945*, Paris, Seuil, 1976.

Les Procès de la Radio, Paris, Albin Michel, 1947

Henry Rousso: *La collaboration*, Paris, MA Éditions, 1987

Robert Rumilly: *Maurice Duplessis et son temps, tome 2*, Montreal, Fides, 1973

Robert Speaight: *Vanier. Soldier, Diplomat and Governor General. A biography*. Collins, Toronto, 1970.

Léon Strauss: *Nouveau dictionnaire de biographie alsacienne*, Strasbourg. Not yet published.

Pierre-Henri Teitgen: *Faites entrer le témoin suivant. 1940-1958. De la Résistance à la Ve République*, Rennes, Ouest France, 1988

Pierre Elliott Trudeau (edited by): *The Asbestos Strike*

Dominique Veillon: *La Collaboration. Textes and débats*, Paris, Le livre de poche, 1984

Archival sources

Quebec National Archives in Quebec City
René Chaloult papers
Maurice Duplessis papers

Archives of Laval University
Philippe Hamel papers

Canadian Jewish Congress Archives
Jacques Dugé de Bernonville file

Archives of the St. Vincent-de-Paul Fathers
Father Simon Arsenault papers

National Archives of Canada
Louis Saint-Laurent papers
Jacques Dugé de Bernonville file
Georges Vanier papers

Archives of the St. Joseph Seminary in Three-Rivers
Maurice Duplessis papers

Quebec National Archives in Montreal
Robert Rumilly papers

Archives of the Archdiocese of Rimouski
Archives of the Université de Montréal
Jean Bruchesi papers
Simon Wiesenthal Centre in Toronto Archives
Jacques Dugé de Bernonville file
Archives of l'Union française (Montreal)

Jesuit Archives
Émile Bouvier papers
Arthur Dubois papers
Silicosis file

Interviews/correspondence

A.B.
François Bédarida
Jeannette Chaloult*
Henri Des Garets
Yves Des Garets
Gabriel Dorget
Philippe Dorget
Yvette (Baulu) Germain*
Guy Hamelin
Jean Houpert
Julien Labedan
Marinette Labedan
Renaude Lapointe
Michel Mohrt
Philippe Montel
M$^{gr.}$ Laurent Morin*
Roger Ouellet
Dom Guy-Marie Oury
Gérard Pelletier*
Father Jean d'Auteuil Richard, S.J.
Simone (Bovet) Rumilly*
Père Louis Soltner, O.B.
Pierre-Henri Teitgen
Émile Tourigny*
Roland Reifenrath
Maurice Riel
Geneviève Seigneur*
Jean-Paul Vinay

*Deceased

Sounds of Silence:
The Memory of World War II
in Quebec

The Good War

For those who fought on the Allied side during World War ll it was, in Herbert Mitgang's phrase, "The Good War," and for those who were too young to fight in it, but lived through it — my generation — it remains, quite simply, the war. Say "the war" to anyone born before 1935 and he or she knows you don't mean the Korean War or Vietnam, but that world conflict in which civilization was at risk. It was the forces of darkness that were being engaged, and that were, furthermore, terrifyingly triumphant for too long a time."[1]

This is how World War II is remembered in the the memoirs of its participants and witnesses, and in the mainstream historiography of the Western World. This image has been confirmed by the various vectors of memory, movies, novels, memoirs and scholarly works that have built over the years a communal memory of this most important event of the twentieth century.

World War II is relatively recent history and many of its aspects were and still are touchy subjects. In the aftermath of the war, Charles de Gaulle successfully established the myth of the French as a nation of Resisters to the Nazi oppressors; over the years the memories of the war would evolve, but the Nazis remained the bad guys, and the

French predominantly Resisters and good guys; others were only bit players. As late as 1972, the fate of the Jews in France during the occupation of that country was cautiously ignored by French historians.

World War II provides an interesting example of the management of memory in Quebec. As a rule of thumb the twentieth century is neglected by Quebec historiography, and World War II is almost ignored. For example, in the most widely used history book in colleges and universities in Quebec, *Histoire du Québec contemporain*, the authors devote to World War II less than four pages which they place under the subtitle of "l'intermède de la guerre" – the interlude of the war – as if it were not an event worth studying in itself, but a mere blip in the general course of events in Quebec.[2]

It has been said that memory is the "structuring of forgetfulness."[3] Forgetfulness is not the only tool that can be used to shape memory. Apologia, euphemism, omission, half-truth and lie can also be used; they were used in the memoirs of many French Canadian public figures who were barely twenty years old when World War II broke out. These memoirs were written by some of those French Canadians who rose to political prominence and therefore felt they had a reasonable hope of being read. For many future French-Canadian leaders in various fields who were coming of age at that time, World War II, the League for the Defence of Canada and the Bloc populaire canadien provided initial political involvement. Jean Drapeau, future mayor of Montreal; Pierre Elliott Trudeau, future prime minister of Canada; Gérard Filion, future publisher of the daily *Le Devoir* and vice president of the Canada Council for the Arts; Gérard Pelletier, future minister in the Trudeau government and future Canadian ambassador in Paris, all became involved in varying degrees with the

Bloc populaire canadien and came under the influence of its secretary general (and president of the provincial wing from 1944) André Laurendeau, successor to Gérard Filion as publisher of *Le Devoir* and future president of the Royal Commission on Bilingualism and Biculturalism. As followers of the Bloc populaire they all opposed conscription. André Laurendeau wrote a book about his experience with the Bloc populaire during the war under the title: *La crise de la conscription*,[4] thus recognizing at least that World War II was a significant element of the political environment of the times.

On the other hand, neither Georges-Émile Lapalme, future leader of the provincial Liberal Party during its years in the wilderness nor René Lévesque, future premier of Quebec opposed conscription. Lévesque wore the American uniform and worked for the Office of War Information while Lapalme, too old to enlist, continued his work as a lawyer and a politician.

These memoirs have been chosen for study because it is through the prism of their sketchy remembrances that the official memory of World War II came into existence. To include many other vectors of memory of World War II would have required more than one chapter and hopefully someone will fill the many gaps left by this modest attempt to understand the management of memory in Quebec. Laurendeau, Filion, Trudeau, Pelletier, Lapalme and Lévesque are not representative of French-Canadian society as a whole, because no group in any society can claim such an attribute. They were highly educated, having gone through that breeding ground of the French-Canadian elite, the classical college. Some of them – Laurendeau and Filion for example – had lived for a while in Paris.

Many memoirists readily acknowledged that World War II was a momentous event in their young lives. For Pierre Elliott Trudeau, two bombshells marked his teen-age years – the death of his father, and the war.[5] He felt "that it might constitute the most dramatic adventure the men of my generation would ever confront."[6] René Lévesque, at the time an intermittent law student about to be expelled from Laval University, called it "the great adventure of our generation."[7] Gérard Pelletier saw it as a "cataclysm, the universal conflagration"[8] that shaped his generation.

André Laurendeau remembered that on that fateful Friday, September 1, 1939 when Germany invaded Poland, his overriding concern was that the war would spread and that French Canadians should avoid any participation in it.[9]

Laurendeau almost immediately plunged into political action. On Monday September 4, he attended a meeting at the Maisonneuve Market in Montreal, organized under the aegis of Paul Gouin and the resurrected nationalistic Action libérale nationale, a splinter group of the provincial Liberal Party established in 1934 that eventually merged with the provincial Conservative Party led by Maurice Duplessis and made possible his election in 1936. René Chaloult, provincial member for Kamouraska and father of the Quebec flag gave a fiery speech against participation in the war. He received thunderous applause from the crowd that began to shout:

"We won't go."

"We don't want the war."

"The Jews and bankers – it's them that started it."

"It's suicide for Canada."

"Down with the Empire! Down with the war!"[10]

But French-Canadian nationalists could not stop Canada participating in the war and an unspoken agreement took place between them and the federal government: "We agreed to submit to participation; they agreed to limit participation to voluntary service."[11]

The Good Life

For many people in the province of Quebec, the war quite simply meant that the good days were back. Georges-Émile Lapalme remembers that World War II brought an economic resurrection, eliminating unemployment. This economic expansion was defined in Saint-Paul-l'Ermite, in the riding of l'Assomption, by the building of the biggest factory of explosives in the British Empire and by the erection of the military camp of Joliette. The best lands were expropriated by the federal government and manpower flooded in, men and women, whom unemployment had shaken to their roots and who now smiled again.[12] According to Gérard Filion, as soon as Canada entered the war, people felt that the end of economic hardship was near. Foreseeing what would happen in Europe, factories started to boom again. The demand for food was greater than ever.[13]

Mordecai Richler, too young to serve, was nevertheless shaped by the war, and especially by his guilt: the war years were incomparably good, he writes, and the exodus from the St-Urbain Street area to Outremont began in earnest.[14]

For Laurendeau, the unease is made more acute because of the parallel that can be easily drawn between Canada and Europe during the war: "Sometimes in those days I would shut my eyes and think of the misfortune of men on the battlefields and in the bombed cities of

Europe.(...) The comfort of our life sickened me, just as it makes us ashamed in the West now."[15]

The Fall of France

Gérard Pelletier, reminiscing about his stay in Paris in 1946, goes on at length about the significance of Paris for his generation. The first trip to Paris was of paramount importance, amounting almost to a rite of passage for young educated French Canadians:

"How to express in few words the deep yearning that possessed almost all of us since childhood to leave Quebec, to leave Canada.(...) Our intellectual pole was France.(...) Our reading, be it literature, politics, sociology or history (except the history of Canada) brought us inevitably to Europe. Our *maîtres à penser, à voir et à sentir* were Claudel, Péguy, Tocqueville, Mounier, Maritain, Michelet, Malraux, Braque or Picasso. Dead or alive, they were all somewhere else. And it is to that somewhere else that we had a burning desire to go."[16]

Gérard Filion was in Paris in 1937. He witnessed firsthand the experience of the Front populaire with Léon Blum as prime minister, and felt the spectre of war looming in the East. He visited Berlin the day after May 1, when Hitler had turned that celebration into a grandiose manifestation of the glory of National Socialism.[17] While in Paris, he met with his friend André Laurendeau.[18]

For all these reasons and some others as well, the fall of France had deep repercussions in the province of Quebec, especially among intellectuals and university students. Father Georges-Henri Lévesque, Dean of the Faculty of Social Sciences at Laval University did not waste any time and established with Marthe Simard what he believed to be the first Free French Committee in the world.[19]

In May 1940, Pierre Elliott Trudeau had just begun to study law at the Université de Montréal. "Obviously, I could not let myself be unaware of something everyone else was discussing.(...)" he writes cautiously in his *Memoirs*.[20] The battle of Britain and the blitz of London were understandably the first and foremost topics of conversation among his fellow students, but he claims he remained indifferent to their concerns and does not even bother to report the content of these discussions.

The day the Germans marched into Paris, René Lévesque was strolling with friends on Quebec City's Grande-Allée. It was spring, the air was soft and through the open windows of the posh houses they could hear the "sober and moving" commentary of the great journalist Louis Francoeur.[21]

On the very same day, Georges-Émile Lapalme witnessed two reactions that in his mind summarized the reactions of French Canadians: a protonotary, deeply affected and concerned, told him that on the previous day, a judge had burst into tears in front of him. Another friend of Lapalme said that the damned English would beg for peace as soon as the first bomb was dropped on their heads.

André Laurendeau was deeply attached to France for more than intellectual reasons and this made the fall of France all the more painful: his father had lived there; and he and his wife had lived for two years in the Latin Quarter where their first child was born. He had memories and friends[22] like Emmanuel Mounier, Father Paul Doncoeur, Émile Baas.

He became sick off and on for weeks, suffering migraine headaches which were a symptom of the depression that had plagued him in the early 1930s.[23]

Guilt, bad faith and silence

Father Doncoeur, a Jesuit who had befriended the Laurendeau couple in Paris and blessed their apartment, for one,
did not mince words: in June 1940 when Pétain asked for
the armistice, he wrote Laurendeau: "Your present attitude is without greatness. I believe it to be lacking in
intelligence. I can see why you want to disengage yourself
from France but you must know the mortal price of neu-
trality. As for Canada, do not believe that you are safe from
this odious Hitlerian power."[24]

For Laurendeau, guilt and shame soon gave way to a
solid dose of realpolitik: the war would end soon. Although admirable, the resistance shown by Mother England was foolhardy and de Gaulle was ignored. When
everything was said and done, Hitler had won.[25]

In the wake of the fall of France and the resistance of
England, the Mackenzie King government had a law
passed in Parliament instigating national registration for
all Canadian citizens and conscription for service on Canadian soil. There was no noticeable protest from French
Canadians or, for that matter, from nationalists of various
stripes. Trudeau felt that the war really did not command
attention.[26] However, Laurendeau and others saw alternative possibilities: people could protest against registration
as Montreal mayor Camilien Houde had done by simply
refusing to register.[27] But neither Laurendeau nor like-
minded people followed Houde on the path of civil disobedience. Even though registration presented an excellent
opportunity to exercise the kind of civil disobedience dear
to Gandhi who had allegedly been an inspiration to
Laurendeau,[28] he did not start such a movement in Quebec, but spent his energy in the League for the Defence of

Canada and the Bloc populaire canadien. Disgusted with himself, he felt he had let France down while it was going through what he called "its greatest hour of distress." He registered, then felt he had betrayed himself, not to say anything of his friends in France.[29] The motives for him and others refusing to avenge France "never became totally clear," claims Laurendeau.[30] They might have been clear but difficult to state bluntly after the war: Laurendeau and his friends supported Marshal Petain and his National Revolution and did not want to fight against him.

Pétainism and Fascism

Pétain is the main riddle of the memoirs under study here. Neither Trudeau, nor Pelletier, nor Filion have anything to say about Pétain. Not a single word. They had dreamed of going to Paris since they were young, felt deeply attached to France – in their own words – but have nothing to say about the occupation of France and Marshall Pétain. Neither Laurendeau, nor Trudeau, Pelletier, Filion, Lapalme and Lévesque had anything of any substance in their comments about these issues. These momentous events barely elicited a reaction, if one is to believe their memoirs.

Did they support Pétain's regime or not? Did they believe it would last? Were they shocked or pleased? How did their ideas on the topic evolve over the years, if they did at all? What did Laurendeau think of the future of a Nazi-dominated Europe, of the future of the Free France movement, or of the resistance of England he had mentioned earlier?

The only thing certain is that they could not possibly have had no thoughts on these subjects. Their silence truly speaks volumes and reverberates out through their memoirs.

The 21 year- old René Lévesque claimed he ended up siding with de Gaulle, a highly unpopular position in Quebec City where thinking people had been "ecstatic about Mussolini" and "had flirted with the strong man of the Reich," only to swing "en masse" to Pétain's side in 1940[31]. According to Lapalme all of French Canada instantly became Pétainist. He claimed that he, however, was for de Gaulle from the first hour.[32]

Laurendeau denies that his fellow nationalists supported Marshall Pétain while mentioning in the same breath that Pétain was admired in French Canada and that he and his friends[33] latched on to Pétain because they felt so "terribly isolated – intoxicated with solitude." Surprisingly, he pleads ignorance of the fate of Frenchmen and Jews in order to explain why he and his friends were uncritical of Pétain's regime. They discarded what information they had as "British propaganda."[34]

If one is ready to believe that the nationalists were willfully unaware of Vichy propaganda, which is highly unlikely, one finds it hard to believe that they knew nothing of the conditions Pétain governed under, nothing of the fate of Frenchmen and Jews. From the letters Laurendeau had received from his friends at the beginning of the war in which they exposed their plight and their unshakable conviction that this was a just war, and by sheer common sense, Laurendeau could have guessed that being at war and living under occupation were not joyful situations. He wrote about the great distress of France during 1940 and then claimed that he knew nothing about France's conditions during the war.

Maréchal, nous voilà!

Pétain's omnipresent absence is a determining vector of memory of World War II in Quebec. Historians have often been too willing to give credence to the structuring of forgetfulness of memoirists. The history of *Le Bloc Populaire Canadien* by Paul-André Comeau is a good case in point.[35]

It is truly amazing to realize that among the most politically active nationalists at the time, that is, members of the Bloc populaire, a majority of the 152 former members who answered a survey in the summer of 1968 claimed to not know whether their party had supported Marshal Pétain. To the question: Was the Bloc Populaire pro-Pétain?, the proportion of the 152 respondents who did not know was a stunning 55.4%; 28.3% answered Yes; 15.2% answered No. To the four other questions concerning the ideology of their party, the proportion of "Do not know" responses hovers between 9.6%, e.g. (Was the Bloc populaire anticommunist?) and 15.1% (Was it antisemitic?).[36] This is clearly a case of collective amnesia.

Never stating clearly that the Bloc populaire took a pro-Pétain stance, historian Paul-André Comeau nevertheless mentions numerous instances of enthusiastic support for Pétain and praise for Salazar on the part of the leaders of the Bloc.[37]

However, these statements and instances of support for Pétain and Salazar did not rally a majority within the Bloc itself. Far from it, confidently maintains Comeau: barely 30% of the respondents were more or less favourable to Marshal Pétain. Eager to downplay the support for Pétain, he writes that perhaps the veil of passing years has incited some of them to forget their views of that time.[38]

In fact his assertion is built on a strange interpretation of
the data he gathered. A look at his survey of former
members of the Bloc Populaire Canadien shows that the
"some" who might have forgotten was a solid majority of
55.4%, as shown previously. Furthermore, 28.5% answered
that the Bloc was favorable to Marshall Pétain – and not
"more or less" favorable to him as Comeau wrote.

Quebec under the fascist yoke

Beyond forgetfulness, one could claim that it was Quebec,
not France that lived under the fascist yoke. We knew
nothing of the fate of Frenchmen during World War II,
argued Laurendeau, yet at the same time Quebecers suffered a similar terrible fate.

As early as November 1940 Laurendeau wrote a
booklet entitled: *An Alert to French Canadians!*[39] Centrali-
zation is the real threat to Canadian unity, he reminds his
readers. Because Premier Godbout accepted the amend-
ment to the constitution by which the province gave
jurisdiction over unemployment insurance to the federal
government, Laurendeau wrote that: "The sovereignty of
Quebec is endangered."[40] Nevertheless an inspirational
example shone in Europe: One of the first steps taken by
Pétain was to give the French provinces back a little bit of
their past freedoms.[41]

One has the impression of reading a description of
the siege of Leningrad. "We are a besieged people living
in a fortress. The besieging forces deprive us of food. We
are going to starve to death unless we make a daring sortie
– in order to recuperate our provisions".[42] Fear permeated
the lives of French Canadians: "We are living under the
dictatorship of fear."[43]

There is a name for that kind of dictatorship, as an increasingly strident Laurendeau wrote: "It is fascism in a velvet glove. We have the thing itself: let's have the courage to call it by its very name."[44] Like Europeans, French Canadians experienced "the feeling" of occupation by a foreign power and they too suffered, claims Laurendeau:

"During the war, many French Canadians in Quebec had the feeling that they were living in an occupied country. The English were the occupiers, they were the ones who dictated our conduct and prevented the national will from freely asserting itself. Our own politicians were collaborators. In comparison with Hitlerized Europe, it was a benign occupation. Thanks to King's moderation the yoke remained bearable. All we risked were our liberties, and here again the threat seldom became a reality. But its very existence was enough to poison one's life."[45]

Writing in 1962, Laurendeau timely claimed that French Canadians suffered not only the evils of occupation but the ones of colonization as well: "In my opinion, the French-Canadian attitude can best be seen in the context of the phenomenon we now call "decolonization".[46]Their bitter solitude in the world was suffocating.[47]

Conscription, Jews, Prostitutes and Tramways

On January 22, 1942, it was announced that a plebiscite would be held concerning conscription on the following April 27. Mackenzie King's government would ask Canadians to be freed from its promise not to establish conscription.

Gérard Filion remembers attending a meeting at *Abbé* Groulx's home with the directors of the League of National Action – Ligue d'Action nationale – a few days after January 22. Of course, Laurendeau also attended that meeting at which the League for the Defence of Canada was born and he was made principal executive officer. The newspaper *Le Devoir* gave its continual and full support to the subsequent activities of the League. Thanks to Gérard Filion, *La Terre de chez nous*, an important weekly widely read by farmers, showed the same support.

At that first meeting at *Abbé* Groulx's place, it was agreed to organize a demonstration to oppose conscription at the Saint Jacques Market. Filion offered his help.[48] It was the first public meeting organized by the League for the Defence of Canada; according to Laurendeau, about 10,000 people attended. It soon became clear that the fascism of the federal government, under the guise of unemployment insurance, was not the only danger to the province of Quebec. At the Saint Jacques Market demonstration held on February 11, 1942, three other threats to French Canada materialized: the Montreal Tramway Company, prostitutes and Jews.

Things were quiet, boring, almost mournful, to tell the truth, relates Laurendeau, who goes on to express his heartfelt gratitude to students for breaking into a riot: "Luckily the students outside saved the day."[49]

With the loudspeakers not working properly, the speaker's voice was drowned out by the din of the nearby streetcars. Some demanded that the streetcar route be changed. Of course, nothing of the kind happened. Demonstrators began to throw bricks at the streetcars and windows were smashed. Forgetting the streetcars for a moment, some protesters raided a lavish whorehouse.[50] Others started to chant: Down with *The Gazette*! Down with the Jews![51] Eighteen people were arrested, eight policemen injured.

The day after, in his capacity as secretary of the League for the Defence of Canada, Laurendeau was summoned before the chief of police. Laurendeau wrote "I wondered why," although it might not be difficult to understand why Chief Dufresne wanted to see him the day after a riot had broken out at a meeting of the League for the Defence of Canada leaving eight of his policement injured. An infuriated Chief Dufresne screamed during the meeting, and repeatedly thumped his fist on the desk.

Laurendeau denied having incited anyone to violence and replied in all seriousness to a purple-faced Chief Dufresne : "But you, you'd better stop Montreal Tramways from sending empty streetcars around to sabotage our meetings. And try to discipline your men."[52]

At a youth rally held at the Jean Talon Market on March 24, Jews were again the target of an agitated crowd. International Jewish finance and Jews were jeered along with the Toronto Two Hundred, *The Gazette* and the Tories. Gérard Filion, Jean Drapeau and a union leader named Landon Ladd were speakers.

Astonishingly, Laurendeau claims in 1962 to remember a tirade by Ladd in response to the anti-semitic slogans, even though no newspaper has recorded it. Jews are our brothers and they have suffered enough, was allegedly the main line of Ladd's argument. A roar of applause supposedly greeted his speech.[53]

Notwithstanding Ladd's alleged tirade, deeds quickly followed words. A small group of people armed with sticks screamed out: "Kill them! Kill them!" Jewish shops had their windows smashed. Another riot broke out. Laurendeau believed that the mayhem was the work of the former blackshirts of Adrien Arcand, the French-Canadian fascist leader who had been in the same internment camp as Camilien Houde.[54]

In fact, it was not the first time that anti-semitic incidents occurred in the demonstrations of the League.

Shouts of "Down with the Jews" greeted the outbreak of the war, as we have seen. Reluctantly, Laurendeau granted that the followers of the League for the Defence of Canada might have been vaguely antisemitic. He suggested that this was due in part to the economic crisis that had made French-Canadian shopkeepers jealous of their more successful rivals, and in part to religious hostility and the "disconcerting habits" of these foreigners which bred astonishment and revulsion.[55] Furthermore, claims an apologetic Laurendeau, French Canadians had no monopoly on this prejudice, and Canadians Jews did not help their case by declaring themselves in favour of a Yes vote in the plebiscite and by joining forces with the Anglos to soundly defeat the Bloc populaire candidate Jean Drapeau in the Outremont by-election in 1942.[56]

In August 1943, a young multilingual lawyer named Paul Massé ran as a candidate for the Bloc populaire in the riding of Cartier. Massé rhetorically asked in one of his speeches: "What right do these people [Jews] have to ask us to get killed, to ruin our country, because they have suffered?"[57]

That kind of speech, coupled with the inconsiderate use of crude words such as *youpins,* best translated as "kikes", angered English-speaking journalists who quickly dubbed Paul Massé a racist and an anti-semite.[58]

When the doors of Dachau, Buchenwald and Bergen Belsen opened, Comeau, never at a loss for understatement, wrote "the misunderstanding will be tragic." He probably meant that had Massé known about the Final Solution, he would have used milder language, say "unassimilable Jews" instead of "Kikes."

In Comeau's understated account, similar incidents kept occuring which showed a certain uneasiness.[59] The newspaper *Le Bloc* wrote that "a vote for Godboutsky is a vote for Abraham, Isaac and Jacob...". The notion of a Jewish conspiracy became a *leitmotiv* during the entire time of the war,[60] and some Bloc populaire sympathizers did not hide their deep aversion to everything Jewish.[61]

One punch is pulled after another: when denouncing the coming to Canada of "yids of conscription age," a collaborator of the Bloc showed "at the very least ignorance of the history of those refugees who had migrated through by way of France, Spain and Portugal before touching Canadian soil."[62] As late as 1944, someone wrote the following – "frankly acid prose" – in the newspaper *Le Bloc*: "It is true that Jews come here in huge numbers and starve us to death in order to teach us how to live."[63]

The historians' apologia is matched by the amnesia of former members of the Bloc populaire canadien. When asked in the summer of 1968 if the Bloc populaire had been anti-semitic, their answers read as follow: 7% answered "Yes", 77.9% answered "No" and 15.1% said that they did not know. So 77.9% answered "No," notwithstanding the evidence reluctantly gathered by Paul-André Comeau.

The conscription crisis that never was

It might be surprising to realize that only 5.4 per cent of former members of the Bloc populaire gave resistance to conscription as the reason for joining that party. Comeau writes that the plebiscite of April 1942 probably played a much greater role in their decision than is suggested by the numbers, without explaining his assertion. This might be more wishful thinking than reality. Conscription is the least important reason given for joining the ranks of the Bloc populaire: "Hatred of old political parties tirelessly invoked by the speakers of the Bloc" is the reason given by 16.9 % of 152 former members who answered the survey,

23.1% answered that the influence of friends or the pressure of events pushed them to join the Bloc populaire. Nationalist feelings accounted for 16.9%. The numbers mean that hatred of political parties in the name of nationalism was much more appealing than fighting conscription.

There was indeed more to the Bloc populaire and to World War II than the single issue of conscription. Attributing his own feelings to all French Canadians living in Montreal, Pierre Elliott Trudeau concurred that more was at stake than just conscription:

> "But if you were a French Canadian in Montreal in the early 1940s, you did not automatically believe that this was a just war. We still knew nothing of the Holocaust and we tended to think of this war as a settling of scores among the superpowers. And then, of course, there was the conscription issue."[64]

The last sentence reads as an afterthought. Even before conscription became an issue, the righteousness of the Allied cause was very much in doubt. Another uneasy question arises: Would nothing less than the Holocaust have moved him and his friends towards taking action? Would it have convinced them that this was a necessary war? It is doubtful. If the Nazi and Vichyite persecutions of the Jews prior to the Holocaust, coupled with the Nazi occupation of Europe, had not elicited any compassionate reaction on their part, and if the immigration of Jews to Canada was firmly opposed, how on earth could the "Final Solution" have caused a change of heart? Would Laurendeau, Trudeau and like-minded nationalists have risked their lives on the battlefields of Europe for the Jews? Furthermore, knowing about these persecutions like the rest of the world, the crowds continued to oppose participation and subsequently conscription. Meanwhile, the newspapers *Le Bloc* and *Le Devoir*, like Bloc populaire candidates and the crowds they addressed still continued to make anti-semitic statements.

Trudeau and Pelletier are curiously laconic about conscription. The first, disgruntled by the plebiscite that he saw as a broken promise to French Canadians by the Mackenzie King government, made such a fiery speech at one of Jean Drapeau's rallies during the by-election in Outremont that it landed him on the front page of *Le Devoir*: "That was, I believe, my only participation in the politics of that era."[65] Pelletier has this much to say: "Canadian politics had never interested me except briefly during the conscription crisis because of my admiration for André Laurendeau".[66] Did he engage in any political activity? Why did he admire André Laurendeau? One sentence summarizes his activities and views during what he had earlier in his memoirs called "the universal conflagration" that had shaped his generation. He does not say anything more about his stance on the war, on Pétain, on conscription or on Laurendeau.

So, if there was more to World War II than the issue of resistance to conscription, what could it be? For one, the battle against conscription provided a smokescreen under cover of which to fight the old pre-war demon of democracy. Treading carefully on the minefield, Paul-André Comeau mentioned that *The Gazette* branded the Bloc populaire as more or less pro-fascist because the dean of the party and of the nationalist movement, Henri Bourassa, gave the title of true Christian states in the modern world to fascist Italy and Spain.[67]

Granted, acknowledges Comeau, that the weekly *Le Bloc* did not help its case by publishing numerous articles praising "Salazar the Great" in response to accusations

leveled by the English newspapers against the Portuguese
head of state, whose sympathies might not have been, in
the careful words of the historian, on the side of democracy.[68] The Liberal daily *Le Canada* leveled similar
charges of fascism against the Bloc populaire.

   Nazi propaganda had an ally in the Bloc populaire:
on February 18, 1944 the Voice of the Reich sent the
following message on shortwave: "Paris-Canada, Paris-
Canada, here is the Voice of the Reich. French Canadians
– rally around the Bloc populaire and you will overcome
all obstacles."[69]

   The following excerpts of an article published in the
May 27, 1944 issue of of Le Bloc, are quite faithful –
although cooler[70] – to a speech André Laurendeau gave ten
times: "In the past we have seen the province terrorized to
the point of being reduced to silence. Those days are over.
And those who are responsible are going to pay ."[71]

   Liberal politicians, especially the premier of Quebec,
Adélard Godbout, would pay dearly. The Bloc populaire
had become, warned Laurendeau, "the instrument of the
legitimate revenge of Canadians against their corrupt masters." Democracy would be put to rest once and for all to
make room for a National Socialist regime:

> "From the people of this country we ask for a generous
> collaboration. With their help we will put an end to the
> nightmare of the old party system and at last inaugurate a
> social and national regime that will treat men like men and
> cease to hunt them down like beasts."[72]

   Maybe the Voice of the Reich broadcasts were on
target.

   For the modern managers of Quebec's collective
memory, the Bloc and its sympathizers cannot be branded
fascists or as having had fascist leanings. According to

Paul-André Comeau, they simply behaved like the majority of their compatriots who could not instantly break free from an ingrained conservatism.[73] Exit fascism, enter the benign and reassuring terms of conservative nationalism.

It is noticeable that in the historian's explanation, boundaries are eradicated between French Canadians and the proponents of a certain ideology and style of political action. The titles of André Laurendeau's biographies are illuminating in that respect: *André Laurendeau et le destin d'un peuple*[74] – "André Laurendeau and the fate of a people" – *André Laurendeau, un intellectuel d'ici*[75] – "André Laurendeau, a homegrown intellectual." The single person seems able to represent the collective in these titles, but if anyone suggests that some members of a group, in this case the Bloc populaire canadien, were fascist, it is sometimes assumed that one has implied that all French Canadians were. It is an effective tool for censorship. It is an equally effective tool for apologia: individual responsibility is buried under a collective responsibility. So Pierre Elliott Trudeau writes of his views as typical of the ones held by French Canadians living in Montreal in the 1940s. It should be possible to discuss the particular affiliations of significant figures without being understood as having passed any kind of judgment upon a whole group.

Some French Canadians held different views of the war: Louis Saint-Laurent did not wait to learn about the Holocaust to express a different opinion: in a speech he delivered on April 10, 1942, he denounced at length the Nazi ideology and emphasized that total war might be the only way to overcome the enemy.[76]

Whether sharing this view or not, a sizeable number of French Canadians volunteered. According to Laurendeau, most French Canadians had a relative or a friend serving as a volunteer and he personally knew many conscripts and volunteers, but he claims he cannot describe their experiences or feelings because he didn't know the military establishment as such.[77] Why only the latter could properly inform him on that particular topic remains a mystery. He respected the volunteers because they were risking their lives, but did not find their example inspiring.[78] Jean-Louis Gagnon, for example, did volunteer, and his memoirs show the remarkable trajectory of a fascist youth, with the about-face during the Spanish civil war and his subsequent decision to enlist on the side of the Allies.[79]

Memory has crystallized around the issue of conscription largely for self-serving reasons. Laurendeau could cast himself in a prominent role during the valorous struggle of French Canadians against a fascist central state, making himself and his nationalist allies the precursors of the enlightened elite of the Quiet Revolution. Furthermore, for Laurendeau and his young followers, it drew attention away from their probable support for Marshal Pétain, their – at best – neutralist stand since the very beginning of World War II, and the attraction they felt for fascism and for an array of European dictatorships with strong Catholic overtones.

Laurendeau expresses a lingering doubt about his involvement in the resistance to conscription in a statement whose harshness is barely tempered by a question mark: "In the full and formal sense of the term, conscription never occurred. Was this whole long story then nothing but a sinister farce? "[80]

The Big Lie

In his own words René Lévesque finally enlisted because of a "ravenous hunger for war experience," and "perhaps a desire to defend democracy."[81]

This is not exactly true. René Lévesque conveniently failed to mention his numerous attempts to dodge military service. In November 1943, he passed the ritual medical examination. Earlier, he had paid a visit to his family doctor, Dr. Paul V. Marceau, who found him in very poor health. Of course, the army did not buy the story, all the more since Dr. Marceau usually exercised his skills on corpses. On November 22, army doctors placed René Lévesque in the "A-1" group. His military training was to begin two weeks later. He put pressure on his boss at Radio-Canada to help him escape enlistment. To no avail: on December 15, he learned that his *ordre de mobilisation* stood. René Lévesque then frantically tried to enlist as a war correspondent, Radio-Canada exerted still more pressure, and his military training was postponed to January 10, 1944. On that fateful day, he did not show up and made one last attempt to get another deferment. On January 14, Phil Robb of the Office of War Information offered him a position with the American Psychological Warfare Department. René Lévesque's friends were understandably envious: he would be a well-paid reporter without having to go through military training or carry arms.[82]

He was happy to cover his small share of the combat, sometimes being aware that his life was in danger.[83] He experienced gut-wrenching fear, saw and heard a childhood friend die and pitied the German troops "who were only a wan shadow of the supermen of 1940 and 1941."[84]

He went through the terrible experience of being among the first to liberate the concentration camp of Dachau.

The ever-bickering former French presidents Paul Reynaud and Édouard Daladier refused to grant him interviews. But another chance encounter occurred soon afterwards and it was with none other than Hermann Goering himself. René Lévesque remembered vividly the details of the historic event he was witnessing: how Goering was dressed – a simple khaki uniform, the resplendent epaulettes of a *Reichsmarschall*, a chestful of decorations –; how the platoon leader behaved – "in a couple of passes worthy of a fencer, he ripped away all that glitter. A few buttons popped off, too, and became souvenirs along with the rest of paraphernalia"–; how Goering reacted, the words he uttered:

> Shaken, Goering lost his hesitant smile, came to attention, and without a word, let himself to be roughly shoved onto a bench standing in the field. During the next few minutes he silently endured the scatological inquisitions the GIs reviled him with, for example (with expurgations): So that's the great Marshall, huh! Great? That thing? Hell, he's just a great pile of shit!"

> Taking advantage of a pause in the proceedings, he made a short speech in quite acceptable English, which ran more or less as follows: "You can do what you like with me. I have no illusions and nothing to complain of. I just find you very ill-bred. But I beg you, don't make our people go on suffering. They have already more than paid for whatever the world, rightly or wrongly, may hold against them. If there is more to pay, it is I and others like me who should pay the price.

> At that particular moment one couldn't help finding him impressive, if not exactly convincing. Under the carcass of the old ruffian there still lurked a spark of the heroic young

pilot of World War I. It was doubtless this resurgent pluck
that made him a leader of the impossible defence at the
Nuremberg trials, cynical but fearless right up to the very
last choice – cyanide instead of the rope."[85]

There is just one problem with this stirring account:
not a word of it is true. On the day he launched his book,
Lévesque issued a statement admitting both an omission
and a mistake in his memoirs. He had omitted to recant
his previous account of having seen the corpses of Mussolini and his mistress hanging in a street in Milan.[86]

Then comes the confession that he had not witnessed
the first minutes of the surrender of Hermann Goering:
"As for the error I am still incapable of explaining, it is the
appearance of Hermann Goering, to which I was a witness
– but in reality, 15 or 20 minutes after other people... My
apologies to the readers, even if, after 40 years, such a lapse
is perhaps inevitable."[87]

On the eve of D-Day on the outskirts of Southamp-
ton, René Lévesque met some rain-soaked young soldiers
who were about to leave for the landing on the beaches of
Normandy: they laughed too loud and their long silences
spoke much louder than words:

> "I wouldn't be with them, though I was their age. That
> bothered me, made me vaguely ashamed. I was relieved
> not to be storming those bloody beaches, but at the same
> time I felt a mixture of envy and regret at the fact that I
> would miss seeing what was to be the apotheosis of our
> times.(..) I had missed the big rendez-vous."[88]

In the autumn of 1944, Pierre Elliott Trudeau was a
new student at the world-class Harvard University "where
it was impossible not to grasp the true dimensions of the
war."[89] Was it because of a lack of information that he had
not "grasped the true dimensions of the war" while he was

a student at the University of Montreal? Or was it because his professors at Harvard University, many of them German refugees, held very different views on the war from those of André Laurendeau and Jean Drapeau? Besides, what does he mean by "true dimensions of the war?" The least said the better, it seems. But like René Lévesque, he felt that he too had missed the big rendez-vous: "I realized then that I had, as it were, missed one of the major events of the century in which I was living."[90]

Federal Liberal Member of Parliament Georges-Émile Lapalme saw the war against Japan candidly for what it was from a Liberal MP point of view: an electoral godsend. The Conservatives committed political suicide in Quebec by promising conscription pure and simple, and eased the way for the Liberal Party's re-election. "In the vertiginous grandeur of that time, interest is the real meaning of our actions."[91]

The struggle against Duplessis

Two years later Trudeau joined Gérard Pelletier in Paris. Having failed to fight the good war in their youth, they would lead another worthy struggle, with Maurice Duplessis as the Villain and with the Great Darkness as the decor. Not very consciously, if one is to believe Pierre Elliott Trudeau, they began their fight against the regime of Maurice Duplessis and dreamed vaguely of starting a magazine.[92]

Gérard Pelletier wrote that his generation had the impression of living in an endless winter with no sign of thaw in sight.[93] The Asbestos strike of 1949 and the founding of the monthly *Cité libre* (1950) marked the beginning of their decade-long struggle against the Duplessist oppression and the Great Darkness.[94] These events took place more than four years after World War II.

For Gérard Pelletier, the rehabilitation of Maurice Duplessis by the recently elected Parti Québécois in 1977, when they decided to display his statue in front of the National Assembly in Quebec City was analogous to rehabilitating Adolf Hitler or Marshal Pétain:

> "(...) it is a tribute that René Lévesque paid to the Chief and his clique that day. After all, the Germans did not build a monument to honor Hitler nor the Frenchmen to honor Marshal Pétain of 1940. As far as the Soviets are concerned, they began to dismantle the monuments of Stalin right after his death."[95]

The old despot was elevated to the pantheon of arch-villains of the 20th century by some of the memoirists dealt with in this essay; he functioned there as a focal figure to enable them to redeem retrospectively the failures of their misguided youth. The men who were young in 1940 would build their public personae and careers by focusing on their opposition to Duplessis in the late 40s and 50s, avoiding as much as possible their public activities during World War II.

They were not young anymore in the 50s and the missed opportunity of their youth haunts their memoirs. That missed opportunity is compounded by the shame, in retrospect, of having stood for Pétain, Salazar and Mussolini and to have turned their backs on France when the Panzers rolled in. Not only did they not fight the good war, they stood on the wrong side of the fence. In this respect, Laurendeau might have gone a step further than his young friends: his open calls for a National Socialist regime in Quebec as late as 1944 show that the fascist attraction he felt as a member of the Jeune-Canada in the 30s had not totally lost its grip on him. His assertion that Quebec suffered the fate of a Nazi-occupied country might have been tinged with wishful thinking.

Conscription is the face-saving event around which forgetfulness has been structured. Anti-semitism, fascism, Pétainism, attraction for an array of European dictatorships are the sounds buried beneath the wall of silence that the architects of collective memory have carefully constructed around World War II in Quebec.

Bibliography

Paul-André Comeau: *Le Bloc populaire, 1942-1948,* Montréal, Québec/Amérique, 1982

Sous la direction de Robert Comeau et Lucille Beaudry: *André Laurendeau. Un intellectuel d'ici.* Sillery, Presses de l'Université du Québec, 1990

Gérard Filion: *Fais ce que peux,* Montréal, Boréal, 1989

Jean-Louis Gagnon: *Les Apostasies.* Tomes 1 et 2, Montréal, Éditions La Presse, 1985, 1988

Pierre Godin: *René Lévesque. Un enfant du siècle,* Montréal, Boréal, 1994

Donald J. Horton: *André Laurendeau French-Canadian Nationalist 1912-1968,* Toronto, Oxford University Press, 1992

André Laurendeau: *La crise de la conscription 1942.* Montréal, Les Éditions du Jour, 1962

René Lévesque: *Memoirs.* Translated by Philip Startford, McClelland and Stewart, Toronto, 1986

Georges-Émile Lapalme: *Le bruit des choses réveillées,* Montréal, Leméac, Collection Vies et Mémoires, tome 1

André Laurendeau: *Alerte aux Canadiens Français,* Montréal, Éditions de l'Action nationale, 1940

Georges-Henri Lévesque: *Souvenances,* tome 1, Montréal, Éditions La Presse, 1983

Paul-André Linteau, René Durocher, Jean-Claude Robert: *Histoire du Québec contemporain,* Édition révisée, Boréal, Montréal, 1989

Brian McKenna and Susan Purcell: *Drapeau.* Clarke, Irwin & Company Limited, Toronto, Vancouver, 1980

Denis Monière: *André Laurendeau et le destin d'un peuple*, Montréal, Éditions Québec-Amérique, 1983

Gérard Pelletier: *Les années d'impatience 1950-1960*, Montréal, Éditions Stanké, 1983

Mordecai Richler (Edited by): *Writers on World War II, An Anthology*, Alfred A. Knopf, New York, 1991.

Henry Rousso: *The Vichy Syndrome, History and Memory in France since 1944*, Harvard University Press, Cambridge, Massachussetts, London, 1991

Pierre Elliott Trudeau: *Memoirs*, McClelland and Stewart, Toronto, 1993

A Tale of Two Statues:
Authorianism and Fascism in Quebec

It was the newest of times. It was the oldest of times. It
began with the strangest of occurrences, when Maurice
le Noblet Duplessis, autocratic Premier of the province of
Quebec from 1936 to 1939, and subsequently from 1944
until his death, went into a posthumous political wilderness after his death in Schefferville in 1959. Omnipresent
in the public life of the province during his long reign, he
became, almost overnight, Quebec's ultimate political taboo.

It is not that the affront was intentional from the
start. During his hundred-day tenure as Premier, Paul
Sauvé — Duplessis' immediate and short-lived successor
at the helm of the *Union Nationale,* the party Duplessis had
founded and headed — had dutifully paid his respects by
passing a law allocating $30,000 to build a statue of his
predecessor. The famed sculptor Émile Brunet completed
the eleven-foot work of art two years later.[1] Then the
mystery began in earnest, for the bronze statue of *le Chef,*
as Maurice Duplessis was known, disappeared for 16 years.

In the field of social memory — however blurry the
concept may be — there is little room for innocence.
Created, re-created, successful or unsuccessful, hidden or
displayed, symbols reveal something of the intentions of
the few over the multitudes and are, as such, largely
teleological.[2] The Republican Calendar (*Calendrier répub-
licain*) created during the French Revolution—more pre-

cisely and tellingly during The Terror — with the grandiose mission to mark the beginning of a new Era in the history of mankind, lasted exactly twelve years, two months and twenty-seven days.[3] Eternity is not as naive as the human ego. Social memory's futile attempts to marshall time to its service are inevitably defeated.

In terms of imposed cultural icons, the modest kilt — whose origins are anything but Scottish — was infinitely more successful than the Republican Calendar and nowadays is the *par excellence* icon of Scottish folklore.[4] An even happier fate befell Dollard des Ormeaux, the French Canadian hero whose actual deeds were vague enough to become the stuff of legend. He lived, appropriately enough, in New France, French-Canadian historiography's Lost Paradise. According to legend, he died heroically in 1660 with sixteen other young men, fighting the Iroquois at Long-Sault. He was resurrected during the second half of the 19th Century under a purely imaginary physiognomy by artists and historians eager to instill some patriotic fervor into their complacent compatriots.[5] His reputation continued to grow in the following century. Between 1910 and 1930 Dollard was immortalized in a series of heroic monuments bearing a striking resemblance to their sculptor, Alfred Laliberté at the age of 25. They were displayed in Montreal's Parc Lafontaine and at Carillon in Long-Sault where Dollard and his companions reputedly fought and died heroes' deaths. A bronze bust of Dollard by Laliberté was reproduced in plaster and offered as a Canadian history prize in schools. Better yet: he made it into the calendar. The ultimate Imperial holiday, Victoria Day (May 24th), became La Fête de Dollard in Quebec.

Unsurprisingly, there was nothing spontaneous about the patriotic fervor intermittently surrounding Dol-

lard des Ormeaux during the years 1910-1930. It originated at the extreme right of the political spectrum under
the aegis of both the *Action française* — named after the
French *Action française* of Charles Maurras — and a less
extreme youth organization called *l'Association catholique
de la jeunesse canadienne-française*. The main force behind
the myth of Dollard was *Abbé* Lionel Groulx, leader of the
Action française, historian and propagandist with relentless
energy and himself a future nationalist icon in Quebec.
That he laid the founding myths of the French-Canadian
nation and crusaded tirelessly for the adoption of national
symbols like the fleur-de-lys flag does not strike anyone
as particularly original. Long-established nation-states,
minorities striving for statehood and like the working-
class, all have relied on intellectuals to craft the memories
that would legitimize their claims.[6] But Groulx would not
be statisfied with that conventional a role. An ode to
Dollard written during what could only have been an
acute outburst of patriotic fever reads as follow:

> Call us with your virile charm, with your heroic tone. We
> would lift to you hands trembling like palms, ardent with
> the ambition to serve... And for the defence of French and
> for the defence of Catholicism, if you command, O Dol-
> lard, O intoxicating and magnetic leader, we will follow
> you to the supreme holocaust.[7]

If the defense of the French language and Catholicism was part and parcel of a nationalism with traditional
overtones, the same cannot be said of the "supreme holocaust" which Groulx saw engulfing French Canadians
who eagerly followed the ghost of an invented hero. This
usage provides hints to a much darker side of Groulx's
nationalism that would, along with the saga of the Duples-

sis statue, become emblematic of the working of social memory in modern Quebec in the following decades.

The whereabouts of Duplessis' statue remained shrouded in mystery for many years. In 1961, Premier Jean Lesage grudgingly acknowledged that it had arrived from Paris, but he refused to have it exhibited. Members of the National Assembly remained resolutely mute on the topic. To add insult to injury, the *Union Nationale,* which had unexpectedly regained power in 1966 under the leadership of Daniel Johnson Sr., turned its back on its founder by refusing to end the statue's purgatory. Political leaders of every stripe seemed to agree that the symbol par excellence of *la Grande Noirceur,* the Great Darkness, should not be rehabilitated during the heyday of the Quiet Revolution.

The Union Nationale government commissioned an inquiry to probe into the location of the statue. To no one's great surprise, it achieved no results. A less inhibited journalist took the matter into his own hands and traced the accursed statue, by then covered with dust and cobwebs, to the basement of a warehouse belonging to the Sûreté du Québec, Quebec's provincial police force. Was this finally the the end of its undignified exile? Not by far. In 1969, only a photograph of the sculpture's head was made public by the Montreal daily *La Presse.* The ever-faithful Sûreté du Québec would remain the custodians of the monument to their former boss for another eight years.

That, in the 1960s and 70s, the Quebec political class and intelligentsia were so uncomfortable dealing with the immediate past points to a feature of social memory, that it is a much more circumscribed and fragmentary phenomenon than social scientists would like it to be. That in 1960 the Union Nationale came very close to being reelected proves little, except that a sizeable part of the electorate held no grudge against the recently deceased

Duplessis or his party. But to politicos and pundits en-
snared in the myth of the Quiet Revolution — heralding
the dawn of a new era of modernization and openness in
Quebec — Duplessis and the era he embodied, the Great
Darkness, provided a useful device with which to contrast
the former.

Yet this taboo proved too convenient a means for
Quebec society to escape scrutiny of its recent past and face
some uncomfortable facts. Like the Conquest, in the Sixties the Quiet Revolution and the Great Darkness became
mythical milestones of the French-Canadian saga in
North America, even though the changes wrought might
not have been quite the dramatic battles of Good versus
Evil, Oppression versus Liberation, and Obscurantism
versus Enlightenment painted with more romanticism
and teleological concerns than the search for truth. One of
the most astounding feature of the Quiet Revolution was
the exponential growth of the province's state apparatus
and, according to some, the empowerment of a new tech-
nocratic class replacing the clergy.[8]

The central issue of the 1962 provincial election was
the nationalization of Quebec's remaining privately-
owned electric utilities, and was championed by René
Lévesque, then Minister of Natural Resources, and later
co-founder and leader of the Parti Québécois. The slogan
used to promote it was "Maîtres chez nous!" or "Masters
in Our Own Home!" coined some three decades earlier by
none other than Lionel Groulx when he wrote with André
Laurendeau the manifesto of the Jeune-Canada movement and used by none other than Maurice Duplessis in
a speech delivered in January 1938.[9] Groulx and Duplessis
had invented nothing: the same slogan had been used by
the pro-fascist *Action française* of Charles Maurras in Paris
in the years 1924-1926 when Pierre Héricourt wrote a

column in its monthly entitled: *Sommes-nous encore les maîtres chez nous?* (Are we still Masters in our Own House?) where he denounced the Dollar-roi (King Dollar).[10]

The very idea of nationalizing electricity originated in the Thirties when Action Libérale Nationale, a nationalistic splinter group of the Liberal Party close to *Abbé* Groulx, saw it as the way of reversing the discrepancy between the economically mighty Anglo-Saxons/Americans and the conquered and deprived French Canadians. This mythical milestone of the Quiet Revolution came directly from the rhetoric and ideology of the Thirties. And while the architects of the new state were hastily denying any connection with Duplessis and the era he embodied, they were giving renewed impetus not only to his legacy of "provincial autonomy" but also to the famed expression of Lionel Groulx: *Notre État français, nous l'aurons.* ("We will have our French State!") that he had used in June 1937 at the Congrès de la langue française held in Quebec City. After *Maîtres chez nous* there would be *Égalité ou Indépendance,* the constitutional platform of Union Nationale under the leadership of Daniel Johnson Sr.

When Lionel Groulx died in 1967 at the age of 89, writes the historian Ramsay Cook, business in the National Assembly was adjourned so that all MNAs could pay homage to the great nationalist historian.[11] The prolific author and professor of history at the Université de Montréal from 1915 to 1949 was also an indefatigable political agitator, feared in the thirties by the established political parties but with a considerable following among university students, professionnals, and clerics. It is interesting to note that when Groulx gave his famous 1937 speech, Maurice Duplessis was among the dignitaries conspicuously absent. Ironically, Groulx owed his remarkable post-Duplessis surge in popularity to, of all things, the Quiet Revolution, a movement he opposed heart and soul. University buildings, a college, a mountain, several streets and an important metro station would be named after him.

History would have it that Duplessis owed the end of his purgatory and Lionel Groulx the dramatic rekindling of his memory to the recently-established and promising political party which had taken power on November 15, 1976, the Parti Québécois. Seemingly dedicated to making Quebec an independent country, the PQ could fondly recall the former Premier's reassuring message of "provincial autonomy," which could be conveniently linked to their platform of "sovereignty-association" as a step on the road to an independent Quebec. Eighteen years after his death Duplessis' hour of glory had finally come: On September 9, 1977 his statue left the Sûrété's infamous basement and was placed permanently in front of the Quebec National Assembly, where an assembly of dignitaries from the Parti Québécois, the Quebec Liberal Party and the remnants of the Union Nationale paid homage to Maurice Le Noblet Duplessis.

The ghost of Maurice Duplessis was called to duty for some obvious reasons. Sheer political expediency was transparent in the Parti Québécois' strategy: many constituents were still attached, if not to the Union Nationale, then at least to the memory of its founder. With an upcoming referendum on the constitutional status of Quebec, the PQ hoped that invoking the ghost of Duplessis might cajole some voters into unusual boldness. Furthermore, despite the Quebec elite's tradition of political endogamy, many former members of the Union Nationale had nevertheless become Parti Québécois MPs.

However there is more to the display of the statue than meets the eye. Duplessis provided legitimacy to a political option feared by a very sizeable portion of the electorate. Days prior to the statue's exhumation, the Parti Québécois had included a resolution in its program to promote the "autonomy" of Québec while waiting to achieve sovereignty-association, if not full independence (not to be confused with one another, of course). These arcane formulae are more than mere plays on words or expressions of the notorious and often irritating ambivalence of Quebecers toward their constitutional future. Rather, they point to a political class unable to squarely face a political option and its probable consequences, but who cannot help but toy with it while at the same time denying that they really had entertained it. Simultaneous denial and admission is at the core not only of the political process but also of social memory in Quebec for the last thirty years.

That Lionel Groulx was conveniently born in 1878 and dead by 1967 did not escape the attention of the Parti Québécois and the nationalist intelligentsia craving for heroes capable of inspiring circumspect French Canadians into the adventure of sovereignty. It was Lionel Groulx's turn to be summoned to show them the road to the Promised Land. Ten years after his death, and one day after St. Jean-Baptiste day, on June 25, 1977, Premier René Lévesque unveiled a plaque to the memory of Groulx in front of his last residence on Bloomfield Street in Outremont, the bastion of the French-Canadian bourgeoisie. Groulx was an "Éveilleur national" or "National Awakener," according to René Lévesque, who went on to add, correctly from his political standpoint, that Groulx had revived the one science that a young nation needed most: history. Later, Denis Vaugeois, himself a historian and Parti Québécois MNA for Trois-Rivières — Duplessis' old riding — gave a fiery nationalist speech in front of the

Canon's grave with the fleur-de-lys flag fluttering behind him in the wind. No cliché was left out of his homily: the valorous fight of Quebec to remain faithful to its identity, the uncertainty of the future, the hostility of the federal government, the menacing presence of foreigners on the province's soil, the pernicious influence of outsiders, and Quebec's everlasting quest for independence.[12]

In 1978 —the centennial of Lionel Groulx's birth— a flurry of commemorative events were held: two contests on his work were organized in high schools and Cegeps throughout the province, sponsored by the Ministry of Education. Exhibits at the National Library of Quebec, testimonial movies and special television programs, celebratory dinners, masses, and a book were devoted to the memory of the late "national historian." Chance decidedly was on the side of Groulx. His followers were eager to grasp every opportunity to remind their forgetful compatriots of the late priest, and they stumbled across the perfect occasion when an extension of Montreal's subway system was completed the same year. A major terminus station was named after Groulx due to their efforts. It was an enduring memorial impossible to ignore.

Many of these events were quite well attended: 100 people showed up for the unveiling of the plaque, 300 people joined Louis O'Neill, Minister of Cultural Affairs and Maurice Cardinal Roy, archbishop of Quebec for a testimonial dinner held on January 22, 1978 and 600 people gathered for the opening of the exhibition at the National Library presided over by Camille Laurin, Minister of State for Cultural Development. The notables leading the charge for sovereignty of the "young nation" were a certain caste from a certain past: graduates of the Catholic classical colleges, professors, members of liberal professions, priests and former priests, all in their mid-forties or fifties, they were on the whole reminiscent of the French-Canadian elite during the Duplessis era. Duplessis, whose statue had been exhumed only the year before.

The 1980 Quebec referendum saw the victory of the side rejecting sovereignty-association. One year later the Société Saint-Jean-Baptiste came forward with a project to commission a statue of Groulx to be erected in Montreal. The venerable society had pushed Groulx's luck a fatal notch too far, however. On October 17, 1981, on *Noir sur Blanc*, a popular public affairs TV program with a confrontational bent, guest Pastor Claude de Mestral, stated simply that Groulx had been an anti-semite and a fascist and consequently the memory of such a dubious personage should not be so honored. The economist François-Albert Angers, one of Groulx's disciples, heartily agreed with the first part of the statement, but wondered aloud what could possibly be wrong with fascism. In the wake of the newspaper polemics which followed, the project simply petered out. Instead, two years later a travelling exhibition dedicated to Groulx criss-crossed the province.

The polemics of 1981 sound like a dress rehearsal for the events that erupted exactly a decade later around the very same issue, and provide a striking example of the denial-admission complex underpinning social memory in Quebec. Most of arguments advanced would not change from one decade to the next: Groulx was a saint, wrote professor Jean Ethier-Blais, and the malevolent people who point out his racism are the same as those who oppose *le déroulement organique de notre histoire* ("the organic unfolding of our history"),[13] i.e. independence, sovereignty-association or whichever term is politically current at the time. Other peoples have been anti-semitic and fascist and have perpetrated much worse deeds than French Canadians ever did, witness the Germans, and yet nobody accuses them of collectively being racist in the present. "You know what angers me most," Blais fumed rhetorically. "European writers who occasionally indulged in antisemitism — i.e. Valéry and Mallarmé during the Dreyfus affair — are nowadays admired and have streets named after them. And yet Groulx's enemies would deprive him of his statue?"

Another line of argument was that the economic depression of the thirties led French Canadians, and especially the intelligentsia, to embrace Fascist Italy and Charles Maurras' extremist right-wing nationalism with open arms, but they felt no attraction toward German-style Nazism.[14] In 1991 the question of fascism in Quebec again resurfaced, involving not just Lionel Groulx, but his close ideological satellites: the Jeune-Canada youth movement, the nationalist monthly *l'Action nationale*, and the prestigious newspaper *Le Devoir*.[15] Astoundingly enough, the controversy has been periodically resurfacing since then, with no end in sight. It bears the usual trademark of Quebec social memory, simultaneous denial and admission, only this time around its seems more lasting and more vehement. Apologetic statements and exculpatory incantations again abound. "Groulx never said what he said, well, maybe he said it, but only twice." "Furthermore, everyone everywhere was saying what he never said but said only twice." And finally, "What he never said but said only twice he had learned in his breviary." As if that made a difference!

Many welcomed what amounted to a resounding failure of social memory engineering. It was claimed quite disingenuously that Groulx — fascist or not — was unimportant because so few Quebecers knew who he was anyway. They were all too ready to forget the tremendous efforts made to ensure that Quebecers would remember him.

When over the course of ten years during the thirties, *Le Devoir* printed countless times on its front page that Jews were dirty, stinking, criminals, mentally ill, trash of the nations, democratic garbage, Tartars (sic) infected with semitism, living in lice-ridden ghettos, with big crooked noses and crooked fingers, that they were fierce communists — "Goering accuses the 'band of Moscow Jews.' The Prussian prime minister attributes the spread of the Communist threat throughout the world to Soviet agitators" trumpteted *Le Devoir* in bold type[16]— while they were simultaneously "fierce capitalists," the same newspaper demanding that they be forcibly deported from Canada to Palestine, "*Le Devoir* did not really mean it," according to its apologists. *Le Devoir*, like Groulx, apparently never really meant what it had reiterated hundreds of times over the course of a decade.

The driving force behind this denial-admission complex is a simultaneous attraction to and yet embarassment about authoritarianism and/or fascism. The attraction cannot be muted by the taboo, only mitigated through embarassment. Again, we witness the same attitude in the Thirties. Groulx and *Le Devoir*'s journalists often resorted to pen names to express their most outrageous anti-semitic and fascist front-page utterances. Furthermore, they could not help but reveal the charade by their choice of totally implausible and transparaent pseudonyms. Groulx favored names related to Dollard des Ormeaux and his companions, while *Le Devoir* indulged in such absurd names as Nemo (as in the Jules Verne character), *Le Grincheux* ("The Moaner") *Pierre Kiroul* ("Rolling Stone"). They asserted and denied their authorship at one and the same time.

In the end, the Quiet Revolution was not quite so revolutionary or so new. It was the undertaking of young technocrats led by aging ideologues, a generation with ambition but devoid of imagination, that relied on its elders for epics and heroes. Their elders, in turn, were looking backward to find themselves, their past, their youth, the Fascist 30s and the Great Darkness, and found themselves unable to reinterpret their history in a newer, more liberal guise. Slogans, heroes, myths and symbols of the Quiet Revolution came from the thirties. If all "usable past" is more or less a faithful mirror of its creators aspirations, in the case of contemporary Quebec it certainly reveals the hidden and shameful longings of an isolated group trapped in the past. How else to explain the saga of statues which are commissioned, then comically hidden away or never erected?

Modern Quebec is a place of shameful and half-baked heroes. If 19th-century nationalists boldly and naively invented heroes and wrote epics of nostalgia for the lost grandeur of New France, their 20th-century counterparts came up with only two: Dollard des Ormeaux and Lionel Groulx, and the former was a re-creation of the latter. Duplessis did not become a hero but got a statue all the same. Groulx became a hero all the same but did not get a statue. Le Chef was immortalized in bronze because he was a more appropriate and a more presentable figure for modern Quebec, autonomist but not independentist, autocratic but not fascist, a Salazar of the North, dictatorial, bombastic and pragmatic. *Abbé* Lionel Groulx was a Führer animated by nihilistic hatred, not just of Jews but, in true Nazi fashion, of French Canadians as well. He denounced his own people as "an insult to mankind," and he burned with a fierce need to forcibly "reeducate" them into Supermen and Gods. The fires that consumed him would, in any case, surely melt the bronze of any statue.

Bibliography

Esther Delisle: *The Traitor and the Jew*. Montreal, Toronto: Robert Davies Publishing, 1993.

James Fentress and Chris Wickham: *Social Memory*. Oxford U.K. and Cambridge U.S.A.: Blackwell, 1992

Guy Frégault: *Lionel Groulx tel qu'en lui-même*. Montréal: Leméac, 1978.

Hubert Guindon: *Quebec Society. Modernity and Nationhood*. Toronto: University of Toronto Press, 1988.

Eric Hobsbawn and Rerence Ranger (edited by): *The Invention of Tradition*. Cambridge: Cambridge University Press, 1983.

Denis Martin: *Portrait des héros de la Nouvelle-France. Images d'un culte historique*. Montréal: Hurtubise HMH, 1988.

Pierre Nora (sous la direction de): *Les lieux de mémoire*. Paris: NRF, Gallimard 1992.

Catherine Pomeyrols: *Les intellectuels québécois: Formation et engagements 1919-1939*, Pars-Montréal: L'Harmattan, 1996.

Loony tunes: Quebec and the ROC

GLOSSARY

Loon: *A web-footed black and white fish-eating diving bird.[1]*

Loony: *A Canadian dollar, so called because of the loon engraved on the Canadian one dollar coin.*

Peso of the north: *Nickname of the loony in reference to the devaluated currency of Mexico.*

ROC: *The Rest of Canada*

Wishful thinking: *The attribution of reality to what one wishes to be true or the tenuous justification of what one wants to believe.[2]*

It is unusual for an essay on the province of Quebec to open with a glossary. But in the fateful year of 1995 nothing was that simple anymore in Quebec and the ROC, if it had ever been. An indication of the crisis facing the country was that even truisms were failing us when we needed them most. With a coming referendum on sovereignty in Quebec, Canadians on both side of the psychological fence dividing Quebec from the ROC, were focused on more pressing matters than that of the country falling apart. In those days the loony loomed large in everyone's mind. Those days were loony days.

Back in the old days, that is for the last 35 years, essays about the province of Quebec for foreign audiences were the easiest to write. Their narrative was of the ready-to-read sort, a fairy tale built upon rock-solid truisms. The saga of a nation of six million French-speaking people living in North America surrounded by 300 million English-speaking people was definitely intriguing, if not stirring. As in any good narrative, the sequence of events was unchangeable: First, the Golden Age, then the Catastrophe and the Irruption of the Villain followed by the return to the Lost Paradise with Independence.

Therefore, the essay would begin with the Conquest, that fateful battle lost in 1760 on the Plains of Abraham by the French army at the hands of the British who brought the colony of New France under their rule. A proud fledgling nation became an embattled minority. There would follow a rather long lament on the Confederation of 1867, when modern Canada came into being,[3] presented either as a betrayal that had to be redressed, or a pact between two nations — the French and the British — living under a constitutional arangement that had to be undone. Warming up to the crescendo, earlier authors would gloss over the following century to concentrate on the long fight for independence — or the question of separatism, if you want to call it that — of that valiant minority, with its lofty dream of turning a province into a sovereign country. Not that most of it was true, far from it: but it was plausible — plausibility being the cardinal virtue of any enduring truism — and no more was asked. If truth be told, this narrative was not tailored just for foreign readership: it is the very essence of the historical vulgate that has flourished in Quebec for the last 38 years.

However plausibility is not truth. The French colonists who settled in the wake of Jacques Cartier, Canada's disputed official discoverer who was really looking for India, did not necessarily speak French, if only because the vast majority of people in France in the 17th century did not themselves speak French but a variety of dialects.[4] Moreover they were at best nominally Catholic. A cursory glance at French Canadians living in the province of Quebec in the 20th century reveals that the vast majority of them are French-speaking and Catholic, — 83% in 1995 — so it still makes seemingly perfect sense to claim that it has been so since their alleged ancestors settled in North America. The myth of the origins of the French Canadian nation persists and it remains very potent to this day.

The most that can be ventured about the Conquest is that it was a catastrophe for some, a blessing for others and mattered little for a large number. If the sin of anachronism was ever committed in writing history, it was by historians and pundits who turned the Conquest into a Catastrophe, which provided them with a rationale for their thirst for power. The Conquest as Catastrophe gave them their *raison d'être*: they would lead French Canadians in their fight to re-establish New France in the 20th century, that is, to make the province of Quebec a sovereign country.

The intelligentsia of the province began by providing their compatriots with a new denomination: Quebecers. From now on they would be called Quebecers and not French Canadians as had been the case since roughly 1867. That was the final change in a series of names that occurred during Canada's short history: From *Canadiens* (born in New France) vs French (*métropolitains*, i.e. born in France), to *Canadiens* vs British (after New France had become a British colony) to French Canadians vs English Canadians (after the Confederation of 1867) to Quebecers vs Rest of Canada since about 1960. Notice that references

to Canada (in connection to Quebec) or to the French
language have disappeared.

This absence points to another feature of nationalism in Quebec: contrary to widespread assertion and belief, and against all common sense, nationalism in Quebec
is not built upon the defence of the French language.
Language is a smokescreen. Anyone who has the stamina
to read the abundant nationalist literature published in
the last quarter-century will be struck by the fact that the
French language is **not** the defining characteristic of a
Quebecer. Although an English-speaking person can
hardly be considered a Quebecer, being French-speaking
does not necessarily make one so either. The Quebec
government and its various agencies decide who is a Quebecer and who is not, according to blurry and often contradictory parameters based upon the fancies of civil
servants and specialists in social sciences; it is a fertile
ground for absurdity. For example, Quebecers have been
defined as bearers of French *tradition*, peasant stock deeply
rooted in the national soil, close to life and to nature.[5] The
myth of origins could be easily contradicted. For example,
the Quebec government has excluded people of French
origin (that is to say, French nationals) from the "nation"
of French Quebecers, and has instead inadvertently included them among the "other" cultural communities
living in Quebec.[6]

The current narrative of Quebec history was devel-
oped after 1960. That year is another mythical milestone
in the French-Canadian saga in North America. In 1960,
the Liberal Party of Quebec saw the end of its long purgatory and came back into power, defeating the once all-pow-
erful but then vacillating Union Nationale which had
formed the government 16 consecutive years (1944-1960)
as well as for a brief stint before the war. These years were

soon dubbed the Great Darkness because of the iron hand of the autocratic Premier Maurice Duplessis who effectively ruled the province as his private fiefdom. It provided a useful, if carefully unexplored, contrast to the new era dawning in Quebec: the Quiet Revolution.

Canada distinguishes itself by its proliferation of oxymoronic terms. Consider the following: Progressive Conservative Party, Quiet Revolution, Sovereignty-Association, Community of Communities. Even more astounding is the fact that these oxymorons make sense to us — if to no one else — and keep pundits busy crafting their exegeses.

One might be surprised not so much by the Quiet Revolution oxymoron as by the significance given to it in Quebec and the ROC. It has often been presented as The Watershed in Quebec history: a priest-ridden society, ruled by an autocratic corrupt political power, steeped in backwardness, followed by enlightenment, modernization, freedom and economic bounty for the born-again Quebecers. The Quiet Revolution was a mere prelude to the Mother of all Watersheds: Independence.

The most striking feature of the Quiet Revolution was the exponential growth of the state apparatus. Ideally, Quebecers would seize the state apparatus and use it to make their way into the modern capitalist economic world, heretofore closed to them by hostile foreign — Anglo-Saxon and American — capitalists. There occurred a massive transfer of power — on a scale unparalled in the entire world — from the Church to the State. Almost overnight, priests and nuns became civil servants, mixing with young up-and-coming technocrats and teachers fresh from universities. The Ministry of Education was established in 1964, so that future generations would never suffer the rate of illiteracy that had plagued their parents and grandparents.

Nationalization of electricity had been the Holy Grail of Quebec nationalism in the twentieth century. Natural resources make you free! René Lévesque, former journalist and future president of the Parti Québécois (Quebecers' Party)[7] and Premier of Quebec, then the Natural Resources Minister in the Liberal cabinet, campaigned on that theme in 1962. The Liberals were re-elected, with a mandate to nationalize the remaining privately-owned electricity companies. The Montreal office of the premier was and still is very tellingly located on the top floor of the Hydro-Québec building. Over the next decade, various state agencies were created to exploit steel, asbestos, and whatnot while other agencies were created to eradicate social wrongs. For example, the Société d'Assurance Automobile du Québec (State Autombile Insurance Agency) was created to allegedly protect car drivers from the scandalous greed of capitalist insurance companies.

More than thirty years after the Quiet Revolution, collective redemption through the State no longer seems possible. Quebecers are experiencing some very sobering moments. The Ministry of Education is a resounding failure: the francophone drop-out rate in high schools hovers around 40 percent, and the rate of illiterate and functionally illiterate people is rising to alarming levels. The problem is not confined to the province of Quebec, to be sure, but it is more acute here. In any given year, students in Quebec spend fewer hours in school than students in the ROC.

Hydro-Québec has seen its public image abroad tarnished by the successful public relations campaign of Aboriginals who worried about their living conditions if the huge hydroelectric project of Great Whale was carried out. For economic rather than ecological reasons, Great Whale was abandoned in 1994. American states subsequently reneged on their contracts to buy electricity from Hydro-Québec. Conversely, in 1997, Hydro-Québec cut off power in some areas of the province in order to keep sufficient reserves to honor its contracts with US clients. The great dream of national liberation by exploiting natural resources has been fading away for the last 15 years along with millions of wasted loonies.

The existence of SAAQ has paradoxically decreased the chances of a fair settlement for its insured. Its record would make any ruthless private insurance company green with envy. Furthermore, the important financial surplus it generated is never, never returned to the insured, but is pocketed by the state, awash in debt. Clients of the SAAQ have even had to take collective recourse in class-action suits, against "their own" insurer.

Last, but not least, the provincial state is on the brink of bankruptcy. It owes 70 billion loonies, many to foreign lenders, with loans repayable in US dollars, Francs, Deutschmarks or Yen. After Quebec credit had been put "under surveillance" by the Wall Street brokerage firms Moody's and Standard and Poor's for some months, the credit rating on Quebec bonds was finally lowered, making it more expensive for the Quebec Government to float loans.

The problems facing Quebec and the ROC are strikingly similar: both federal and provincial states once saw natural resources as the key to economic development and to more independence from the all powerful United States of America. For example, the federal National Energy Policy was concocted and Petro-Canada — the jewel in its crown — established in the 70s precisely for that purpose.

Canada mustered the allegiance of its citizens and of the provincial barons during World War II by allowing the overlapping of federal and provincial powers — mainly in the fields of health and education — and by making Canada as distinct from the United States as possible by adding a whole array of social programs.

The federal and provincial governments could not, however, sustain financial and ideological competition with each other. The debt of the federal and provincial goverments totaled, as of 1994, 750 billion. Now Quebec and the ROC are about to apply identical remedies to their financial predicaments. Many state agencies which have not made a profit in ages nor, sad to say, have neither warded off America's economic grip on the the ROC nor brought Quebec much closer to economic self-reliance, have been privatized.

None of Canada's cherished symbols is beyond the axe of a panicky government fretting under the eyes of edgy foreign creditors. Canadian National Railways, a company owned by the federal government which has symbolized to Canadians the notion that all areas of the country are somehow linked together, has been partially privatized. The sacred cow of subsidies to prairie farmers for the transportation of wheat has been sacrificed on the altar of deficit reduction. The very existence of the Canadian Broadcasting Corporation — the centrepiece of Canadian radio and television broadcasting policy in both official languages — is imperiled by successive and never-ending rounds of budget cuts. Petro Canada, the cornerstone of Canada's grand energy policy was put up for sale. No more mega-projects financed by the federal government would be undertaken. Massive transfers of powers from the federal government to its provincial counterparts have been initiated. Quietly, with barely more than a whimper, Canada has been giving way to entrenched regional kingdoms.

In Quebec there was an incredible and surrealistic situation where sovereignist parties scored remarkably well in both federal and provincial elections yet a majority of Quebecers rejected sovereignty. The sovereignist Bloc Québécois was the official opposition in federal parliament in Ottawa for a whole term, and the Parti Québécois was and still is in power in Quebec. Moreover in an unprecedented attempt to count the chickens before they have hatched, the PQ submitted a draft bill of sovereignty to the National Assembly, where it passed handily since that party had a solid majority of seats. In 1995 Quebec was going to become a sovereign country, at least on paper, and for real if a majority of voters supported the bill in a referendum. The first article of the draft bill read as follows: "Quebec is a sovereign country."[8] Then it went on to specify that a sovereign Quebec would use the beleaguered but nonetheless reassuring loony; that the current joint "economic space" would remain intact; that Quebecers would remain Canadian citizens, holding Canadian passports if they wished. The referendum question itself read as follows: "Are you in favour of the Act passed by the National Assembly declaring the sovereignty of Québec? YES or NO"[9] Under the influence of Lucien Bouchard, the charismatic leader of the Bloc Québécois, the question was changed to make it more enticing and palatable to Quebecers. It became: "Do you accept that Quebec becomes sovereign after having formally offered Canada a new economic and political partnership, within the framework of the bill respecting the future of Québec and the agreement of June 12, 1995? Yes or No."

Pierre Elliott Trudeau, Prime Minister of Canada for 16 years, built his political carreer on the conviction that

French Canadians should feel at home everywhere in
Canada and not just in the province of Quebec.[10] The late
René Lévesque held the opposite position, that French
Canadians could feel at home only in Quebec, because it
is the only place in North America where they constitute
a majority.[11] That clash of visions and the ensuing constitutional imbroglio has generated a wealth of magic formulas deemed solutions. Their nomenclature is quite
impressive:

Separation
Secession
Independence
Sovereignty
Hyphenated sovereignty-association (political sover-
eignty with an economic union with the ROC)
Non-hyphenated sovereignty association (political
sovereignty not necessarily with an economic association
with the ROC)
Cultural sovereignty
Particular status
Profitable federalism
Renewed federalism
Asymmetrical federalism
Flexible federalism
Administrative federalism
Status Quo
Partnership

Predictably enough, at least according to reliable
surveys, people don't grasp these subtle distinctions. According to now-retired McGill University professor of
sociology Maurice Pinard, a sizeable number of Quebecers
cling tenaciously to the idea that they will elect MPs to the
federal parliament once Quebec is sovereign.

"While the meaning of separation may be understood, the same is not true for sovereignty. In particular many see it as maintaining political ties with the rest of Canada. Thus, according to a March 1992 CROP survey, 31% of respondents mistakenly believed, among other things, that a sovereign Quebec 'would still be part of Canada,' and 14% did not know; similarly, 20% thought that Quebecers 'would still elect members of Parliament to Ottawa,' and no less than one quarter of respondents in favour of 'Quebec sovereignty,' opted, in reply to another question, for Quebec 'to remain a province of Canada' rather than 'to become an independent country.' "[12]

On the eve of the 1995 referendum, a survey showed that 49 percent of Quebecers who said they would vote Yes to sovereignty nevertheless wished to remain Canadian citizens in a sovereign Quebec. Of the people who said they would vote Yes, 17 percent specified that their support did not give the Parti Québécois a clear mandate to achieve independence; two Quebecers out of three wanted to keep the Canadian dollar.[13] Yiddish wisdom might summarize Quebec's conundrum as follows: Sovereignty, schmovereignty, why not, as long as we remain Canadian citizens!

However inelegant it would be to mock the bewilderment of "ordinary" Quebecers in the face of separation cum renewed federalism, the following personal anecdote is illuminating. I attended a dinner with some distinguished professors in the fall of 1994. One of the enlightened academics sitting at the table was expounding the virtues of asymmetrical federalism for Quebec and everyone was nodding — whether in agreement or in indifference — when taking my courage in both hands I asked him to explain the difference between the asymmetrical federalism that he was so fond of and sovereignty-association. He could not answer except to state the obvious: it was far from being clear and needed to be discussed a lot further. I was left wondering how these arcane discussions could possibly make sense to my fellow citizens who had other more pressing matters on their minds, such as the fate of the loony.

One might wonder what remains to be explained and understood 18 years after the first referendum on sovereignty (1980); 28 years after the October Crisis, when the British Consul James Richard Cross and Quebec Minister of Labour Pierre Laporte were kidnapped and Laporte murdered by the *Front de Libération du Québec,* which was devoted to establishing a socialist and independent Quebec; 30 years after the establishment of the Parti Québécois, 31 years after the founding of the Mouvement Souveraineté-association — the forebear of the PQ — and 36 years after the establishment of the first separatist political party, the Rassemblement pour l'Indépendance nationale. In other words, what is there to debate and expound after more than a quarter of a century spent discussing the constitutional status of the province of Quebec inside or outside Canada? All the debate has produced is a lengthy nomenclature of obtuse constitutional options and a cottage industry of intellectuals of all kinds pondering the issue.

Understanding the issue at stake is — fortunately or unfortunately — not required in order to discuss them at length, if not ad nauseam. The ensuing confusion always calls for more discussions and this keeps the intellectual cottage industry thriving. Regional commissions on the future of Quebec held public hearings at the beginning of 1995. Although headed by sovereignist commissars, these commissions had little choice but to report the consider-

able worries of citizens about sovereignty and their confusion over the issue.

With the expected momentum for sovereignty remaining more elusive than ever and amidst increasing
confusion, Premier Jacques Parizeau engineered the creation of yet another commission. He turned to prominent
citizens to muster support for his party's constitutional
option. Sign of the times, even that attempt petered out.
Like their less prominent fellow citizens, heads of organizations were to submit a "grocery list" — a list of demands
— to the increasingly disgruntled commissars. "Were you
not ardent nationalists just three years ago?" the commissars thundered. To which the outraged VIPs invariably
replied: "We will not allow anyone to doubt the strength
of our nationalist commitment! Never! But you have to
understand our predicament: we need more information
about what a sovereign Quebec would be. Such an important decision cannot be made while there is still a lot of
confusion around the issue. Meanwhile what we really
need is: 1. more money; 2. more power; 3. more of this; 4.
and more of that." Every day bemused citizens witnessed
these surrealistic exchanges. And became more confused.
They were, however, permitted to express their puzzle-
ment in a poem and run the chance of having dinner with
the Premier and his overbearing wife at their official
residence if they won the weekly contest organized by a
local radio station in Quebec City.

The heart of the matter may be that French Canadians did not want then, and indeed never have wanted a
complete secession from Canada. To appease their fear,
nationalist politicians and their faithful pundits — who
may not want it either — have asserted a form of secession
so qualified that it bears only a vague resemblance to itself.
First, drop the dreaded words Separation and Inde-

pendence. Dilute them in the blissfully blurred concept of sovereignty. Then promise your distrustful compatriots they will remain Canadian citizens if they wish to, they will keep their Canadian passports, will use the battered but nevertheless trusted loony and will be allowed to work in the ROC if they wish to.

It is true too that the orthodoxy born out of the Quiet Revolution is wearing thin. There may be no good explanation for this except that 35 to 50 years might be the average lifespan of any orthodoxy. Dessicated nationalism may give the illusion of importance because of the noise it makes. But the show does little to mitigate the fact that the ideas put forth are repetitive and shallow. For example, the state will spearhead the economic development of Quebec; Quebec is oppressed by Ottawa; Quebecers should be sovereign like any "normal" nation; Quebecers are the last colonized people in the Western world; and so on and so forth. The passion that made up for the weakness of the orthodoxy's logic and the imprecision of its terms is waning. We can say about Quebec what was said of the last days of the Austro-Hungarian empire, when theatre plays made more sense to people than politics. On the eve of the 1995 referendum and now, citizens here watch with indifference the same ballet danced by skillful but dispirited dancers. The spark is not there anymore. The passion is as worn out as the public finances.

The real suspense still centers around the number "70," which has acquired over the years a sort of supernatural significance here. It does not refer to the percentage of votes necessary to validate the secession of Quebec, but to the exchange rate of the loony with the American dollar. Will the financially challenged loony finally drop below 70 American cents? It since has. Newspaper headlines in Quebec and the ROC did not tell of the coming historical referendum, but of the frightening downward fluctuations of the loony, which was frantically flapping its wings to avoid drowning in red ink, and the ensuing attempts of the central Bank of Canada to rescue it. Very much in the headlines, too, were — and still are — cuts, cuts, cuts in public spending.

Quebecers may be the world champions of wishful thinking. Since 1960, Quebec is always referred to as Quebec and never as the province of Quebec. Every public agency and organization in the province has the "national" epithet. The "P" word has become a dirty word. There is Quebec and there is the rest of Canada, as if Quebec was not part of the country. To top it all off, there is a law about to make Quebec sovereign in words if not in deed. The idea of the province being sovereign on paper only may yet prove satisfactory to these gold medalists of wishful thinking who say: Let's retain our illusions without facing the unpleasant consequences of reality. Why not have the best of both worlds?

Yvon Deschamps, a famed Québécois humourist best summed it up when he stated that what Quebecers really want is an independent Quebec in a strong and united Canada. Under, may we add, the ever watchful eye of Wall Street.

Th...Th... Th... Th... Th... That's all, folks!

Notes

NAC: National Archives of Canada
ANQ: Archives nationales du Québec

Introduction
1. André Laurendeau, *La crise de la conscription 1942*, Éditions du Jour, Montréal, 1962.
2. *Le Devoir*, 4 February 1944.
3. André Laurendeau, *op. cit.*, p. 155.

Sleepless in Quebec City
1. Confidential file 862. 20211-T. K. Eschmann. All of the reports on Father Eschmann mentioned in this chapter come from this dossier.
2. Rollin R. Winslow to Adolf A. Berle, 12 July 1940.
3. Rollin R. Winslow, 27 September 1940, report n° 163.
4. Federal Bureau of Investigation, Department of Justice, Washington, D. C. J. Edgard Hoover to the Honorable Adolf A. Berle Jr., Undersecretary of State, US Department of State, 29 march 1941.
5. Strictly confidential file 851. 20210-Légion des Anciens Combattants/The Menace of Vichy in French Canada.
6. Rollin R. Winslow, 25 February 1942, Report n° 406.
7. Rollin R. Winslow, 5 March 1942, Report n° 413.
8. Rollin R. Winslow, 9 March 1942, Report n° 416.
9. "French Canadian Nationalist Movement Communist Activities Within Quebec Province," National Archives of Canada. J. A. Pouliot, district supervisor for the chief postal censor, Québec, 26 June 1941. S. T. Wood to J. M. Bernier, private secretary to the Minister of Justice, 17 July 1941. *L'Événement-Journal*, 18 June 1941.

10. Gregory S. Kealey and Reg Whitaker (editors), *RCMP Security Bulletins, The War Series*, Part II, 1942-1945, St. John's Canadian Committee on Labour History, 1993, p. 63.

11. Rollin R. Winslow, "The Menace of Vichy in French-Canada," 5 March 1942, Report n° 413.

12. *Ibid.*

13. Rollin R. Winslow, 27 February 1942, Report n° 408. The following excerpts come from the same report.

14. This new organization is probably the League for the Defence of Canada, founded in the days following Prime Minister Mackenzie King's 22 January 1942 annoucement of a referendum asking citizens to free him from his promise not to impose conscription.

15. Confidential file 851. 20200-Albert Briand, Rollin R. Winslow, 23 March 1942, Report n° 433. "Subject is the owner of Albert Briand Fils, commissioned merchants and general store in Saint-Pierre and of Quality Supplies Limited of St. John's, Newfoundland. ," p. 1. "On 18 January 1941, Mr. Briand, his wife Mary Deminiac Briand and several friends (Miss Olano, P^r and Mrs. Henry Claireaux and Miss Fontaine) arrived in Halifax from Saint-Pierre on the SS Caribou. ," p. 2.

16. Rollin R. Winslow, 1 7 April 1942, Report n° 447.

17. Winslow does not mention which police force interrogated Briand.

18. "French-Canadian Nationalist Movement/Communist Activities Within Quebec Province." NAC, Ottawa, report by constable Victor Dubé, 17 March 1942.

19. This Iron Guard is a different organization from the Iron Guard of Adrien Arcand's fascist Parti d'Unité nationale.

20. Confidential file 800. 20242/5, Rollin R. Winslow, 9 April 1942, Report n° 443.

21. *Ibid.*

22. On *l'Action libérale nationale*: Patricia Dirks, *The Failure of l'Action libérale nationale*, McGill-Queen's University Press, Montreal & Kingston, London, Buffalo, 1991, pp. 84-145.

23. Rollin R. Winslow, *op. cit.*

24. Rollin R. Winslow, 23 April 1942, Report n° 452.

25. *Ibid.*

26. "French-Canadian Nationalist Movement / Communist Activities within Quebec Province," Canadian Press Censor to Inspecteur A. Drysdale, 13 March 1942.

27. *Ibid.* Letter to Commissioner S. T. Wood, RCMP, Ottawa, 13 March 1942. We did not use Raymond Chouinard's name here because it was struck by the censor. However, the suspect's name does sometimes appear. If we include information concerning the Iron Guard found in US State Department archives and in Quebec newspapers, it seems evident that the suspect alluded to in the RCMP reports is Raymond Chouinard.

28. *Ibid.* , report of sergeant J. E. E. DesRosiers, 17 March 1942.

29. A probable supposition: J. -Ernest Grégoire, former mayor of Quebec City.

30. *Ibid.*, report by H. A. R. Gagnon to Commissioner, RCMP, Ottawa, 25 March 1942.

31. *Ibid.* , report by constable Victor Dubé, 12 March 1942, p. 5: "This diary contains the dates, code names and secret locations of meeting places, as well as the names of those present and speakers."

32. Rollin R. Winslow, 9 April 1942, Report n° 443.

33. *Op. cit.* , report by constable Victor Dubé, 13 March 1942: "It is obvious that they knew that publishing these stories would immediately suggest to those involved in this business the need to destroy incriminating evidence, for their own protection." See also *Le Soleil* 11, 12,19 March and 21 April 1942.

34. S. T. Wood to the Honorable Louis Saint-Laurent, Minister of Justice, Ottawa, 30 March, 1942. See *Le Soleil,* 11 March 1942: "Police seize subversive documents in our city" and 12 March 1942: "R. Chouinard involved in another judicial affair ," where the same events that took place on the dates mentionned in the RCMP reports name Raymond Chouinard as the suspect.

35. *Le Soleil,* 12 March 1942: "Chouinard involved in another judicial affair," p. 3. *"Nom non divulgué* appeared in Court at 2 p. m. only to learn that his sentencing was adjourned until 9 a.m."

36. Report by constable Victor Dubé, 12 March 1942, p. 5.

37. *Le Soleil,* 19 March 1942: "Two months' imprisonment," p. 10. Also Rollin R. Winslow, 9 April 1942. He also believes the two-month sentence to be cumulative for all of the crimes.

38. Rollin R. Winslow to Pierrepont Moffat, American diplomat, American Legation, Ottawa, 19 May, 1942.

39. Rollin R. Winslow, 23 April 1942, Report n° 452.

40. Rollin R. Winslow to Pierrepont Moffat, *op. cit.*

41. Jacques Normand, *Les nuits de Montréal,* Éditions La Presse, Montréal, 1974, p. 183.

42. Jacques Normand, *De Québec to Tizi-Ouzou,* Stanké, Montréal, 1980, p. 50-56.

43. Rollin R. Winslow, 30 April 1942.

44. Gregory S. Kealey and Reg Whitaker (editors), RCMP Security Bulletins, The War Series, *op. cit.*, pp. 62-63.

45. Rollin R. Winslow, 11 June 1942.

46. Gregory S. Kealey and Reg Whittaker, *op. cit.*, p. 40.

47. Rollin R. Winslow, 23 March 1942.

48. Rollin R. Winslow, letter to Pierrepont Moffat, American diplomat, American Legation, Ottawa, 19 May, 1942.

49. Rollin R. Winslow to Pierrepont Moffat, 15 May 1942.

50. Rollin R. Winslow to Pierrepont Moffat, 30 April 1942.

51. *Ibid.*

52. *Ibid.*

53. *Ibid.*

54. *Ibid.*

55. Pierrepont Moffat to American Foreign Service, 21 May 1942.

56. Henry Torrès, "The Fifth Column in French Canada," memorandum received by the State Department, 19 May 1942 .

57. Confidential Memo, Federal Communications Commission, Foreign Broadcasts Intelligence Service, report n° 18, 19 August 1942, p. 1.

58. *Ibid.*, p. 3. Vichy to North America, 27 May, noon, "Address to French Canadians," recording n° 13219.

59. *Ibid.*, p. 4. Vichy to North America, 16 June, midnight to 12:18, read by Geneviève d'Orville, title: "To My French-Canadian Friends," recording n° 02525.

60. *Ibid.*, p. 5. Vichy to North America, 15 May, 23:40 to 23:50, "War and Diplomacy," recording n° 8505. The misunderstood or mispronounced name is that of Dostaler O'Leary.

61. *Ibid.*, p. 8, Vichy to North America, 10 July, midnight to 00:07, title: "Feminine Chronicle," presumed reader Geneviève d'Orville, recording n° 14250.

62. Confidential file 800. 20211-Oliver, Gerard Joseph; J. Edgard Hoover to Adolf A. Berle, 6 August 1942.

63. Rollin R. Winslow, 14 August 1942, Report n° 494.

64. *Ibid.*

65. Rollin R. Winslow, 15 August 1942, Report n° 495.
66. *Ibid.*
67. *The Quebec Chronicle Telegraph,* 19 November 1941, p. 3.
68. Rollin R. Winslow, 20 November 1942, Report n° 545.
69. *Action catholique,* "French Canada wants to be happy," 19 October 1942 and "Freedom needs the support of French Canada," 20 October 1942.
70. Rollin R. Winslow, o*p. cit.*
71. Rollin R. Winslow, 27 November 1942, Report n° 547.
72. Rollin R. Winslow, 2 December 1942, Report n° 552.
73. *Ibid.*

A Strange Sort of Hero

1. Dominique Veillon, *La Collaboration, Textes et débats,* Le livre de poche, Paris, 1984, p. 462.
2. Pascal Ory, *Les Collaborateurs 1940-1945,* Éditions du Seuil, Paris, 1976, p. 150
3. *Ibid.* , p. 251.
4. Herbert R. Lottman, *The Purge,* William Morrow and Company Inc., New York, 1986, p. 33.
5. Created on 2 June 1943.
6. Pascal Ory, *op. cit.* , p. 251.
7. Some authors maintain that Jacques Dugé de Bernonville was a real count, others discount that affirmation. According to the Association of mutual assistance of the French Nobility, Jacques Dugé de Bernonville comes from an obscure family with no ties to the nobility (cf. Georges Tombs, "How a war criminal found haven in Quebec," *The Gazette,* 24 September 1994, p. B6). In this book, I use the names Jacques Dugé de Bernonville and Jacques Bernonville because, nobility or not, he was known under them.
8. François Bédarida, "Historien du présent," *La Presse,* 2 September 1995.
9. For another account of the facts and acts of Jacques Dugé de Bernonville au Québec, see : Yves Lavertu, *The Bernonville Affair (1948-1951),* Robert Davies Publishing, 1996. We compiled this account by adding information discovered in the many archives combed for our research and from interviews conducted with eye-witnesses.

10. Pierre *Assouline: Simenon,* Julliard, Laurédit inc. , Paris, 1992, pp. 314-315.

11. *Ibid.* , p. 327.

12. *Ibid.*

13. *Ibid.* , p. 368.

14. *Ibid.* , p. 370.

15. Georges Vanier papers, NAC.

16. *Ibid.*

17. *Ibid.*

18. Pierre Assouline, *op. cit.* , p. 370.

19. *Ibid.* , p. 338.

20. Conversation with the author, 16 February 1995.

21. Herbert R. Lottman, o*p. cit.* , p. 113.

22. On 15 February 1945, an arrest warrant for Doctor André-Charles Emmanuel Boussat was issued by the prefecture of police of Agen. On 3 July 1945, he was condemned *in absentia* to life at hard labour by the Court of the Département of Lot-et-Garonne, had his wealth confiscated and his citizenship stripped for collaboration with the enemy.

23. Vera Murray, "The Crimes of Julien Labedon", report produced for *The Fifth Estate,* CBC, summer 1984.

24. Report on Jean Bonnel, 4 March 1949, Jacques Dugé de Bernonville Dossier, NAC.

25. They were far from being the only ones: in April 1946, more than 1400 potential immigrants visited or wrote to the Canadian embassy. G. L. Magnan writing for Canadian ambasador Georges Vanier, advised the secretary of State for External Affairs that: "At this time, two staff members are working with correspondence and visitors requesting information on entering Canada and finding work there. In fact, it is quite often impossible for two officers to interview all the daily visitors and to respond to letters received by the embassy. We have noticed that the busiest days immediately follow radio or print reports or official and semi-official references concerning Canadian interest in immigrants." NAC

26. Robert Speaight, *Vanier. Soldier, Diplomat and Governor General. A biography,* Collins, Toronto, 1970, chapters 13-18. Deborah Cowley and George Cowley, *One Woman's Journey. A Portrait of Pauline Vanier,* Novalis, Université Saint-Paul, Ottawa, 1992, chapter 11.

27. "General Vanier, Canadian ambassador in Paris, was a great friend of France; General de Gaulle held him in high esteem. Right from the Liberation, our two families were tied together by a reciprocal affection made even easier by the fact that one could hardly imagine a more cultivated, distinguished and charming woman than Pauline Vanier." Vanier accompanied Teitgen to Angers and subsequently visited many regions of France, which allowed him to report to the Canadian government that the fears entertained in some quarters that France was in a state of anarchy where the Communists dominated the liberation committees, were unfounded. Pierre-Henri Teitgen, *Faites entrer le témoin suivant, 1940-1958. De la Résistance to la Ve République,* Ouest France, Rennes, 1988, pp. 200-220.

28. Meeting on 20 June 1984.

29. Appeal Court, Poitiers, 26 January 1949.

30. Author's conversation with Henri Des Garets, 28 June 1997.

31. Author's conversation with Yvette Germain, 30 April 1996. Author's conversation with Yves Desgarets, 23 February 1997.

32. The real Vincent Des Garets died in December 1996.

33. Conversations with the author, 6 and 19 October 1995.

34. Author's conversation with Geneviève Seigneur, 24 June 1984, and with Yvette Germain, 30 April 1996.

35. Maurice Vincent to Robert Rumilly, 4 September 1946, Robert Rumilly papers, ANQ.

36. Maurice Vincent to Robert Rumilly, 7 September 1946, Robert Rumilly papers, ANQ.

37. On 14 February 1947, the Canadian External Affairs Department advised its immigration officer in Paris that Keyserling's visa was approved. Victor Keyserling file, Louis Saint-Laurent papers, NAC.

38. Court of Justice of the Seine Département, decision of 6 December, 1945 regarding the informational procedure n° 8202 . Victor Keyserling file, Louis Saint-Laurent papers, NAC.

39. "I am one of those Frenchmen who believed themselves to be "fascists" (without much liking the name) and who, one day in 1945 or even earlier, realised that they were in fact liberals." Michel Mohrt, quoted in Pierre-Marie Dioudonnat, "*Je suis partout*, 1930-1944," *Les maurassiens devant la tentation fasciste,* La Table Ronde, Paris, 1973, p. 408. Michel Mohrt wrote a dozen or more articles for

Je Suis Partout in 1943. He also published two books: *Les intellectuels devant la défaite de 1870* (1942) and *Montherlant l'homme libre* (1942) and in addition, wrote for free zone papers like *Idées* and *Écho des étudiants*. Pierre-Marie Dioudonnat, *Les 700 Rédacteurs de Je Suis Partout*, Sedepols, Paris, 1993, p. 65.

40. Michel Mohrt, *Mon royaume pour un cheval*, Albin Michel, Paris, 1949.

41. Telephone conversation with Gabriel Dorget, 8 July 1995.

42. Robert Rumilly, "Second speech on the Bernonville Affair," never given, 1948, Robert Rumilly papers, ANQ.

43. Simon Arsenault to Frédéric Dorion, 30 October 1948, Robert Rumilly papers, ANQ.

44. Julien Labedan to Robert Rumilly, 25 May 1948, Robert Rumilly papers, ANQ.

45. Georges-Benoît Montel, *Souvenirs et Commentaires d'un homme libre*, inédit, p. 39.

46. *Ibid.*

47. Julien Labedan to Robert Rumilly, 25 May 1948, Robert Rumilly papers, ANQ.

48. Robert Rumilly to Jean Bonnel, 20 May 1947, Robert Rumilly papers, ANQ.

49. Jacques Benoît (de Bernonville) to Robert Rumilly, 22 May 1947, Robert Rumilly papers, ANQ.

50. Mgr. Ferdinand Vandry to M. Louis Saint-Laurent, 25 August 1947, Louis Saint-Laurent papers, NAC.

51. "(. . .) but Senator Dessurault to whom I spoke about the matter told me that Jollife had informed him that he would settle the matter." Louis Saint-Laurent to Mgr Vandry, 27 August 1947, Louis Saint-Laurent papers, NAC.

52. Jacques Benoît de Bernonville to Jean Bruchesi, 10 January 1948, Jean Bruchesi papers, Archives de l'Université de Montréal. "I have just submitted a request to Ottawa to use my real name and to obtain a permanent resident visa. I am confident that the decision will be favorable, having been unofficially told this will be the case." Jacques Benoît de Bernonville to René Chaloult, 23 January 1948, René Chaloult papers, ANQ.

53. Jacques Benoît de Bernonville to Jean Bruchesi, 10 January 1948, Jean Bruchesi papers, Archives de l'Université de Montréal.

54. "Having had the pleasure of knowing Mr. de Bernonville and of having met him on many occasions, and knowing full well his record of service in France, I do not hesitate to recommend him to you." Jean Bruchesi to the Commissioner of Immigration in Ottawa, 14 January 1948, Jean Bruchesi Papers.

55. Senator Dessurault to Louis Saint-Laurent, 24 February 1948, Louis Saint-Laurent papers, NAC. To Frédéric Dorion, Saint-Laurent apparently said that he heard about Dr. Montel from Senator Dessurault and from Mgr Vandry, who had written to him on the matter. Saint-Laurent had asked the assistant of Commissioner of Immigration Jollife not to take any decision on the case without consulting him. He heard nothing further on the matter. Robert Rumilly to Mgr Vandry, 25 February 1948, Robert Rumilly papers, ANQ.

56. Philippe Hamel to Robert Rumilly, 24 September 1948, Robert Rumilly papers, ANQ.

57. Mgr Ferdinand Vandry to J. A. Glen, Minister of Mines and Natural Resources, 23 February 1948, Louis Saint-Laurent papers, NAC.

58. "I also met with Mgr Maurice Roy, who was supposed to see Mr. Saint-Laurent in Ottawa yesterday. He assured me that he would bring up the case of Dr. Montel. I will get back in touch with Mgr Roy within the next few days." René Chaloult to Robert Rumilly, 23 February 1948, Robert Rumilly papers, ANQ. "Permit me to remind you of the Montel affair. If it would be possible to settle this case before Mgr Vandry's return, we would please him greatly, and please his Excellence Mgr Roy as well." Senator P. H. Bouffard to Guy Sylvestre, secretary to the Minister of External Affairs, 9 August 1948, Louis Saint-Laurent papers, NAC,

59. Mgr Philippe-Servule Desranleau to Louis Saint-Laurent, 6 March 1948, Louis Saint-Laurent papers, NAC.

60. René Chaloult to Robert Rumilly, 23 February 1948. "I believe we must not hesitate to use this last recourse *in extremis*." Robert Rumilly papers, ANQ.

61. Robert Rumilly to René Chaloult, 26 February 1948, Robert Rumilly papers, ANQ.

62. Robert Rumilly to René Chaloult, 27 February 1948, Robert Rumilly papers, ANQ,

63. "Did I tell you, in our conversation, that I talked with Houde about the cases of the French exiles threatened with deportation. "We

must save them," said Mrs. Houde, and they discussed an immediate campaign, with Duplessis and yourself. I was obliged to restrain
them because of what I had been told by Mgr Vandry and Dr.
Montel." Robert Rumilly to René Chaloult, 13 April 1948, René
Chaloult papers, ANQ.

64. Report by General Vanier to Louis Saint-Laurent, 22 April 1948,
Louis Saint-Laurent papers, NAC. Several days later, the French
ambassador to Canada, Francisque Gay, confirmed to Mgr Vandry
that he had received word from the Ministry of Foreign Affairs in
Paris assuring him that the French Government had no intention
of requesting Montel's extradition.

65. "It was the Communists that chased us from France." Interview
with Mme Seigneur, *La Presse,* 23 February 1949.

66. Secretary of State for External Affairs at the Canadian Embassy,
Paris, France, 24 February 1949, Jacques Dugé de Bernonville file,
Simon Wiesenthal Centre, Toronto.

67. G. P. Vanier to the Secretary of State for External Affairs, 4 March
1949. "I include a memorandum (Paris, 26 February) that I asked
D. W. Munro to prepare in order that you may know in detail the
reaction of the French authorities." Jacques Dugé de Bernonville
file, Simon Wiesenthal Centre, Toronto.

68. Memorandum from D. W. Munro to Ambassador Georges Vanier,
26 February 1949, Jacques Dugé de Bernonville file, Simon Wiesenthal Centre, Toronto.

69. E. R. Hopkins to Ross Martin, 26 February 1949, Jacques Dugé de
Bernonville file, Simon Wiesenthal Centre, Toronto.

70. Georges Vanier to the Secretary of State for External Affairs,
telegram, Paris, 12 March 1949, Jacques Dugé de Bernonville file,
Simon Wiesenthal Centre, Toronto.

71. "The enclosed report by Mr. Hopkins presents a serious problem.
It would, I believe, be desirable to submit into the record the
transcriptions of the judgement when we reply to Mr. Stewart's
motion, but it would be difficult to justify without the explicit
consent of the french government. I wonder if it would not be
prudent to ask Maybank, when he returns from Winnipeg, to show
the transcription to Stewart and to explain the entire situation to
him?" J. W. Pickersgill, memorandum to the Prime Minister, Jacques Dugé de Bernonville file, Simon Wiesenthal Centre, Toronto.

72. *Le Devoir,* 31 September 1948. "With the exception of Bernonville, the government has not shown much interest in expelling these men (Montel, Boussat, Labedan, Huc). The latter seem to have been nothing more that average supporters of the Pétain regime, except for Bernonville who apparently was the most active collaborator with the authorities of the German occupation." Secretary of State for External Affairs to the Canadian High Commissioner, London, 18 October 1948, Jacques Dugé de Bernonville file, Simon Wiesenthal Centre, Toronto.

73. Debates of the House of Commons, official transcript, 9 February 1949, p. 3103.

74. Canadian Embassy in Paris, R. M. MacDonnell (for the Ambassador), 20 March 1950, Jacques Dugé de Bernonville file, Simon Wiesenthal Centre, Toronto.

75. Embassy of Canada in Rio de Janeiro to Under-secretary of State for External Affairs, 30 September 1955. Other reasons: certain documents in the dossier were not legally usable. Embassy of Canada in Rio de Janeiro to Under-secretary of State for External Affairs, 25 October 1956. The Brazilian Supreme Court will not extradite an individual facing the death penalty in his country of origin. Jaques de Dugé de Bernonville file, Simon Wiesenthal Centre, Toronto.

76. Robert Rumilly to René Chaloult, 15 April 1948, René Chaloult papers, ANQ.

77. Louis Saint-Laurent to Philippe Hamel, 13 September 1948, Louis Saint-Laurent papers, NAC.

78. *Action catholique,* 21 September 1948, "L'Action catholique: Mr. Dessurault's reply to Mr. Rumilly," Robert Rumilly papers, ANQ.

79. Keenleyside, in a meeting with other bureacrats, would insist that: "In fact, the immigration service recommended that all four be deported, and the decision to allow them to remain in Canada was the sole responsibility of the Minister and of Cabinet." Prime Minister's office to Jack Pickersgill, 18 October 1948, Jacques Dugé de Bernonville file, Simon Wiesenthal Centre, Toronto.

80. Robert Rumilly to René Chaloult, 21 October 1948, René Chaloult papers, ANQ.

81. Philippe Hamel to Robert Rumilly, 24 September 1948, Robert Rumilly papers, ANQ.

82. Order-in-council PC 4186, passed on 16 September 1948 and PC 4468, passed on 5 October 1948.

83. "The RCMP said that they had been informed that the Victor Keyserling who is in Canada is identical to the individual who was a Sturman in the SS "Kurt Eggers" regiment and that he apparently fled clandestinely to Spain in April 1947 to escape arrest by the French police for his activities in the SS, and not to escape deportation to the Soviet Union as he prentented." A. L. Joliffe to Jules Léger, secretary to the Prime Minister, 7 September 1949, Louis Saint-Laurent papers, NAC. "Now, beacuse I was on the list of the only *Volksdeutsche* war correspondents, the SS Kurt Eggers group, I learn that in principle I am not eligible for admission to Canada, having technically belonged to the German armed forces." Victor Keyserling to Louis Saint-Laurent, 11 August 1949, Louis Saint-Laurent papers, NAC.

84. "I must make it clear that I am also still a Latvian, and consequently, the Germans considered me to be Alsatian, that is to say draftable and obliged to submit to all military obligations (. . .) I found, as an editor for Radio-Paris, a refuge where I could escape these German military obligations, and as such it was not because of political or other convictions that I worked there." Deposition given by Victor Keyserling at the trial of Jean Hérald-Paquis, in *Les Procès de la Radio,* Albin Michel, Paris, 1947, pp. 188-189.

85. Madeleine Thibaudeau to Louis Saint-Laurent, 17 September 1949, Louis Saint-Laurent papers, NAC.

86. Madeleine Thibaudeau to Jules Léger, Thursday evening (undated letter), Louis Saint-Laurent papers, NAC.

87. Jules Léger to Louis Saint-Laurent, 10 September 1949, Louis Saint-Laurent papers, NAC.

88. Victor Keyserling to Jules Léger, 28 September 1949, Louis Saint-Laurent papers, NAC.

89. Jules Léger to Édouard Rinfret, Minister of the Postal Service, 12 September 1949, Louis Saint-Laurent papers, NAC.

90. Jules Léger to Madeleine Thibaudeau, 6 October 1949, Louis Saint-Laurent papers, NAC.

91. Robert Rumilly to Victor Keyserling, 31 December 1948, Robert Rumilly papers, ANQ.

92. Victor Keyserling to Robert Rumilly, 1 March 1949, Robert Rumilly papers, ANQ.

93. Robert Rumilly to Victor Keyserling, 9 March 1949, Robert Rumilly papers, ANQ.

94. Victor Keyserling to Robert Rumilly, 7 March 1949, Robert Rumilly papers, ANQ.

95. Robert Rumilly to Victor Keyserling, 9 March 1949, Robert Rumilly papers, ANQ.

96. *La Presse,* 9 September 1948.

97. Report on Jean Bonnel, 4 March 1949, Jacques Dugé de Bernonville file, NAC.

98. Jean Bonnel to Philippe Hamel, 4 October 1948, Philippe Hamel papers, Archives de l'Université Laval.

99. Jacques Dugé de Bernonville to Philippe Hamel, 14 November 1948, Philippe Hamel papers, Archives de l'Université Laval.

100. Jacques Dugé de Bernonville to Philippe Hamel, 12 April 1949, Philippe Hamel papers, Archives de l'Université Laval.

101. Canadian Jewish Congress press clippings, 15 May 1951, Jacques Dugé de Bernonville file, Canadian Jewish Congress archives.

102. Robert Rumilly to René Chaloult, September 12, 1949. René Chaloult papers, ANQ.

103. Father Simon Arsenault to Robert Rumilly, 8 December 1949, Robert Rumilly papers, ANQ. Joseph Kerhulu to Robert Rumilly, 15 September 1950, Robert Rumilly papers, ANQ.

104. Robert Rumilly to René Chaloult, 12 September 1948, Robert Rumilly papers, ANQ. René Chaloult to Robert Rumilly, 16 September 1948, Robert Rumilly papers, ANQ.

105. René Chaloult to Robert Rumilly, 12 September 1948, Robert Rumilly papers, ANQ.

106. René Chaloult to Robert Rumilly, 7 March 1951, Robert Rumilly papers, ANQ.

107. Mgr Félix-Antoine Savard to René Chaloult, 23 February 1953, Robert Rumilly papers, ANQ.

108. Philippe Hamel to M. L. Gagné, 17 December 1948, Philippe Hamel papers, Archives de l'Université Laval.

109. "La liberté religieuse à l'immigration," *Le Devoir,* 21 September 1948.

110. "I need not emphasize to you how cruel a deportation would be for the de Bernonville family, already tortured by the long delays. I presume that a kind of warning in *Le Devoir* would put a stop to it. If one of you would take it in hand, it would be a good thing."

Robert Rumilly to André Laurendeau, 12 August 1949, Robert Rumilly papers, ANQ. "You can read in today's *Devoir* a brief commentary on the Bernonville affair. The news we have received about it are for the moment contradictory. Nevertheless, I thought it proper to remind the government of what constitutes common sense." André Laurendeau to Robert Rumilly, 19 August 1949, Robert Rumilly papers, ANQ. "I obtained several articles in *Le Devoir.*" Robert Rumilly to René Chaloult, 11 January 1950, Robert Rumilly papers ANQ.

111. Jacques Dugé de Bernonville to Philippe Hamel, 8 November 1948, Philippe Hamel papers, Archives de l'Université Laval.

112. Jacques Dugé de Bernonville to Philippe Hamel, 14 November 1948, Philippe Hamel papers, Archives de l'Université Laval.

113. Paul Massé himself wrote to Louis Saint-Laurent on behalf of Bernonville on 12 September 1948.

114. "Count J. de Bernonville thanks the signatories of the petition to Minister Harris." *Le Devoir,* 2 May 1950.

115. Jacques Benoît de Bernonville to René Chaloult, 23 January 1948, René Chaloult papers, ANQ.

116. 23 February 1950.

117. Mgr Georges Courchesne to Louis Saint-Laurent, 18 February 1950, Louis Saint-Laurent papers, NAC.

118. 7 September 1948.

119. "At the request of his Excellence Mgr l'Archevêque, I have been following the case of Monsieur le comte de Bernonville for some time. I have seen the confidential testimony on his behalf and we here at the archdiocese are convinced that he is a first-rate citizen who never betrayed his country nor disgraced himself." Mgr Albert Valois, diocesan director of *L'Action catholique* to Senator Jean-Marie Dessurault, 8 September 1949. On 21 September 1949, Senator Dessurault gave Louis Saint-Laurent Mgr Charbonneau's letter of support. Louis Saint-Laurent papers, NAC.

120. Alfred Plourde, P. J. Fortier, Lucien Beaugé to Minister of Mines and Resources, 22 September 1948, Louis Saint-Laurent papers, NAC.

121. The mayor of Trois-Rivières to Louis Saint-Laurent, 25 February 1949, Louis Saint-Laurent papers, NAC.

122. Mgr Alexandre Vachon to Louis Saint-Laurent, 17 August 1949, Louis Saint-Laurent papers, NAC.

123. *La Presse*, 9 September 1948.

124. Jacques Dugé de Bernonville to Philippe Hamel, 14 November 1948, Philippe Hamel papers, Archives de l'Université Laval.

125. Telegram from Onésime Gagnon to Louis Saint-Laurent, 24 February 1950, Louis Saint-Laurent papers, NAC.

126. André Laurendeau, "Are the Russians always wrong?" dans *L'Action nationale, Pour gagner la paix*, May 1949, p. 341.

127. Philippe Hamel, *Les responsables de la Deuxième Grande Guerre*, 1948.

128. *Ibid.*, p. 10.

129. *Ibid.*, p. 13.

130. Jacques Dugé de Bernonville to Philippe Hamel, 28 October 1948, Philippe Hamel papers, Archives de l'Université Laval.

131. "M. Chaloult and the Bernonville incident," *Action catholique*, 9 September 1948. "Keenleyside is a freemason," Robert Rumilly to René Chaloult, 29 December 1949, René Chaloult papers, ANQ.

132. Frédéric Dorion, official transcript of the debates of the House of Commons, 24 February 1949, p. 877. CCF Member Alistair Stewart had unsuccessfully pleaded with the Minister of Immigration on behalf of seven Jews who had illegally entered Canada, and who were deported because the minister in question feared creating a precedent. "The precedent is established. I imagine that the minister knew that these fascists were here, but he deported the Jews since they seemed not to have any influential friends." Official transcript of the Debates of the House of Commons, 22 February 1949., p. 795

133. Robert Rumilly to Victor Keyserling, 9 March 1949, Robert Rumilly papers ANQ. "Count de Bernonville must be freed. Is it not true that we welcome here all kinds of scum and riff-raff and foreign trash from the four corners of the globe?" Diary of Claude-Henri Grignon, 25 February 1951, Robert Rumilly papers, ANQ. Jacques Dugé de Bernonville shared these kinds of views. As he wrote to Camilien Houde on 8 September 1948: "The accusations against me smell of anti-Christian, Communist and Jewish machinations. Clues already gathered leave no doubt on that score." Robert Rumilly papers, ANQ.

134. Robert Rumilly to colonel Rémy, 16 August 1950, Robert Rumilly papers ANQ. "Our national associations do nothing. The dirty work is left to a few sharp-shooters. The Jews make a fuss, and the entire

anglo-saxon press and the French-Canadian liberal press come out against the French and we do nothing. How difficult it is to make a people lose its loser's reflex." Phillippe Hamel to Abbé Pierre Gravel, 6 November 1948, Philippe Hamel papers, Archives de l'Université Laval.

135. André Laurendeau, Bloc-Notes, *Le Devoir*, 22 October 1948.

136. Maurice Ferro, "Au Canada Français, autonomisme, conservatisme and neutralisme québécois." *Le Monde*, 16 May 1951.

137. Anatole Vanier to Louis Saint-Laurent, le 14 January 1950, Louis Saint-Laurent papers, NAC.

138. André Payette, *Quartier latin*, 9 March 1951.

139. Le journal of Claude-Henri Grignon, 25 February 1951.

140. Judgment of the Honorable Louis Cousineau, Superior Court, district of Montréal, n° 3395, 21 February 1949, p. 31.

141. *Ibid.*

142. *Ibid.* , pp. 31-32.

143. *Ibid.* , p. 32.

144. Gérard Filion, "Nous sommes-nous battus en vain?" *Le Devoir*, 20 October 1948.

145. Memorandum for the Prime Minister, 1er September 1949, Louis Saint-Laurent papers, NAC.

146. Gérard Filion, *op. cit.* Jacques Rousseau, director of the Montreal Botanical Garden, gives the same warning to Drew via the Honorable Louis Cécile: "This business could be fatal to the interests of Conservatives in Quebec. It is thus important that there be no questions in the House by Conservatives, as such questions would not bring any support to the party." Jacques Rousseau to the Honorable Louis Cécile, City Hall, Toronto, 26 January 1949, Robert Rumilly papers, ANQ.

147. Robert Rumilly to René Chaloult, 21 November 1948, Robert Rumilly papers, ANQ. Rumilly has the impression of having been had by the federal government: "The government thought itself adroit in acquiescing in four cases and refusing de Bernonville. I warned the ministers that they would have "a messy affair" on their hands, and you know what happened. I KNOW that the government regrets today not having given me what I wanted." Robert Rumilly to Victor Keyserling, 31 December 1948, Robert Rumilly papers, ANQ.

148. Louis Saint-Laurent to Mgr Alexandre Vachon, 22 August 1949, Louis Saint-Laurent papers, NAC.

149. Me Bourdon is highly indignant and "made it quite clear that he had also received similar promises." Robert Rumilly to René Chaloult, 23 December 1949, René Chaloult papers, ANQ.

150. Pierre Desjardins, "Canada. Land of freedom and honour," 11 January 1949.

151. Pierre Héricourt to Philippe Hamel, 11 January 1949, Robert Rumilly papers, ANQ.

152. Philippe Hamel to Jacques Dugé de Bernonville, 14. February 1949, Philippe Hamel papers, Archives de l'Université Laval.

153. "On that question, mayor Houde received an appeal from the Ligue des victimes civiques, an association of victims of the purges, formed in Paris, and which was seeking Canadian assistance." Robert Rumilly to René Chaloult, 13 April 1948, Robert Rumilly papers, ANQ.

154. Charles Palpant, social assistant in Saint-Martin Île-de-Ré, to Camilien Houde, 26 April 1949, Robert Rumilly papers, ANQ.

155. Camilien Houde to Mme Henry Coston, 11 May 1949, Robert Rumilly papers, ANQ.

156. Undated letter, E. Gaboriau or Braboriau to Camilien Houde, Robert Rumilly papers, ANQ.

157. Commander A. Quivault to Camilien Houde 25 March 1949. Quivault was back in France after having spent some time in Canada where he met Camilien Houde: "As I told you during our previous meeting last November (after the brilliant speech by Mr. Rumilly to the Young Chamber of Commerce where you presided), I returned to France to fight the good fight." To fight the good fight in Canada, it would be wise to "invite speakers to enlighten French Canadians on the odious acts of the courts of purification." Robert Rumilly papers, ANQ.

158. Robert Rumilly to colonel Rémy, 16 August 1950. Rémy acquiesces to Rumilly's judgement: "You are correct when you say that it is difficult for a French Canadian to introduce the necessary nuances into the discussion of questions stemming from events in our country. Here, already, it is not easy. But little by little, the truth comes to light." Colonel Rémy to Robert Rumilly, 21 August 1950, Robert Rumilly papers, ANQ.

159. Philippe Hamel to Robert Rumilly, 28 August 1950, Robert Rumilly papers, ANQ.

160. Abel Bonnard to the Canadian government, 30 September 1949, Robert Rumilly papers, ANQ.

161. Jacques Dugé de Bernonville to Philippe Hamel, 14 November 1948, Philippe Hamel papers, Archives de l'Université Laval. In his letter of support for Bernonville dated 25 October 1948, Émile Barazer de Lannurien alludes to his past membership in *La Cagoule*(The Hood).

162. René Chaloult to Robert Rumilly, 27 March 1951, Robert Rumilly papers, ANQ; "As far as I can tell, de Bernonville was a bit daft as a result of the injuries he suffered during the 1914-1918 war. He is perhaps a zealot whose ideas are not all shared by the likes of you or me. But he is certainly a hero of World War I (and I weigh my words) and I am sure he did nothing to hurt France or the French, although he may be an anti-semite." Avila Bédard to Philippe Hamel, 6 April 1949, Philippe Hamel papers, Archives de l'Université Laval.

163. Philippe Hamel to Jacques Dugé de Bernonville, 28 March 1951, Robert Rumilly papers, ANQ.

164. Jacques Bernonville to Louis Saint-Laurent, 21 March 1951, Louis Saint-Laurent papers, NAC. De Bernonville's testimony before Superior Court of Quebec, 6 June 1951, Jacques Dugé de Bernonville file, NAC.

165. Jacques Bernonville to Louis Saint-Laurent, 16 March 1951, Robert Rumilly papers, ANQ.

166. Jacques Bernonville to Jean Bruchesi, 8 June 1951, Jean Bruchesi paper, Archives de l'Université de Montréal. "All of the missions I fulfilled were ordered by my hierarchical and legitimate superiors, and concerned specific periods and limited objectives. Certain missions were of a delicate and confidential nature and, given the leaks and the risks run by certain persons in France, I am not able to name names without the authorization of those involved; some of these people may be difficult to reach." Jacques Dugé de Bernonville, confidential notes, 2 May 1950, Robert Rumilly papers, ANQ.

167. Jacques Dugé de Bernonville, confidential notes, 21 September 1950, p. 4, Robert Rumilly papers, ANQ.

168. They were published in *Le Petit Journal* on 12 September 1948.

169. "Our investigation revealed that Bernonville is an individual who took part in particulary disdainful acts of collaboration during the occupation of his country and for which he was condemned to death *in absentsia* for treason by the Court of Toulouse on 8 October 1947. Apparently, he was responsible during this time of collaboration for having given over many of his loyal compatriots to his temporary German masters, which acts, we believe, led to their deaths (. . .) we believe that de Bernonville is certainly not the type of person who should go free in this country." Go. B. McClellan, *Special Branch* officer to Commissioner of immigration, Ministry of Mines and Ressources, Ottawa, Ontario, Jacques Dugé de Bernonville file, NAC.

170. Court of Justice of Toulouse, 22 January 1949.

171. Jacques Dugé de Bernonville to Jean Bruchesi, 8 June 1951, Jean Bruchesi papers, Archives de l'Université de Montréal. "The police also mentioned German documents: receipts for monies received by me. I was mandated by a Vichy Minister to maintain surveillance on a small group of Frenchmen that the Germans wished to arm, but I remained involved with this for a very short time, and never knew what became of them because the Germans thought me suspect and Vichy entrusted me with another mission." Confidential note of Jacques Dugé de Bernonville, 2 May 1950, Robert Rumilly papers, ANQ.

172. P. T. Baldwin (chief, division of admissions) to superintendent of translation, Ottawa, 28 May 1951, Jacques Dugé de Bernonville file, Simon Wiesenthal Centre Archives.

173. McKenzie Porter, "De Bernonville," *Maclean's*, 15 November 1951.

174. Pierre Asselin to Bernonville, 19 March 1951, Louis Saint-Laurent papers, NAC.

175. Bona Arsenault to Robert Rumilly, 18 December 1950, Robert Rumilly papers, ANQ.

176. Bona Arsenault to Dr. Lionel Chevrier and to Robert Rumilly, 14 February 1951, Robert Rumilly papers, ANQ.

177. Robert Rumilly, personal note, end of February 1951, Robert Rumilly papers, ANQ.

178. Jacques Dugé de Bernonville to Jean Bruchesi, 8 June 1951, Jean Bruchesi papers, Archives de l'Université de Montréal.

179. Jacques Dugé de Bernonville to Jean Bruchesi, 12 September 1951, Jean Bruchesi papers, Archives de l'Université de Montréal.

180. Jacques Dugé de Bernonville to Jean Bruchesi, 7 February 1968, Jean Bruchesi papers, Archives de l'Université de Montréal.

18I. Jean Bruchesi to Jacques Dugé de Bernonville, 1 December 1959, Jean Bruchesi papers, Archives de l'Université de Montréal.

182. Jacques Dugé de Bernonville to Jean Bruchesi, 5 July 1962, Jean Bruchesi papers, Archives de l'Université de Montréal.

183. Bertram Gordon, *op. cit.* , p. 161.

184. Jacques Dugé de Bernonville to Jean Bruchesi, 5 February 1960. Jacques Dugé de Bernonville to Jean Bruchesi, 5 July 1962. Jacques Dugé de Bernonville to Jean Bruchesi, 17 September 1962. Jean Bruchesi papers, Archives de l'Université de Montréal.

185. Jacques Dugé de Bernonville to Jean Bruchesi, 11 April 1962, Jean Bruchesi papers, Archives de l'Université de Montréal.

186. Léon Strauss, *Nouveau dictionnaire de biographie alsacienne,* Strasbourg. Not yet published. Unless otherwise indicated, the pre-war biographical information on Paul Erwin Eberhard Reifenrath comes from this work.

187. Léon Strauss: Antisemitism in Alsatia during the thirties. XVII-I[th] colloquium of the Société d'histoire des Israélites d'Alsace et de Lorraine, Strasbourg, 10 and 11 February 1996. Texts compiled by Anny Bloch. "Here is how he presented the Jewish question in Alsatia: the Jews lived off the inhabitants like parasites, feeding themselves from their substance. Just as a horse can endure a certain number of fleas in its hide, Alsatia is capable enduring its allotment of undesirable Jews."

188. *Ibid.*

189. *Ibid.*

190. Renaude Lapointe, *L'histoire bouleversante de Mgr Charbonneau,* Éditions du jour, Montréal, 1962, p. 85. Many accounts confirm this information.

191. Maurice Duplessis papers, ANQ, Québec. Also Conrad Black, *Maurice Duplessis, 1944-1959 Le pouvoir,* Éditions de l'homme, Montréal, 1977, p. 378, note 19. It was Duplessis, using his secretary Auréa Cloutier as an intermediary, who gave this information to Jean Bruchesi. According to Black, who took his information from Auréa Cloutier, Canon Cyrille Labrecque and Father Arthur

Dubois had met Paul-Éverard Richemont at the Centre Pie XI in Montréal. *Ibid.* , p. 350.

192. Jean Bruchesi, *Souvenirs à vaincre,* Hurtubise HMH, Montréal, 1974, p. 90. The canon in question quite is likely Canon Cyrille Labrecque, as the rest of the story reveals.

193. The Timmins group controlled Hollinger Consolidated Gold Mines, which allowed it to also control Hollinger North Shore Exploration Co. and Labrador Mining and Exploration Co. Ltd. Burton Ledoux, "La silicose, de Saint-Rémi d'Amherst à l'Ungava," *Relations,* École sociale populaire, Montreal, March 1948.

194. Jean d'Auteuil Richard, editor of *Relations,* "Les victimes de Saint-Rémi sont nos frères," éditorial, *Relations,* March 1948.

195. Adélard Dugré, "La silicose: rectification," *Relations,* July 1948, pp. 193-194. The comings and goings around and consequences of the publication of this rectification, as interesting as they are, cannot be adequately treated in the framework of this text.

196. On 13 February 1949 at Asbestos and on 14 February 1949 at Thetford Mines.

197. Gérard Dion, *La grève de l'amiante*, Memoir presented to the Royal Society of Canada, fourth series, vol. XVII, 1979. This text shows that the asbestos strike was fundamentally an ideological struggle.

198. Conrad Black, *op. cit.* , p. 360.

199. This organization "considered itself the Canadian equivalent of the Association of Catholic employers and engineers of Belgium. However, the position of the API on structural reform was far from being as progressive as that of its Belgian counterpart. It aligned itself above all on the conservative wing of this association whose main spokesman, Thomas Lhoest, was often invited to Quebec to caution local employers ." Gérard Dion, *op. cit.* , p. 34.

200. Here is an excerpt of the convocation: "Worrisome events are taking place in the Province of Quebec. There is a malaise everywhere. Everyone who is aware is anxious. People ask themselves with a definite fear what tomorrow will bring. Bedlam is perhaps at our door. It is high time for employers to take stock of the situation and to decide what positions to take to save free entreprise." *Ibid.,* p. 36.

201. Collection of documents on the 1949 Asbestos strike compiled by the Confederation of Christian workers of Canada, tome 1, File on the Asbestos strike, Archives of the Rimouski archdiocese.

202. *Ibid.* , p. 3.

203. *Ibid.* , p. 4.

204. *Ibid.* , p. 97.

205. *Ibid.* , p. 14.

206. *Ibid.* , p. 27. The letter is dated 22 August 1949.

207. Trudeau, Pierre Elliott (editor), *La grève de l'amiante,* Éditions du Jour, Montréal, 1970, p. 259, note 27. Also Appendix 11, "Le rapport Custos."

208. Maurice Duplessis paper, ANQ. Conrad Black, *op. cit.* , pp. 351-352.

209. "But in November 1949, Canon Cyrille Labrecque was in Beauport, taking care of the affairs of the foundation of a religious order. The record of the order for 13 November 1949 confirm his presence there. How could he be in Rome at the same time?" Other reasons Sister Fecteau had for doubting that "L" was Canon Labrecque : "He never wrote using a typewriter (with which the letter was composed) but by hand, with a very fine pen. His French was impeccable, but the letter contains grammatical errors and does not at all correspond to his style of written expression." Letter from Sister Jeanne Fecteau, archivist, to the author, 25 October 1995.

210. Édouard Gouin, "Pour la réconciliation nationale," *La Presse,* 27 November 1948. Jean-Marie Poirier, "Aider les Français à s'unir," interview with Abbé Édouard Gouin, *La Presse,* 27 November 1948. Robert Rumilly, "Sur une conférence de M, Robert Rumilly," *Le Devoir,* 7 December 1948. Édouard Gouin to Robert Rumilly, un-dated letter, Robert Rumilly papers, ANQ. Robert Rumilly to Édouard Gouin, 16 December 1948, Robert Rumilly papers, ANQ. Édouard Gouin, "La libération en France," *Le Devoir,* 4 January 1949.

211. Renaude Lapointe, *op. cit.* , p. 83.

212. *Ibid.* , p. 81.

213. Alex Carter, *A Canadian Bishop's Memoirs,* Tomiko Publications, North Bay, 1994, pp. 110-111. He recounts a time when, working at the chancery of the archdiocese, he informed Charbonneau of the existence of a movement within the Quebec clergy to have him removed from his functions. In 1949, Mgr Charbonneau made his *ad limina* visit to the Vatican without ever realising the precarity of the situation. *Ibid.* , pp. 104-105.

214. *Ibid.* , p. 108.

215. *Ibid.* , pp. 109-110.

216. Mgr Ildebrando Antoniutti to Maurice Duplessis, 2 February 1950. Quoted in Conrad Black, *op. cit.* , p. 360.

217. Maurice Duplessis to Mgr Ildebrando Antoniutti, 6 February 1950, *ibid.* , pp. 360-361.

218. Mgr Ildebrando Antoniutti to Maurice Duplessis, 15 February 1950, *ibid,* p. 361.

219. On the role of de Richemont in obstructing propaganda unfavorable to Duplessis at the Vatican, see also Robert Rumilly, *Maurice Duplessis and son temps,* vol 2, Fides, Montréal, 1973, pp. 361-362.

220. Paul-Éverard Richemont to Maurice Duplessis, 11 December 1951, Maurice Duplessis papers, ANQ. Quoted in Conrad Black, *op. cit.* , pp. 366-367.

221. Renaude Lapointe, *op. cit.* , pp. 84-85. The letter is dated 4 November 1950.

222. Paul-Éverard Richemont to Maurice Duplessis, 29 May 1950, Maurice Duplessis papers, ANQ. Also Conrad Black, *op. cit.* , pp. 365-366.

223. Maurice Duplessis papers, ANQ. Conrad Black, *ibid.* , p. 357.

224. "Father Dubois is ready to complete the revision of the rectification whose draft I submitted last week, to free myself up for other work." Paul-Éverard Richemont to Émile Tourigny, 29 May 1950. "M. Richemont told me about a short piece of editing he had for me. If I am not disturbed, I should be able to return it to you for the weekend." Father Émile Dubois to Maurice Duplessis, 4 June 1950, Maurice Duplessis papers, Séminaire Saint-Joseph, Trois-Rivières. Mr. Richemont had just left for Rome. The dates of these letters fit with the publication dates of the government's reply.

225. Maurice Duplessis to Paul-Éverard Richemont, June 1, 1950, ANQ. Conrad Black, *op. cit.* , p. 366.

226. Gérard Dion, *op. cit.* , p. 33.

227. Renaude Lapointe, *op. cit.* , pp. 84-85. The letter is dated 4 November 1950. Also, letter from Édouard Gouin, 20 February 1951, *ibid.* , p. 86.

228. *Bulletin de Custos,* Introduction, Maurice Duplessis papers, ANQ.

229. *Ibid.* , p. 1.

230. *Ibid.* , p. 2.

231. *Ibid.* , p. 1.

232. *Ibid.* , p. 3.

233. *Ibid.*

234. *Ibid.* , p. 4.

235. *Ibid.*

236. Édouard Gouin, 20 February 1951. Renaude Lapointe, *op. cit.* , p. 86.

Sounds of Silence

1. Mordecai Richler (Edited by), *Writers on World War 2, An Anthology*, Alfred A. Knopf, New York, 1991, p. XXI.

2. Paul-André Linteau, René Durocher, François Ricard and Jean-Claude Robert, *Histoire du Québec contemporain*, revised edition, Boréal, Montréal, 1989, pp. 124-127.

3. "Because studies reveal that memory, even at the social level, is merely the structuring of forgetfulness." Henry Rousso, *The Vichy Syndrome, History and Memory in France since 1944*, Harvard University Press, Cambridge (É-U), London, (UK), 1991, p. 4.

4. André Laurendeau, *La crise de la conscription 1942*, Éditions du Jour, Montréal, 1962.

5. Pierre Elliott Trudeau, *Memoirs*, McClelland and Stewart, Toronto, 1993, p. 31.

6. *Ibid.*, p. 32.

7. René Lévesque, Memoirs. Translated by Philip Stratford, McClelland and Stewart, Toronto, 1986, p. 84.

8. Gérard Pelletier, *Les années d'impatience 1950-1960*, Éditions Stanké, Montréal, 1983, p. 57.

9. "One felt torn betweenconflicting feelings - horror at Hitler's invasion of Poland, fear that the fighting would spread, the wish to avoid, if possible taking part in it ourselve." André Laurendeau, The Conscription Crisis in *André Laurendeau, Witness for Quebec*, Essays Selected and Translated by Philip Stratford, Macmillan of Canada, Toronto, 1973, p. 17. In his book on the conscription crisis, Laurendeau neglects to mention that: "In 1938, when the Sudetenland had become the main issue, Laurendeau argued that neither justice, nor the law, nor their own best interests called French Canadians to the defense of the Czechs. He went so far as to picture the Germans of the Sudetenland as a beleaguered minority, tyrannised by the central government in Prague. He had changed considerably, in other words, since the time in Paris when he strongly

opposed fascist belligerance during the Spanish Civil War." Donald
J. Horton, *André Laurendeau, French-Canadian Nationalist 1912-1968*, Oxford University Press, Toronto, 1992, p. 91.

10. André Laurendeau, *op. cit.* , pp. 17-18.

11. *Ibid.* , p. 22.

12. Georges-Émile Lapalme, *Le bruit des choses réveillées*, Leméac, vol. 1, Montréal, p. 272.

13. Gérard Filion, *Fais ce que peux*, Montréal, Boréal, 1989, p. 158.

14. Mordecai Richler, *op. cit.* , p. XXIII.

15. André Laurendeau, *op. cit.* , p. 117. He judged it necessary to repeat the same proposition: "War-time finances had eased the aggressivity somewhat. With his family allowance payments, King assiduously courted Quebec." *Ibid.* , p. 153.

16. Gérard Pelletier, *op. cit.* , pp. 37-38.

17. Gérard Filion, *op. cit.* , pp. 138-139.

18. *Ibid.* , p. 139.

19. Georges-Henri Lévesque, *Souvenances*, vol. 1, Éditions La Presse, Montréal, 1984, pp. 315-316.

20. Pierre-Elliott Trudeau, *op. cit.* , p. 32.

21. "We were coming back from class down the Grande-Allée in Quebec City and all the windows were open to the soft spring air. As we walked along we could hear a voice, always the same, reaching our ears from house to house. In that way, word for word, we followed the sober and moving commentary of that excellent journalist Louis Francoeur." René Lévesque, *op. cit.* , p. 82.

22. "For my family and for myself, Paris meant more than the Eiffel Tower and the Folies-Bergère. My father had lived there. My wife and I had lived for two years in the Latin Quarter, and our first child had been born there. France wasn't just a prestigious but distant intellectual symbol: I had French friends and memories." André Laurendeau: *Op. cit.*, p. 40. "'Then it was France's turn-what had happened to Emmanuel Mounier and Father Paul Doncoeur, our concierge, our classmates, and the vegetable woman in la rue Mouffetord? Where would Daniel-Rops, André Siegfried, and Emile Baas go now, and all those young families who had welcomed us when we felt alone in Paris, and those lay sisters from la rue Tournefort who had shared their potato soup with us during my wife's long illness?" *Ibid.*

23. Donald J. Horton: Op. cit., p. 100. "His anguish was even greater because in 1939 he had received letters from Madeleine and Émile Baas reporting that they had been separated by the war declaration, that she was pregnant and he was in the army. They added that Father Doncoeur was most likely a French army chaplain, and made a point of insisting that it was a 'just war.' " *Ibid.*

24. *Action nationale,* June 1940, pp. 434-435. Quoted in Paul-André Comeau, *Le Bloc populaire,* 1942-1948, Montréal, Éditions Québec/Amérique, 1982, p. 61.

25. André Laurendeau, *op. cit.* , p. 41.

26. "Abstaining from any form of of participation in the military was more difficult, however. You were either conscripted into the army, or if you were a student you had to join the Canadian Officers Training Corps. This required us to go to an armoury in the city twice a week to do drills and learn how to handle weapons. (. . .) But apart from these military duties, which I fulfilled like everyone else, the war really did not command my attention." Pierre Elliott Trudeau, *op. cit.* , p. 34.

27. André Laurendeau, *op. cit.* , p. 43. Camilien Houde spent the next four years in the Petawawa internment camp.

28. *Ibid.* , p. 44.

29. "So I went and registered like everyone else. For me it took place in the country. I can still see the little office where I answered my questions and signed my signature before the representative of the State. I came out of there feeling that I had just contradicted and perhaps betrayed myself."*Ibid.*, pp. 4-45. "And yet the spirit of revolt practically never went ot the limit. The internment of Camilien Houde caused, on the whole, few repercussions. (. . .) This was because the exercise of constraint, too, seldom went to the limit, and because, though we possessed little, we still preserved the morale of possessors." *Ibid.* , p. 120.

30. "Perhaps there were other motives that made me and others like me act as we did. Motives that never became totally clear. To choose the moment of France's greatest distress to refuse to collaborate in policies that were intended to avenge her had, it seemed to me, something repugnant about it." *Ibid.*.

31. René Lévesque, *op. cit.* , p. 84.

32. Georges-Émile Lapalme, *op. cit.* , p. 271.

33. Including René Chaloult, accused after the May 19, 1942 meeting of the League for the Defence of Canada at the Saint-Jacques market at which he praised Pétain and said "never" to conscription.

34. "We knew nothing of the conditions he governed under, or what was happening to Frenchmen and Jews in France. The only news we got came with the stamp of British propaganda on it, and we didn't believe it." André Laurendeau, *op. cit.*, p. 88.

35. The Bloc populaire canadien was founded on 8 September 1942 in order to make permanent the League for the Defence of Canada. Paul-André Comeau, *op. cit.* , p. 97.

36. *Ibid.* , p. 191.

37. *Ibid.* , p. 164.

38. *Ibid.* , pp. 164-165.

39. André Laurendeau, *Alerte aux Canadiens français,* Éditions de l'Action nationale, Montréal, 1940.

40. *Ibid.* , p. 24.

41. *Ibid.* , pp. 24-25.

42. *Ibid.* , p. 11.

43. *Ibid.* , p. 23.

44. *Ibid.* , p. 23.

45. André Laurendeau, *op. cit.* , p. 156.

46. *Ibid.* , p. 2.

47. "I sometimes felt the bitter solitutde of my people in the world to the point of suffocation."*Ibid.* , p. 120.

48. Gérard Filion, *op. cit.* , pp. 160-161.

49. André Laurendeau, *op. cit.* , p. 66.

50. "At the corner of St. Laurence and Ontario, the group broke down the doors of one of the city's fanciest whorehouses. The demosntrators invaded the soigné establishment and overturned beds, with clients still hiding underneath the sheets, and smashed the large, gilt-edged mirrors. The were finally expulsed by the enraged Madam and a coterie of her girls." Brian McKenna and Susan Purcell, *Drapeau,* Clarke, Irwin & Company Limited, Toronto, Vancouver, 1980, p. 45.

51. André Laurendeau, *op. cit.* , p. 67.

52. *Ibid.* , pp. 68.

53. "No paper published his words; they remained in my memory because of his accent, because of the risk he knew he was taking,

and because of the initial silence that greeted him and then the applause that shook the room when he had finished." *Ibid.*, pp. 70.

54. *Ibid.* , pp. 71-72.

55. *Ibid.* , p. 72.

56. *Ibid.*

57. *Le Devoir,* 30 July 1943, p. 2. Quoted dans Paul-André Comeau, *op. cit.* , p. 172.

58. *Ibid.* "A mitigating factor for Paul Massé, was the fact that his main adversary, Fred Rose (Rosenberg), was also a member of the Canadian Communist Party, which was also the chief reason for the opposition of the Bloc populaire." *Ibid.*

59. *Ibid.*

60. *Ibid.* , p. 173.

61. *Ibid.* , p. 171.

62. *Ibid.* , p. 173.

63. *Ibid.* , p. 174.

64. Pierre Elliott Trudeau, *op. cit.* , p. 32.

65. *Ibid.* , p. 34.

66. Gérard Pelletier, *op. cit.* , p. 43.

67. Paul-André Comeau, *op. cit.* , p. 165.

68. *Ibid.* , p. 166.

69. *Ibid.*

70. The article might be cooler than the words actually uttered because of censorship. Victor Trépanier of Le Bloc might have behaved as Georges Pelletier of *Le Devoir*: "Georges Pelletier was determined to save nationalist speakers from their own passions. He reported the speeches accurately but left out any excessive language. At the same time he was protecting the paper itself, for a newspaper has a certain legal responsibility for the texts it publishes. Consequently the Member for Lotbinière might well have expressed opinions Le Devoir did not record." André Laurendeau: *op. cit.*, p. 101

71. *Ibid.* , p. 114.

72. *Ibid.* , p. 115.

73. Paul-André Comeau, *op. cit.* , p. 166.

74. Denis Monière, *André Laurendeau et le destin d'un peuple,* Éditions Québec-Amérique, Montréal, 1983.

75. Robert Comeau and Lucille Beaudry (editors), *André Laurendeau. Un intellectuel d'ici,* Presses de l'Université du Québec, Sillery, 1990.

76. André Laurendeau, *op. cit.* , pp. 87-88.

77. *Ibid.* , p. 93.

78. *Ibid.*

79. Jean-Louis Gagnon, *Les Apostasies. Tome 2, Les dangers de la vertu*, Éditions La Presse, Montréal, 1988.

80. André Laurendeau, *op. cit.* , p. 119.

81. René Lévesque, *op. cit.* , p. 84-85.

82. Pierre Godin, *René Lévesque. Un enfant du siècle*, Boréal, Montréal, 1994, pp. 127-130.

83. René Lévesque, *op. cit.* , p. 92.

84. *Ibid.* , p. 95.

85. René Lévesque, *op. cit.* , pp. 99-100.

86. "What I forgot, in the first place, was a footnote for page 135 where I confessed, notably, to having somewhat embellished my brief encounter with Mussolini when I returned home from the war at age 23. I had in truth arrived at the horrible scene of his execution after the event, and not during, as I had said. This youthful sin, not unusual at the time even though it is no excuse, haunted me until when, reading the account written in a history book by Jean Provencher, I decided never to repeat the story again." Robert MacKenzie, "Lévesque rectifies tales of Goering, Mussolini," *Toronto Star*, 16 March 1986. See also, Benoît Aubin, "Lévesque admits his new book contains a lie," *The Gazette*, 16 October 1986.

87. Robert MacKenzie: "Lévesque rectifies tales of Goering, Mussolini." *Toronto Star*, March 16, 1986.

88. René Lévesque, *op. cit.* , p. 90

89. Pierre Elliott Trudeau, *op. cit.* , p. 37.

90. *Ibid.*

91. Georges-Émile Lapalme, *op. cit.* , p. 288.

92. Pierre Elliott Trudeau, *op. cit.* , p. 45.

93. Gérard Pelletier, *op. cit.* , p. 56.

94. *Ibid.* , p. 47.

95. *Ibid.* , p. 97.

A Tale of Two Statues

1. Clément Fontaine, "Duplessis has emerged from purgatory, but not the statue's sculptor, Émile Brunet," *Perspective*, 20 August 1977, pp. 6-9. The details concerning the statue's perigrenations come from this article.

2. James Fentress and Chris Wickham, *Social Memory,* Blockwell, Oxford (UK) and Cambridge (É-U) 1992, p. 134.

3. Bronislaw Backzo, "Le calendrier révolutionnaire. Décréter l'éternité." in Pierre Nora (editor), *Les lieux de mémoire,* NRF, Gallimard, Paris, 1992, vol III, Les France, p. 39. The revolutionary calendar was abolished on 1 January 1806.

4. Hugh Trevor-Roper, "The Invention of Tradition: The Highland Tradition of Scotland" in Eric Hobsbawn and Terence Ranger (editors), *The Invention of Tradition,* Cambridge University Press, Cambridge, 1983.

5. Denis Martin, *Portrait des héros de la Nouvelle-France. Images d'un culte historique,* Hurtubise HMH, Montréal, 1988, p. 100. The information on the celebrations in honor of Dollard des Ormeaux in this paragraph come from the same book, pp. 101-103, and from Catherine Pomeyrols, *Les intellectuels québécois, formation and engagements 1919-1939,* L'Harmattan, Paris, Montréal, 1996.

6. James Fentress and Chris Wickham, *op. cit.* , pp. 134-135.

7. Excerpt from "Si Dollard revenait," a speech given at the Monument national on 31 January, 1919. Quoted by Guy Frégault, in *Lionel Groulx tel qu'en lui-même,* Leméac, Montréal, 1978, p. 137.

8. Hubert Guindon, *Quebec Society. Modernity and Nationhood.* University of Toronto Press, Toronto, 1988.

9. Cité dans *Le Devoir,* 10 September 1977.

10. Catherine Pomeyrols, *op. cit.* , p. 306.

11. Ramsay Cook, "The Remembrance of All Things Past," preface to: Esther Delisle, *The Traitor and the Jew,* Robert Davies Publishing, Montréal-Toronto, 1993, p. 12.

12. Denis Vaugeois, "Hommage au chanoine Groulx," *Le Devoir,* 4 June 1977, p. 17.

13. "Les carnets de Jean Éthier-Blais," Le Devoir, 31 October 1981, p. 24.

14. Raoul Roy, "Lionel Groulx mérite un monument," *Le Devoir,* 21 August 1981, p. 13.

15. The controversy concerned my book: Esther Delisle, *The Traitor and the Jew. Anti-Semitism and the delirium of extremist right-wing nationalism in French Canada, 1929-1939.* Robert Davies Publishing, Montreal, Toronto, 1993.

16. *Le Devoir,* 30 November 1936.

Loony Tunes

1. *Le petit Robert*, 1977.
2. Merriam Webster's Collegiate Dictionary, 10th edition, Springfield, Massachusetts, p. 1358.
3. Newfoundland joined the federation in 1949.
4. Eugene Weber, *Peasants into Frenchmen. Modernization of Rural France 1870-1914,* Stanford University Press, Stanford, 1976.
5. "Deeply anchored in the soil, close to nature and life, Québécois of French tradition had to learn, because of their isolation, to relativise the artifice of human endeavour. They kept their peasant ways (...)." Gouvernement du Québec, *La politique québécoise de développement culturel,* Éditeur officiel du Québec, Québec, 1978, p. 49.
6. *Ibid.* , p. 54.
7. Founded in 1968 through the union of the Mouvement souveraineté-association (MSA) and the Ralliement national (RN), which were then joined by the Rassemblement pour l'indépendance nationale (RIN).
8. *Bill respecting the future of Quebec,* Quebec Official Publisher, Québec, 1995, p. 12.
9. Government of Québec, A *Guide to your participation in the commissions on the future of Quebec,* Quebec Official Publisher, Québec, 1995, p. 16.
10. Pierre Elliott Trudeau, *Federalism and the French Canadians.* New York, St. Martins Press, 1968.
11. René Lévesque, *An Option for Quebec,* Toronto, McClelland and Stewart, 1965.
12. Maurice Pinard, "The Secessionist Option and Quebec Public Opinion, 1988-1993," *Opinion,* vol. 2, n° 3, June 1994, p. 3.
13. Jean Paré, "Noui au Canada, Non à Ottawa," *L'actualité,* vol. 20, n° 4, 15 March 1995, p. 51.

Appendix I

**A selection of facsimile reproductions
of documents located by the author
at the National Archives in Washington, D. C.**

N EDGAR HOOVER
DIRECTOR

Federal Bureau of Investigation
United States Department of Justice
Washington, D. C.

March 29, 1941

PERSONAL AND CONFIDENTIAL
SPECIAL MESSENGER

Honorable Adolf A. Berle, Jr.
Assistant Secretary of State
Department of State
Washington, D. C.

My dear Mr. Berle:

　　　　　With reference to our previous correspondence
concerning Father Theodor Karl Eschmann and Father P. C.
Wahle, your reference A-B, I wish to advise that information from a confidential source has disclosed that
Father Eschmann has not received any mail for over six
weeks and since his residence in Ottawa he has received
only a few letters from students of Laval University at
Quebec where, as you know, he was formerly a professor.

　　　　　Father Eschmann's conduct has been reported as
most satisfactory and he has not received any visitors
or communicated with any persons in Ottawa where he is
presently associated with the Dominican Order.

　　　　　　　　　Sincerely yours,

　　　　　　　　　J. E. Hoover

CANADIENS ! PRETEZ VOTRE ARGENT !

Oui! Canadiens, prêtez votre argent afin que la R.A.F. puisse aller tuer vos frères de France, parce que les aviateurs anglais ne peuvent pas survoler l'Allemagne qui est trop bien défendue, ils iront en France exercer leur "bravoure" sur des populations civiles innocentes, ils tueront 650 de vos frères français et en blesseront 1500, aiderez-vous à accomplir ce meurtre crapuleux ?

Le Gouvernement canadien vous a demandé de prêter votre argent pour aider à écraser l'Allemagne, vous avez répondu d'une façon éloquente à cet appel et la population française n'a-pas été la dernière à faire son devoir, mais les Canadiens-Français savaient-ils que leur argent servirait à tuer d'autres Français ?

Si quelques usines françaises travaillent pour le compte du Reich, c'est parce qu'elles y sont forcées. Il faut tout de même que les ouvriers français mangent, mais, il serait sans doute vain de parler de la faim aux dirigeants de la guerre en Angleterre, eux qui pratiquent encore "la vie comme d'habitude", (the usual life) et les oppresseurs de Londres se moquent pas mal que "la brave aviation britannique" se livre à des massacres sur des femmes de France et sur des enfants français; ce sont eux qui en ont donné l'ordre.

C'est, paraît-il, "France-Libre" qui a conseillé aux Anglais d'attaquer la France; ces maudits juifs auraient mieux fait de se battre en France au printemps de 1940 au lieu de se sauver à Londres et à New-York avant même que la bataille prenne une mauvaise tournure pour les armées françaises.

L'ANGLETERRE CHERCHE QUELQU'UN !

Ce que l'Angleterre cherche, c'est quelqu'un qui voudra bien faire la guerre pour elle, afin que les oppresseurs judéo-anglais puissent conserver leur emprise sur les esclaves-coloniaux.

Nous ne reconquerrons pas la Malaisie pour les Malais ou pour le peuple britannique, mais pour que Sir John Hart et es rackeeters puissent continuer d'exploiter les populations de Malaisie et conserver leur controle du caoutchouc à travers le monde. (Abbé Coughlin dans "Social Justice")

CANADIENS, REVEILLEZ-VOUS !

Les Allemands tuent en France des communistes qui se rendent coupables de sabotage, mais, les Anglais tuent sans discernement les femmes et les enfants. l'Allemagne, avec ses tactiques de "guerre moderne" a tué 10 fois moins de monde pendant cette guerre qu'elle en a tué en 1914-18, mais les Anglais semblent avoir conservé leur brave méthode de 1763, et l'attaque sur Paris dépasse en "saloperie" l'attaque des Japonais sur Pearl-Harbour, seule la dispersion des Acadiens fut plus criminelle que ce raid du 3 mars sur Paris et l'on sait qui en furent les auteurs, certainement pas les Allemands.

CANADIENS-FRANCAIS QUI NE VOUS ETES PAS LAISSES CONQUERIR MORALEMENT DEPUIS L'INVASION DE 1763, NOUS VOUS DEMANDONS D'ECRIRE AUJOURD'HUI MEME A VOTRE DEPUTE A OTTAWA POUR LUI DEMANDER DE FAIRE PART AU PARLEMENT CANADIEN DE VOTRE INDIGNATION DEVANT LE MEURTRE QUE LA R.A.F. VIENT DE COMMETTRE SI FROIDEMENT SUR LA FRANCE.

CANADIENS ! SOUVENEZ-VOUS DU RAID SUR PARIS le 3 mars 1942.
CANADIENS ! SOUVENEZ-VOUS DE L'ACADIE !

On vous dit "Souvenez-vous de Hong-Kong", c'est sans doute une annonce pour la Sainte-Enfance, quant à nous qui sommes sérieux, comme Hong-Kong ne nous rappelle que de mauvais souvenirs, nous vous disons "Oubliez-le au plus tôt".

LA GARDE DE FER: Faites partie de notre garde, nous sommes déja des centaines et demain nous serons des milliers, nous jouons cartes sur table. Dieu nous aidera...

VIVE LA FRANCE !!

La Garde de Fer.

AMERICAN CONSULATE

Quebec, Canada, April 9, 1942

CONFIDENTIAL

SUBJECT: QUEBEC'S "IRON GUARD"

1—1055

THE HONORABLE

THE SECRETARY OF STATE

WASHINGTON

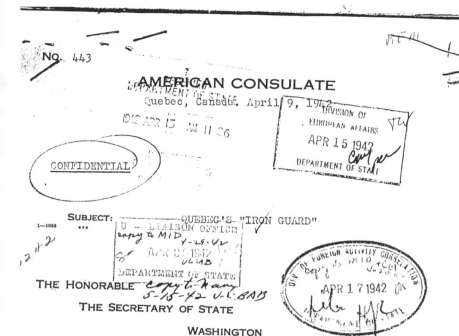

SIR:

I have the honor to refer to the arrest and conviction
of one Raymond CHOUINARD for printing and distributing subversive "Iron Guard" pamphlets at an anti-conscriptionist
meeting held in Quebec on March 8, 1942.   The youthful
Chouinard was given a sentence of only two months for his
part in the affair, presumably because of the general belief that he had not drafted the circular (see Enclosure
No. 1 for translation) and as "higher-ups" had not been
caught.

Following Chouinard's arrest the Royal Canadian Mounted Police raided the homes of some of his associates, the
first being Laureat TARDIF.   At Tardif's home valuable evidence was collected in the form of notebooks and a diary
which gave in minute detail the activities of the extreme
nationalists and named all the "higher-ups" but, before the
police could raid the homes of the leaders, a local radio
station announced that raids were in progress and the entire
organization was put on its guard; consequently subsequent

indications that the subversive elements here are extremely well organized.

The trial of Tardif for having received from Chouinard and having distributed some of the circulars, was
concluded on Tuesday, April 7, 1942 (see Enclosure No.
2) and judgment will be rendered on April 14. Though
the evidence found in Tardif's home showed him to have
been engaged in activities of a very subversive character
over a period of three years, there is a general belief
that he will not be sentenced to prison though in all
probability he will be sent to a military camp for a time.
He was defended by Antoine Rivard, who is one of the most
able lawyers in the city and also one of the leading nationalist extremists.

The diary and notebooks of Tardif show that the following persons are the leaders (Committee) of the nationalist group with which he has been associated:

> Abbe Lionel Groulx of Quebec
> Rene Chaloult, member of the Provincial
>   Assembly
> Paul Bouchard of Quebec (now in Mexico)
> J. E. Gregoire, former Mayor of Quebec
> Abbe Pierre Gravel, cure of St. Roch's
>   parish
> Philippe Hamel, Quebec dentist
> Oscar Drouin, Provincial Minister of
>   Trade
> J. Ernest Drolet, journalist, of Quebec
> Victor Barbeau, Quebec journalist
> Hermas Bastien
> Demet Baril of Montreal
> Oliver Asselin of Montreal
> Fernand de Haerne of Montreal
> Paul Gouin of Montreal

As a former student at Laval University Tardif re-
ceived his nationalist training from Abbe Groulx, Abbe
Gravel and the German Dominican, Father Eschmann. After
Canada entered the war Abbe Gravel and Abbe Groulx con-